CHRISTMAS 2011

TO MY EDIN,

HERE'S TO C  ...C BIG ONE"!

I LOVE YOU,
MAIRI.

SCOTLAND'S CLASSIC WILD TROUT WATERS

Opposite: The learning ground – Loch Calder.

SCOTLAND'S CLASSIC WILD TROUT WATERS

Lesley Crawford

SWAN·HILL
PRESS

Other books by Lesley Crawford

Fishing for Wild Trout in Scottish Lochs – Swan Hill Press 1996
An Angler's Year in Caithness & Sutherland – Northern Times 1992
Caithness & Sutherland, Trout Loch Country – North of Scotland Newspapers 1991

First published in the UK in 2000
by Swan Hill Press, an imprint of Airlife Publishing Ltd

British Library Cataloguing-in-Publication Data
A catalogue record for this book
is available from the British Library

ISBN 1 84037 092 0

All colour and B&W photography by Lesley Crawford.

Typeset by Servis Filmsetting Ltd, Manchester, England
Printed in Hong Kong

Swan Hill Press

an imprint of Airlife Publishing Ltd
101 Longden Road, Shrewsbury, SY3 9EB, England
E-mail: airlife@airlifebooks.com
Website: www.airlifebooks.com

DEDICATION

To my late Dad 1915–1998 who first encouraged me to fish
and my dear Mum who has supported
all my sporting endeavours, past and present.

Lesley and her brother Howard c.1959 – the adventure begins.

Acknowledgements

I must thank the following persons for their kind assistance in helping me to research this book – Robin Ade, Dick Bolton, Olive Brown, Bob Brighton, Graham Brooks, Paul Buchanan, Geoffrey Bucknall, Graeme Callander, Donald Campbell, Fraser Campbell, Ron Campbell, George Cameron, Charles and Lawrence Court, James Coutts, Robert Dane, Harry Davidson, Alan Derbyshire, Ed Headley, E. W. Hunter, Dick Graham, Ken Howie, Drew Jamieson, Campbell Ketchion, Tony King, Kyle Laidlay, John Lyon, David McDonald, Alastair McKellar, Willie Miller, Mitchells of Pitlochry, Bob Morgan, Shetland Anglers' Association, Anthony Steel, Peter Thomas, Anne Tuscher, Andy Walker, Jack Watson, Jon Watt, Roy Wentworth, Gordon Williamson, Donald Wilson, Jane Wright, Barbara Wyllie.

Also grateful thanks to my family, Ron, Andrew and Ewan for maintenance of straight drifts and even keels.

Contents

Introduction

Since writing *Fishing for Wild Trout in Scottish Lochs* for Swan Hill Press in 1996 I have given much thought as to what constitutes the 'classic' Scottish trout water. Fundamentally it has got to be one which entrances, challenges and occasionally frustrates. Always it will compel you back for more. Trout perfection comes in many forms all of which merge together to make the fishing day. The water may be gloriously scenic or dramatically austere, the fishing may be unusual if not quirky and the trout are forever an exciting, unpredictable and deliciously risky business. Above all classic trout lochs and streams are your constant good friends rather than remote cussed enemies.

Scotland's Classic Wild Trout Waters gives a realistic selection of centres of trout excellence from around Scotland. However before you enjoy, I must lay my catch upon the tray about having to choose 'favourite' or 'best' waters. Like many wild trout enthusiasts, I strongly believe ALL untamed trout havens are special for a variety of complex reasons and to specify one water above others is somewhat unfair. In the modern fishing world where anglers catch pellet fed stockies and 'fisheries' are created from a hole in the ground and a plastic bin liner, it is a privilege to angle for Scotland's premier game fish – *Salmo trutta* – wherever he exists in a natural habitat. What waters to leave out has therefore been a harrowing task and if your preferred venue is not mentioned here, be assured there is no reason for doing this other than the confines of time and space. The overall aim is to give you a nationwide sample of waters recognised for their consistent, high quality brown and/or sea trout fishing. To do this methodically, the cross-section of trout rivers and lochs has been selected using the criteria outlined in Chapter 1 'Special' Wild Trout Waters.

In discussing our precious fish, waters with both sea and brown trout present are mentioned largely in the same breath. Though tactics may vary slightly for the migratory and non-migratory fish, I prefer to look upon them all simply as wonderful Scottish 'trout'. Equally I must draw your attention to the rapidly emerging distinction

The author believes all untamed trout havens are special.

It is a privilege to angle for Scotland's trout wherever they exist in a natural habitat.

between 'wild' and 'native' fish as in the years ahead this issue is likely to gain significance. Though all the trout mentioned in the book can be thought of as 'wild' do remember native trout are unadulterated strains going back thousands of years whereas 'wild' trout can sometimes be second/third generation stocked browns which have begun naturally reproducing. There is a subtle but important difference and in terms of future conservation of a unique species it is vital that we recognise this aspect.

From the limestone lochs of Durness to the racy waters of the Tummel and from the clear open waters of Orkney and Shetland to the majestic pools of the River Tweed, this selection should satisfy the needs of the most discerning of *trutta* aficionados. While providing you with much practical guidance on the local tactics to use, the unique characteristics of each of the fabulous fishing haunts are also highlighted in considerable detail. Lochs and rivers quite literally from one end of Scotland to the other are covered, and, as some anglers can find the transition between the two trout angling environments somewhat taxing, there is a pragmatic section on the fundamental differences between loch and river angling techniques.

Be assured the waters listed are spectacular, enigmatic, historic, and frequently testing. All should inspire you to great things not only in your fishing but also in the way you perceive Scottish trout as a species. As salmon stocks dwindle and American rainbows usurp waters which originally only held native/wild stocks, our wonderful trout will play an ever more central role in maintaining this country's gamefishing heritage. Please treat this sporting fish with the respect and care he deserves and fish with sensible voluntary restraint according to the water concerned. I prefer not use the blanket term 'catch and release' as I believe each trout venue needs a well informed management policy relevant to its own fish populations. Instead I urge you to be prudent and show this exciting sporting quarry the respect he undoubtedly deserves. *'Catch as many trout as you wish but take home only what the water can stand and the table requires'* is my maxim and I hope it might be yours.

Above all it is my intention not only to show you those special angling places, but also widen your perception of Scotland's wild and/or native trout as a whole. Just as there are delights, there are also a variety of problems which must be addressed now and in the future. As we enter a new millennium, it is vital you gain as clear and as candid a picture of the national *Salmo trutta* scene as possible. We already have much to be proud of but all those involved with game fishing must recognise that work will be needed to maintain and, where appropriate, improve what is readily available in Scotland.

If I can increase understanding, light fires of enthusiasm and bring a sureness to your cast then I am half way there . . .

Lesley Crawford
Reay
Caithness

Part One

Classic wild trout waters show a number of
similar, though not identical, features. Part One
looks at these qualities together with various
environmental and social influences which
affect Scotland's trout. Essential tactics and
skills for river and loch trout angling are also
given prominence . . .

River Blackwater.

Assynt Hill Loch – a trout returned.

Chapter 1

'Special' Wild Trout Waters

'What is a demanding pleasure? A pleasure that demands the use of one's mind; not in the sense of problem solving but in the sense of exercising discrimination, judgement, awareness.'

Ayn Rand

Many anglers, whether local or visiting, find themselves compelled to keep returning to certain Scottish trout lochs and/or rivers. Time and time again, they travel the length and breadth of the country to revisit old haunts. It is almost as if the resident trout in specific waters exert some kind of unseen magnetic power giving anglers just enough tantalising glimpses of their fishy charms to forever induce 'just one more cast' here, and another there. Yet, if you ask these same anglers what drives them across continents and time zones, along motorways and country lanes, through fields, up hills or out on the windswept moor, they will normally answer rather vaguely, 'Oh it's the fishing' and leave it at that.

There is no doubt however that, whether on river or loch, it is the quality of Scottish trout angling which holds the fly fisher in its spell, but trying to quantify this in real terms is not an easy task. After a deal of contemplation, I have come up with a selection of factors which contribute toward making those favourite wild trout waters so 'special'. These can be seen as the following:

a) Quality of trout present.
b) Distinctive aspects of the angling.
c) Differing environmental loch/river characteristics.
d) Ambience of the water concerned.
e) Historic links and a sense of place.
f) Presence of sustainable wild trout management.

'Ambience.'

QUALITY OF TROUT

When you mention (often in slightly surreptitious tones!) that a water contains 'good quality wild trout', your fellow angler is almost always likely to understand immediately without further explanation, what that definition means. Normally he will conjure up a mental picture of a well conditioned, golden-flanked fish of around the 1lb mark bucking the rod and fighting hard before coming to the net. However, we can further analyse 'quality' in brown/sea trout by looking at them in terms of their size, their behaviour and their fighting abilities. The trout's general condition, coloration and markings also play a part in making us judge its overall performance. The worth of wild trout is therefore wrapped up in many attributes, biological and physical, plus there is of course that certain 'mystical' appeal about *Salmo trutta* which can never be totally described in the printed word.

To take the *size of trout* first; most anglers will rate any wild trout over 1lb as a respectable fish and a trout in the 2lb plus range as a very worthy prize. If you have been brought up on stocked rainbow trout fisheries these size ranges may seem small, but remember, wild trout have none of the benefits of force feeding with pellets in a safe and soft pond environment. The proportions of our trout are most emphatically

not everything. I have frequently hooked fish of half a pound or less which have arched the rod like the very devil and made me think for a moment I have connected with an all-time leviathan. Compared to farmed trout, naturally reproducing trout may lack weight but they more than make up for this with their dynamic, athletic and considerably less predictable behaviour.

Though many popular guide books have a habit of mentioning it, you should beware of placing too much emphasis on *'average' sizes* of trout. Averages will sometimes give a rough indication of what is present, but they should always be taken with a pinch of salt. Size of trout can greatly depend on what time of year you are fishing the water. In river systems the fish can move up and down stretches for feeding and shelter purposes and thus the location where you contact browns of over 1lb in April may not necessarily hold the same size of trout in July (see also Chapter 7 The River Don). Similar occurrences happen in lochs with the descent of fry and parr into a loch (normally in June) after their birthplace, the feeder streams, have started to dry out. Constantly connecting with these tiny fish can make us draw the wrong overall conclusions about that loch. Thus when an angler tells you that the average size in a certain water is 'brilliant' or has 'only small ones' do ask if he fishes it all year, day in and day out, because trout populations are constantly evolving. It is vital you obtain a seasonal picture as the site of so-called 'hot spots' can alter slightly during the angling year. If you are still in any doubt about the exact size of trout which lurk in your favourite loch or river, visit the spawning streams in late October, November and early December. Almost invariably you will have your eyes opened and see your so-called 'average size' measurements are surprisingly off the mark.

When further judging size of trout present in your chosen water avoid too much emphasis on the 'largest trout' caught there. Though it may weigh a hefty 10lb plus, it may have been caught in the late 1800s or even if caught recently, it may be the only one to come off the water in say five years and may well have been caught on a worm! Age and weight ranges of the indigenous trout population are usually the best guide to the overall health of the fish within a particular water. Superior wild trout waters usually have broad ranges of fish with plenty of trout parr, many over the ½lb class, a good few trout over the pound mark and a selection of leviathans at over 3lb to shock the unsuspecting angler every now and again.

The *behaviour of wild trout* always provides a welcome if sometimes unpredictable challenge for the angler. The study of wild trout behaviour is a subject very close to my heart and through the following chapters of this book it will quickly become apparent that wild trout behave in extraordinarily different ways, sometimes within waters only yards apart.

The latest scientific research indicates that each brown trout population in a catchment area originally had its own unique set of genes designed to assist survival in their specific environment. Most of us already know that Scotland's native brown/sea trout have been around since the last Ice Age but it is only now becoming clearer why trout in certain lochs or rivers can show differing characteristics from others. Of course in some more heavily fished waters, restocking policies have diluted many of the old strains of trout, yet in other more remote waters the local 'strain' which makes the trout capable of adapting to that particular environment remains remarkably constant.

Even more interesting are the apparently differing characteristics between the open water East coast strain of native trout and the more reclusive West coast strain. Research into the apparent genetic differences between trout of the East and West coast of Scotland is still ongoing and a

Trout in certain lochs and rivers will show differing characteristics.

The noble ferox.

variety of differing characteristics are emerging. Going back over many thousands of years Scotland's native trout populations developed along a rough East/West divide. The trout of our East coast, also known as the Baltic strain, more resembled sea trout with a silvery sheen, slight shoaling tendency, exhibiting highly acrobatic displays when caught. The original trout in Loch Leven (a loch once linked to the sea) showed all of these characteristics and gave rise to the term 'Leven' strain. The trout of the West coast differed from those of the East in that they were darker in colour, mainly solitary by nature and fought deep and dour when caught. These exhibited characteristics of what we know today as the 'ferox' strain. Note: it is vital not to dismiss ferox as old spent trout with big heads, dark lank bodies and ugly teeth. Most ferox, even the small immature ones, are noble trout with rich bronze flanks, great physical strength and fighting abilities second to none. Though over thousands of years, the migratory Baltic trout swam around Scotland's shores to mate with the trout of the West coast, a degree of independence of strains still exists. (See Chapter 8 on River Ken for further discussion of brown trout strains.)

Inherent *'migratory tendencies'* also affect wild trout behaviour in both loch and river. It is well known that any trout which has access to salt water can choose to go to sea and therefore become classed as a migratory 'sea trout'. There are however other trout movements of equal importance in freshwater. The urge to reproduce is undoubtedly the strongest migratory influence and at spawning time, trout can be found miles away from their normal stations, cutting redds in offshoot burns, land drains and any inflowing stream where there is a good flow of water and clean gravel. Lesser 'migrations' also occur outwith natural spawning both in lochs and rivers when trout move toward abundant food sources especially when profuse hatches like mayfly or large dark olive are at their zenith, drawing the fish away from their usual safe holds. 'Smolt migrations' are also seen in both flowing and still water. Every year on my own lochs, many small trout are caught (and released back by anglers) in profusion during June and July. These trout are identical in size and age giving the appearance of a shoal and having appeared almost in unison. I am sure they are simply responding to their genetic imprints which compel them to live one stage of their lives in one area then, with maturity, they move on to another. Later in the year these same little trout apparently disappear from the shallow bays and the big boys muscle in again.

One of the best descriptions I have heard of trout behaviour likened the fish to groups of school children. As babies they attend nursery school in the feeder burns; by the age of 2+ they get into primary school by migrating into the edges of the main river or loch. By 3+ they make it the into the more demanding world of secondary school where some mature quickly and establish solid territories while others do not; and if they survive to 4+ they are independent spirits in the prime of adulthood reproducing their own offspring, making their own decisions and generally knowing their place in the local trout hierarchy.

The *fighting ability* of wild trout when caught is also a good indication of quality.

Thankfully very few Scottish trout come tamely to the net, if they have been born and bred in the wild they have developed endless skills in foraging for food and evading threats from predators. Thus when captured they are rarely, if ever, hauled in like a floppy obese pudding; you must look to the stew ponds for that kind of thing. No, they will fight you as much as their size and strength can muster and this is an inherent part of the attractiveness of Scotland's *Salmo trutta*. Often they will vigorously shake themselves free of the fly and in my youth I freely admit to being stung to the core if a brown trout escaped my clutches. Nowadays I am usually a touch more magnanimous. Usually I accept his dash for freedom as all part of the game of fishing – some you win and some you lose!

Fighting qualities are again partly inherited, for example Leven trout behave in slightly different ways from ferox when caught, but ecological factors also play a part. If the trout are under significant stress, for example in waters where there is intense competition for food or in waters which are acidic and mineral deficient, then their combative abilities may be reduced. Equally if the trout suffer parasitic infection, for example with worm infestation, their natural strength can suffer. Unfortunately a 1987 scientific survey of parasites in trout lochs of Caithness and Sutherland told us that worm infestation is a natural occurrence about which we can do very little. It is actually the sign of a well established, largely untouched, truly wild trout population, so we cannot have it both ways!

Without doubt the beautiful *colour and markings* of our trout adds rather than detracts from their overall quality. Variations of hue are almost limitless and depending on your venue you will encounter trout of gold, silver or deep yellow hue with spots either of the sprinkled black and red, black asterisk, or black ringed varieties. Do not be tempted however to place too much emphasis on colour as an indication of the generic strain of trout. Whilst it is true that isolated strains of trout exist with their own particular markings, notably the yellow trout of a particularly remote loch in N.W. Sutherland or the silver liveried trout of Loch Borralie at Durness, most trout will tend to assume the colour of the loch or river bottom for safety reasons. Their colours act as camouflage from predators and are not necessarily an indication of a particular strain of trout. Incidentally Robin Ade (see Chapter 8) adds a thoughtful point on the highly visible parr markings like fingerprints down the flanks of some of our trout. Unlike the Victorians who classed these fish as 'Parr Marked Trout' he reckons these are markings showing a particularly aggressive streak in the trout. The marks act as a warning to other trout to steer clear. Alas, with this country's predilection for restocking, any number of distinctly coloured trout have bred together since the early 1800s and a huge mixture of hues has resulted.

Some anglers look at me with raised eyebrows when I talk of a brown trout's *mystical qualities* but there is undoubtedly something spellbinding about the actions of a Scottish trout. The flash of underwater gold, the graceful rollover on a fly or that fierce pull on the line are all occasions when we suddenly and dramatically become connected to a wild creature. The tussle may be fleeting or it may be prolonged but during that time you are completely focused. Nothing else matters and no other random thoughts intrude or distract. Pure magic by any other name!

ASPECTS OF ANGLING

Every trout water in Scotland will fish in its own particular way but those waters we class as 'special' often show a degree of consistency not found in others. This could simply mean that the water fishes well for most of the year or in particular months like the West Caithness lochs (June and July) or the River Conon (July to September). A degree of consistency should not be confused with an absolute certainty of catching fish – this would become deadly boring – it simply means the water concerned produces good quality trout at reasonably frequent intervals. Equally, consistency can imply that the chosen venue will always provide the angler with constantly challenging fishing capable of stretching the old grey matter to the very limit. Examples of this would include the Durness lochs, certain waters on Shetland and the demanding rivers of the Don or the Tweed.

For me, the amount of challenge a water presents is paramount in my selecting it as a popular venue. I want my fishing to be an intricate pleasure, something which expands my knowledge, increases my awareness and forces me to make decisions. The best, most enjoyable kind of angling is inextricably bound up in acquiring knowledge and acting upon it, be it from good or bad experience. The angler who claims he knows everything there is to know about a water is obviously not fishing the right one. The sport of trout fishing constantly evolves, ever throwing up new aspects for the dedicated fisher to mull over and work on, and that is just how it should be.

Waters considered consistently good usually have become home to a certain style of fishing. For example certain lochs like those of Assynt consistently produce the goods with traditional 'loch style' wet fly fishing whilst rivers like the Don have become acknowledged homes to very small dry flies. Then again certain waters like the Tummel lend themselves to particular styles of nymph fishing. Thus when visiting different venues you have both the opportunity to experiment and try out different methods and see if your local flies and skills can be transposed. This all adds to the drama and if you can share ideas with new angling friends along the way so much the better.

Similarly, familiarity with a water can be a comfort, helping us quickly past those basic decisions on where to start or what fly to use. I treat some of my local waters like old and trusted pals, for example there's no need for me to struggle with tentative social niceties on say Loch Calder, I simply get down there with my floating line and traditional patterns and get on with it. Acquiring local knowledge means you are skill building but 'special' trout waters always have that slightly unpredictable edge to them. Though familiarity with a water saves on initial time and effort in wild trout fishing, it seldom if ever breeds contempt. Included in the forthcoming chapters are a few waters I know intimately yet they are still frequently capable of surprising and delighting me. There are just too many imponderables when you are fishing in a largely untamed environment amidst constantly changing conditions over which you have no direct control.

ENVIRONMENTAL CHARACTERISTICS

Taken as a whole, Scotland abounds in excellent trout habitats. Clear, well oxygenated waters, unpolluted feeder streams and loch or river bases over sandstone, granite, schist, gneiss or limestone mean that trout are well provided for in most respects. Given adequate access to good gravel rich, silt free spawning redds, and a general lack of predation (including over fishing by man) they will flourish and grow. As you visit different trout waters however, you will notice their environmental characteristics can show tantalising

Small but special.

helps to neutralise the effects of acidic peat run off and will help enrich waters. Remember, appearances can be deceptive particularly in remote moorland areas and a little geological research can pay dividends.

It goes without saying that the available natural feeding in a trout water is directly related to its immediate environment. Fertile alkaline environments favour the invertebrates the trout like to consume, highly acidic barren lands do not. Most of the waters described in this book are made 'special' because they are 'environmentally friendly' to trout. The rivers readily nurture algae and this in turn harbours caddis and nymph and a number of the lochs mentioned have marl clays present (marl is a limestone derivative) which make excellent habitats for mayfly. Natural feeding is normally adversely affected where the surrounding environment is 'bare bones' and deficient in minerals. If the water system is also of an acidic nature in apparently barren surroundings, the trout will usually have a much harder time of it.

Also when there is little or no shelter for indigenous insects and invertebrates, for example in the form of weed beds or boulder fields, the trout can have a battle on their hands to survive and thrive. The more energy trout have to expend foraging, the slower their growth rate, particularly in acidic waters where every day is a constant struggle to find enough food. If you compare the growth rates of burn trout in a high peaty mountain stream with the trout of a slower flowing more alkaline lowland water, almost always the less 'stressed out' lowland trout will grow much larger.

The best trout waters have a good number of visible and invisible underwater features which help create a fertile safe haven for trout. In lochs, features which break up the uniformity of the water surface play a critical role in providing food and shelter for the indigenous fish. Thus islands, reefs,

differences even when they lie only half a mile apart. From the fisherman's point of view these features are vital as they determine how and what the trout feed on, the amount of shelter they can obtain and how much competition there is likely to be within a water.

In terms of their environs 'special' trout havens often have something in common. Generally, they will be productive and fertile and very often the water pH is neutral or slightly alkaline in nature. There are often mineral rich deposits in their watersheds and this allows better growth of underwater weed and algae with invertebrate life such as shrimp, caddis and snail all doing well. Although Scotland has its fair share of towering mountains and moorland peat, many lochs are spring fed from a rich mineral/limestone base and a number of rivers also flow over strata of limestone. The presence of limestone in whatever form (marl/shell sand or rock) skerries, promontories, drop offs, old walls and fences, underwater shelves and so on, all help to provide resting stations and act as collecting areas for drifting trout food. It is particularly important to start fishing around these trout holding areas first when faced with an apparently vast expanse of water – think micro environments rather than a vast unyielding horizon. Similarly, though normally a touch more obvious, are the features in a good river such as midstream boulders which break up the flow, pots which collect trout fodder, the head and tail of a pool where the flow funnels together and of course overhanging banks, trees and general vegetation.

On either loch or river, checking out the number of accessible spawning burns (use an OS map if the water is large) will give you a rough indication of the availability of natural spawning areas. In some cases numerous inflowing burns may mean an over-production of small fish with too many trout competing for a finite amount of food.

AMBIENCE

The ambience of a water is less easy to define but nevertheless it plays a central role in judging its appeal. Sometimes you hear a fellow piscator describing a loch or river as somewhere which 'reeks' of trout. What he really means is the venue will have some or all of the obvious fish friendly goodies previously mentioned, and has a certain atmospheric appeal which sets it head and shoulders above the rest. Whether we like it or not, brown / sea trout fishing in Scotland is inextricably bound up in its surroundings and the general character of a fishing spot is often critical to its enjoyment. Your fishing 'vibes' can be an austere ring of sentinel peaks or simply a gentle robe of green agriculture. Whatever it is, the situation of your chosen water will have a profound influence on both your senses and your angling day.

Unfortunately, unless you fish a water all year and get to know each of its changing moods intimately, ambience can seem a very transient thing. For example, in early season our lochs and rivers give the impression of being cold, dark and quite threatening, but visit them in high summer with the vegetation lush and the insect life in full flow and they seem a completely different world. If we accept the run of the

The situation has a profound influence on both the senses and the angling day.

Each area has a character all of its own.

seasons with some equanimity even the darkest days on the water have their own magical allure. Remember the more you fish for wild/native trout in Scotland the more you will find each area taking on a captivating character of its own. Good examples of this include the wilder regions of Lochaber where the trout can be as fiercely inspirational as the massive hills which surround them or the tranquil, clear pools of the Tweed where sleek silhouettes glide between the Ranaculus. Look out for those ambient 'trade marks' for they give many anglers as much pleasure as the indigenous trout themselves.

SENSE OF PLACE

Many of the waters mentioned in forthcoming chapters show historical attachments to various past pioneers of angling. Admittedly to anglers only concerned with today's catches, what

happened in the past may appear to have little or no direct bearing on their angling. Does it really matter that you might be following in the footsteps of the likes of Stewart or Bridgett, Lamond or McDonald Robertson? To those who think in terms purely of their current catch rates it may not, but their trout fishing will be the poorer for it. Tales of pioneering wild trout fishing from eras when tarmac roads were hardly invented and reaching the Northern Highlands took several days, have motivated many of us. Such exciting, slightly eccentric sources of inspiration are seldom found in the clinical dissertations on tackle and techniques so often written in the modern angling press. It may be sentimental but I like to feel a sense of place when I am fishing, it is part of the whole experience and sometimes interesting comparisons emerge on the apparent success or decline of a water.

Fellow trout enthusiast Geoffrey Bucknall put it beautifully as we fished together in the Highlands. He said:

> 'I want the fishing space my Grandad enjoyed, the challenge he faced of deceiving a wild thing which God put in a distant loch. I don't want to beat the lonely stranger I meet, we learn from each other.'

Hear! hear! Geoffrey.

GOOD TROUT MANAGEMENT PRACTICES

Good managerial practices for wild trout are sometimes hard to quantify in real terms. Left alone in an unpolluted, relatively fertile, well oxygenated water with access to clean gravel for spawning, brown/sea trout do very well with the minimum of interference from us. Some of the best 'wild' fishings in Scotland show only the barest of intervention from man,

Angling demand can be intense near main centres of population.

indeed many are mentioned in this book. Management may entail little more than a general monitoring of the trout's progress by catch returns and surveys of the spawning redds. Unfortunately, any apparently successful 'laissez-faire' philosophy gives the disinterested riparian owner (or the fishery manager only concerned with more profitable game fish like salmon), the ideal excuse for not doing anything to sustainably manage his trout stocks. Though Scotland's *Salmo trutta* are generally hardy resolute fish and many populations do well despite occasional lack of interest, it is as well you are aware that, sadly, the attitude which dismisses brownies as vermin still exists in some game fishing regions of Scotland.

Equally, where there is intense demand for angling near the main centres of population, a management policy for trout waters is essential if they are not to become fished out. A good example of sympathetic management of very busy local lochs/reservoirs is that of East of Scotland

Water and further aspects of their successful policies can be seen in Chapter 25 on Loch Talla. On rivers, one need look no further than the River Tweed which has a superb holistic management policy for ALL fish in its catchment area including browns, sea trout, grayling and salmon. (See Chapter 13 The River Tweed.)

Getting the balance right in wild trout management is, however, never an easy task. Sometimes over zealous fishery owners, lessees or angling clubs acting with the best intentions, make ill-thought out decisions to alter the resident fish populations in their waters. Often this involves restocking with non-indigenous species and if the managers are not careful the original character of their water is lost forever. Keen to meet public demand and make their fishery a success they restock to the point of saturation, adding either large farmed browns or worse still mixing rainbow trout amongst the wild fish. If the water is large sometimes the wild stock cope reasonably well with the new additions but often, particularly in small waters, they become stressed by new fish suddenly appearing in their territory. If introduced browns go on to breed with the indigenous trout, important genetic traits which help them survive in that particular water are diluted and in some cases lost forever.

I firmly believe that prudent scientific advice is needed in getting restocking right for in some cases it is not needed at all. Where possible, restocking should be done from locally grown stock, preferably from stripped fish from an 'in situ' hatchery. Using 'local' stock derived from native fish allows the genetic imprints in the fish to continue. Fry additions must be done judiciously according to what the water needs, sometimes electrofishing surveys reveal large numbers of local fry already present (see Chapter 13 The River Tweed). Today it is increasingly recognised that continually throwing more fish into a water does not necessarily mean there will

be more fish for anglers to catch. Indeed, too many trout in small waters actually causes more problems than it solves in terms of competition for a finite food source. Equally, restocking larger lochs or rivers can be a risky business either turning them partially into 'put and takes' or they become a complete waste of resources. A Highland colleague once said to me, 'You would be better standing up in the boat and tipping tenners straight into the loch rather than introducing non-native trout!'

Getting any stock supplements right is definitely a task for the dedicated, far-seeing fishery manager. If in any doubt seek independent advice before restocking and I do mean 'independent' as a number of today's fisheries consultants are also associated with large trout farms and it is naturally in their business interests to recommend restocking as a first option. Happily, restocking is not now seen in quite the light it was in Victorian times when it was classed as the panacea for all ills, but quick fix hangovers do remain.

Singular trout waters show a special degree of care and fundamental to this will

Any restocking should be undertaken with great caution.

be a comprehensive understanding of the indigenous fish populations. In some cases practical managerial intervention is essential, for example in the restoration of natural spawning habitat, the improvement of flow in rivers, the removal of an overgrowth of weed and so on. However, any of these managerial tasks should be undertaken with caution after careful assessment. It is easy to rush headlong into it when expectant anglers declare there are 'no fish left in the loch/river'. Seek advice from a scientific source such as a fisheries biologist if you can, if not at least make a preliminary survey of spawning burn habitat yourself, looking at quality of gravel, speed of flow, any habitat threats like overgrazing, fry numbers and so on.

The angler himself can ask a few astute questions of the permit provider/fishery manager as there is much to be read between the lines. Enquire about the success of natural spawning, just where the wild trout spawn and what mix of fish

Special wild trout waters consistently provide top quality angling.

sizes (from parr to leviathan) are normally present in the water. Ask what the natural feeding is and what methods the trout respond best to, i.e. nymph, upstream dry or traditional wet. Have there been any past additions to stock as many trout lochs had considerable additions of Leven trout placed in them in the 1900s? Also enquire generally about access to the water, the number of day tickets issued, any hazards in or around the water and so on. Good managers will answer these questions without hesitation but if you are met with indifference or blank looks then the care of the wild trout you are about to fish for may well be lacking.

Questions can only go so far however and a little local knowledge if you can obtain it (some locals play their angling cards limpet-like to their chests!) goes a long way in balancing the perspective. Also, conduct investigations on your own, for everything is rarely as it seems with wild trout!

★

Special wild trout waters will therefore consistently provide top quality trout fishing in ambient surroundings. Generations of anglers will have found the fishing to be stimulating and challenging and the care of the wild trout and his environment continues in a practical vein as necessary on these waters. Above all, that special loch or river provides a demanding but pleasurable experience every time you visit it . . .

Chapter 2

Facets of Angling on Scotland's Lochs and Rivers I

'It is a mistake for any fisherman to allow himself to be influenced consciously or otherwise to prefer rivers to lochs.'

W.A. Adamson

ECOLOGICAL & SOCIAL FACTORS AFFECTING SCOTTISH TROUT ANGLING

Scotland is an extraordinary country of mixed landscapes and there is no doubt that the drama of our rugged mountains and green glens is greatly enriched by the myriad of waters which bedeck our lands. From great glacial lochs to scatters of hill tarns; from sweeping rivers to bubbling burns we have freshwater in huge abundance and the trout fisherman is well served on all fronts. Despite the fabulous choice however, many anglers are content to specialise in their fishing, either on rivers or lochs. They will fish a few local waters regularly and perhaps only branch out from familiar territory while on holiday. Of course there is little wrong with this type of angling, often born more out of logistic necessity rather than choice, and

Drama in the hills.

many 'local experts' are made from constantly fishing their home territory in all its moods. However if opportunities arise, the more adventurous amongst us try to strike a balance between familiar and different places, trying out new techniques and novel tackle. Diversification keeps interest high, and the depth of our angling knowledge is pleasurably widened.

There will always be stimulating and thought-provoking dilemmas occurring when the angler moves from fast flowing to still water or vice versa. Various technical differences suddenly appear and these can tax even the most expert trout fisher. Though your experiences in trout fishing may be long and hard won, there is always that short but difficult transition period when you switch between 'loch mode' and 'river mode'. Too many river anglers are prone to freeze when confronted by the vastness of a loch and equally, many loch fishers fail to adjust quickly to the smaller, more enclosed river habitat. I remain convinced that those who claim to move seamlessly from one style to another are either anglers from another world or they are simply not telling the whole story!

As I heartily recommend trying as much of Scottish wild trout fishing as possible, variety being the spice of angling life, there follows some advice based on practical and often hard won experience of the important ecological aspects and skill factors involved in flowing and still water angling.

ECOLOGICAL FACTORS

The trout of loch and river

Essentially there is no physical difference between a loch trout and one that has spent all his days in a river. Nor is there anatomically much difference between a trout which has chosen to go to sea and one which resides in fresh water other than an adaption of metabolism and skin

tone when moving from one medium to the other. The basic anatomy of 'wild' trout will largely be the same no matter what their environment. Historically though the odds are still stacked against this scientific fact. Anglers have been brought up to believe there are great divides between loch and river trout and their diverse habitats. This false belief is further built upon by the current laws covering migratory fish, i.e. sea trout and salmon, and non-migratory brown trout. The law still unnecessarily separates the two (see also the legal section of this chapter).

Actually, our quarry *Salmo trutta*, behaves in many similar ways no matter what his habitat. For example, look at the trout 'pecking order' that you see in streams where the bigger more aggressive trout keep a tight guard on the best feeding territories – it is virtually the same in lochs where the larger trout nearly always dominate the better feeding areas. Trout in both rivers and lochs tend to move into the

Diversification keeps the interest high.

margins to feed in the safer dimming evening light. It's interesting too that trout wherever they dwell will occasionally move into shallows to rest as much as to feed. I have witnessed hefty fish lying up in the loch shallows of an evening, wallowing in the warmer water only inches deep and showing no interest in flies whatsoever. It was just as if they were indeed enjoying a well earned rest and when I walked past they simply swam slowly away, dark shadows in the gloaming. Equally, river trout may also move into shallows appearing to rest in late evening. You could further argue that the river trout swim or hold station facing upstream into the current whilst loch trout do not, yet a loch/lake trout nearly always swims into the wind for maximum oxygen over the gills, the wind being the loch trout's equivalent of a current.

Consider too the principal needs of all wild trout, needs which govern their behaviour no matter what their environment. These are food, shelter from predators, a safe stress-free life and a place to spawn. These fishy requirements are virtually unchanging whether the trout inhabits a freshwater river, a loch or a brackish estuary. Unfortunately our angling fore-bears did not subscribe to scientific fact and a considerable amount of unnecessary mystique built up around trout angling. For example, if you followed the ideals of W. C. Stewart who belittled loch fishing as inferior, you might argue that loch trout are invariably reckless, opportunistic feeders whereas the 'educated' river trout is always a far more selective beast. Not true I'm afraid. No trout are 'educated', they simply follow instincts, sometimes genetic, which urge certain behaviour in certain waters at certain times of year.

Remember too that most trout will like to lie where they expend the least amount of energy for the maximum amount of food. They are opportunistic feeders in the broadest sense. If the prospective food

Trout are opportunistic feeders.

source looks and moves vaguely like something edible, is the right size for them to get their jaws round and does not frighten them, then they are likely to have a go at it. Apart from the broad dietary spectrum of insects, nymphs, larvae, crustacea, eels and other smaller fish, the trout of loch and river will feed (or attempt to feed) on most likely items passing their way. More unusual finds in wild trout's stomachs include partly digested frogs, bits of twig, cigarette butts, water voles, fish farm pellets (often in huge number) and rice pudding. And before you assume the last item was found in a loch trout, the rice pudding was retrieved from a river trout's gut. It seems a local hotel had been careless in its disposal of food scraps and the trout had enjoyed a bounty of starch in the nearby burn.

Occasionally *Salmo trutta*, whatever their locale, go through spells of random unpredictable behaviour. One minute they engage in wanton feeding, throwing all customary caution to the wind, the next they seem deadly dour and impossible to move. Such common threads of fish behaviour are usually linked to seasonal food availability, the prevailing weather conditions and a little bit of '*je ne sais quoi*'. Highs and lows in barometric pressure, changes in air temperature and the degree of light intensity on the water all exert a

River currents act as food and oxygen carriers for the trout.

powerful influence on trout behaviour, stimulating anything from dramatic action to lethargic torpor.

All trout have a 'mind your backs' attitude to life. They like to feel safe and secure away from nasty predators like bigger trout, pike, fish-eating birds, anglers and if at sea, seals. Shelter is therefore vitally important, a place to retreat from threats is essential if trout are to thrive. Competition to grab the best bolt hole and/or territory is generally intense wherever trout lurk. In lochs and rivers with a paucity of good cover and/or underwater shelter features the trout can sometimes be of lesser size, though naturally there are always exceptions to any rule.

Shelter is required in severe conditions. Thus when spates or low water conditions occur, the trout may be forced to move temporarily to different territories to attain food and shelter often some distance away from their normal haunts. It is important not to overlook these mini migrations for they help to further explain why trout are often found in certain parts of the loch or river at certain times of the year but not others.

Similarities in loch or river trout behaviour are constantly seen. Whatever their habitat, from October onward, the urge to spawn becomes all powerful. Though spawning runs may occur at different times according to location, the need to reproduce the species is compelling. Customary caution is thrown to the wind as trout journey back to the stream of their birth. Sometimes this is over many miles, sometimes only a few yards, but all trout whatever their creed feel the urge to continue their lineage.

Though some of these comparisons between our wonderful trout of loch and river may seem common sense, I would urge you to think carefully on them, especially when that river or loch 'mystique' looks like taking over!

Trout habitats

Rivers

Flowing water or the lack of it is the most obvious difference between the habitats of river or loch. In very general terms trout in rivers are more greatly influenced by the flow of the current than trout in lochs. River currents act as food and oxygen carriers and most of the trout's time is

A trout rises and then dives away, taking his food (the fly) with him.

taken up maintaining his station in the current, waiting for its food to be washed down to him either on or under the water surface. In a river, the speed of current will obviously be adjusted by the volume of water present. Heavy rain will mean faster flows and droughts will cause currents to falter, sometimes to a mere trickle. River features like bends, riffles, pots, glides and eddies, fast and slack water will alter flow and act as food collecting points while providing shelter for the indigenous trout. Unseen underwater amenities on the river bed such as rocks, boulders and weed beds are of equal importance and the trout will take full advantage of the 'best' micro habitats (see also Chapter 1). Kingsmill Moore aptly describes the best river trout habitat as being 'an ease between two streams, eddies behind or in front of stones, the tail of a run and the belt of slacker water which often intervenes between current and bank' and I cannot really improve on that.

In fast flowing streams where few aquatic plants can take root, algae growth on stones is critical for this algae provides succour to the small invertebrates the trout like to feed on. Trout in slower flowing rivers usually have something of an easier time of it especially if aquatic plants are lush and full of insect/shrimp fodder. Providing the water does not become over enriched from surrounding agricultural or phosphate build up and the competition with other coarse fish like pike, perch or ruffe is not too great, then the resident trout do well. Not many of Scotland's northern rivers can be said to be slow flowing 'canal like' streams, however southern streams like the Annan or the Tweed are very rich which encourages fast growth rates in fish.

The degree of vegetation around the river also has an significant role to play. Trout like some shade/cover from overly bright light and from predators and of course trees and scrub will also harbour many insects. Excessively overgrazed rivers, where banks are eroded and vegetation rendered to little more than silt and the odd tuft of rough grass, can lose their ability to provide natural shelter for fish. Bank erosion also causes a shallowing out of pools and thereby a further loss of habitat. Conversely, densely overgrown rivers and their feeder streams can obscure natural sunlight thereby inhibiting diverse plant and invertebrate growth with a subsequent knock-on effect on the trout population. Thus the best trout streams are usually those which provide a balanced habitat of light and shade, shallows and deeps,

Unseen influences are at work in larger lochs.

ripples and glides, bends and straights, trees and scrub with a reasonably steady flow of well oxygenated, neutral to alkaline, unpolluted water.

Lochs

The wild trout in lochs are less affected by 'flows', however, it is a mistake to assume that no currents exist in lochs as there are an intriguing variety of water movements in this habitat and these can have a profound effect on how the wild loch trout obtain their food. Take first the physical features like an island, skerray, promontory, reef, ledge, old wall, half submerged fence or inflowing stream. These will break up the uniformity of the loch surface and act like magnets to loch trout. When the wind blows, mini currents and eddies are created by these features and as the water swirls around them micro organisms are collected. Trout stations are often next to these convenient larders. Winds on lochs also create some strange effects including wind lanes, not just those prominent streaks of foamy water which run down a loch in a gale but also those unusual oily patches of warmer water which run out over the loch when the wind changes direction.

Substantial but unseen influences also exist in larger lochs in the form of water layers. In deep lochs a warmer upper layer of water (the epilimnion) sits atop a very cold deep layer (the hypolimnion). In between them is a thermocline which is a zone of rapidly cooling water. In warm still summer conditions these layers become very pronounced, a process known as stratification, whereas in the gales of winter the water is much more mixed in nature. At first glance these water layers seem to be of little relevance to the ordinary fisherman, however, anglers would do well to pay heed to these natural occurrences. For example, after a prolonged period of strong winds, the upper warm water layer is quite literally blown down onto one shoreline thereby exposing cooler water. As trout generally pick up more food in warmer water than they do in cold sterile conditions it could be that the fish with territories in the exposed hypolimnion are having a lean time of it! This fact partly explains the common fisherman's

Lochs often hold many surprises.

tale of all the trout being on the windward shore 'because that is where their food has blown'. There is some truth in this idea but remember if all the warm water has piled up on a shore which normally renders poor feeding, the few skinny residents there may be the only ones to temporarily benefit. It is simply not the case that all the trout population will race down to the windward shore, they are far too territorial for that. Even more intriguing is the fact that, after high winds, the warmer upper-surface layer of water can rock back and forward, a process known as the seiche effect. Thus parts of a loch will appear to change between cold and warmer temperatures. This might all seem a bit technical for the simple trout fisherman, but it could well explain in part the sudden bursts of fish activity in lochs during and after high winds, especially if there is no apparent hatch.

The zooplankton such as daphnia, naturally occurring in many lochs, also play an important role in determining trout movements. Daphnia constitute a vital part of the trout's diet and as these microscopic creatures are light sensitive, tend to rise and fall in the loch according to light intensity. On dull days the plankton rise up toward the surface and trout will follow them, whereas on bright days the plankton go down speedily, followed by the trout. When there are no other surface hatches occurring daphnia provide extra nourishment for trout so the angler should try and anticipate something of the movements of plankton – where daphnia go trout follow!

Unfortunately lochs, just like rivers, can have their fair share of environmental problems. Very exposed lochs also suffer from bank erosion, usually from the scouring action of wind and wave, though livestock can also play a part in destroying surrounding vegetation. Some windswept lochs lack habitat diversity particularly in the form of rooted aquatic plants while others are mineral deficient with poor availability of natural feeding. Lochs can also be affected by pollution whether it be in the form of acidic run off or by over-fertilisation. None of these effects are beneficial to the indigenous trout and therefore the best loch habitats within Scotland can be broadly described as having a good 'bio diversity'. This basically means having a good variety of plant, animal and invertebrate species present which in turn can encourage diverse natural feeding for the trout. Generally, lochs with neutral to alkaline water and a variety of environmental features, especially those which break up wave action, provide the better trout habitats. Lochans are funny things though and even acidic tarns can hold a monster or two – you have been warned!

★

THE LAW ON TROUT ANGLING IN LOCHS AND RIVERS

All trout angling in Scotland is covered by the law in one form or another and this will affect the whys and wherefores of your fishing. There are several important points to note regarding differing aspects of loch and river angling. As you will have gleaned, the laws governing migratory and non-migratory fish are slightly different and it is worthwhile reiterating some of the important points which will affect your wild trout angling.

Legalities of trout river angling

Normally in river systems there will be some form of migratory fish present, for example salmon or sea trout, and therefore your brown trout fishing will be affected by statutes which come principally under the Freshwater and Salmon fisheries Act (Scotland) 1976 and the Salmon Act 1986. From the trout anglers standpoint the most important of these regulations are:

1. It is an offence to fish for salmon (even if you are technically after trout) in inland waters without written permission of the riparian owner of the fishing rights.
2. In inland waters it is an offence to fish other than with rod and line.
3. It is an offence to fish in a fish pass.
4. It is an offence to take or destroy juvenile fish, i.e. fry or smolts or to take gravid fish or spent fish, such as kelts.
5. You can be prosecuted for fishing on a Sunday in rivers where migratory fish are likely to be present.
6. It is an offence to fish with illegal methods such as using any fish roe as a lure or using a set line, i.e. a rod which is not hand held and propped up on a rod rest.

From 'A Description of the Regulations relating to Salmon fishing in Scotland' – R. Williamson OBE. (Scottish Office 1995)

In practice bona fide trout fly fishers on the river rarely fall foul of any of these regulations but it is important that you are aware of them. Some controversy still exists about the Scottish laws governing trout angling in rivers and not without some substance. For example, it is argued by some that if you are fishing only for brown trout, why should you have to pay the price of a more expensive salmon permit? Equally, throughout Scotland there are many rivers containing excellent brown trout but you cannot get on them for love nor money as they are 'preserved' as salmon waters. It is, frankly, galling to see a river full of rising trout yet be told you cannot fish there as there are 'no trout permits available'.

I find it a touch ironic in the light of the massive collapse of salmon stocks, that the bulk of fish left in some of the over priced Scottish 'salmon' rivers are now brown trout. In the future some drastic realignment of river fishing management priorities may be required on certain watersheds if game angling is to continue in any shape or form. There also needs to be a fundamental shift of attitude in some quarters away from the outdated and

often ludicrous concept that all trout anglers are just out to fish so-called 'salmon water' for the cheaper price of a trout ticket. Riparian owners must be made to see that there are plenty of anglers who just want to fish quietly and legally for trout on dry or wet fly. We must move forward from the blinkered view that all trout anglers are out for mass slaughter of all game species. It is frankly insulting and a huge waste of river resources which could generate revenue in the months when salmon are not there in any number. All the rivers mentioned in this book have reasonable rights of access for trout anglers, but this is not universal across Scotland. You should know the full story just in case you get embroiled in some controversial discussion either on the river or in the pub afterwards!

A trout returned on Loch Ness.

Legalities of trout loch fishing

Where there are no migratory fish present on a freshwater loch the following edicts from the civil law of trespass apply:

1. No one has any right to trespass upon the lands of another for the purpose of fishing.
2. No one even if he is lawfully on the bank of a river or loch under right of access, has the right to fish in the river or loch.
3. Members of the public, having neither title nor right, cannot establish a right of fishing by any usage of fishing for however long a period, as against a proprietor having title over which the stream flows.
4. It is an offence (under the Salmon Act) to fish for trout with a set line akin to coarse fishing method where the rod is not hand held.

Extracts from 'The Law of Game, Salmon and Freshwater Fishing in Scotland' – Scott Robinson QC – Butterworth 1990.

To put the first three statements in plain English, the rights to fish for brown trout in lochs rest solely with the riparian owners. Assertions like, 'you can fish here for trout for free' or 'trout fishing is a public right' are false and misleading. Technically the riparian owners are the only ones who can grant permission to fish for wild trout but in practice they often lease out their trout loch to local angling clubs or similar who then do the administration of permits. Fortunately permits for trout loch fishing in Scotland are normally very reasonably priced and if the water is adequately managed and stocks monitored, no one should balk at paying a modest fee to fish for loch trout.

Item No. 4 is very important as several 'fishmongers' have been successfully prosecuted for using multiple set line rods on highland lochs and given a hefty fine. This type of dubious fishing, especially with bait, is very damaging to wild stocks as it is cruelly indiscriminate. The trout normally physically swallow the bait hook and have to be killed no matter what their size. Despite strenuous efforts by the more caring riparian owners, angling clubs and fishery representatives, this type of fishing unfortunately still goes on. If you see multiple set line fishing being undertaken at a fly only loch, it is best not to take matters into your own hands but report it to the fishery managers and/or the police. Sadly many of the 'six rods along the bank' brigade operate in gangs and you might be physically assaulted if you alone try to discourage their antics. Whatever happened to the 'Gentle Art of Fishing' one wonders?

Loch and river trout fishing in areas governed by Protection Orders

In a clumsy attempt to bring together statutory and civil legislation governing wild fish 'Protection Orders' (POs) were introduced into Scotland in 1976. A PO covers a defined catchment area often encompassing a number of lochs and rivers. It is designed to protect the riparian owner's rights of fishing by making it illegal for anyone to fish in the designated area without a permit. In return for this additional legal protection, the riparian owner must increase public access to his waters

and is supposed to take steps to conserve the indigenous fish stocks. Areas already covered by POs in Scotland include Loch Arkaig, Loch Morar, Loch Earn catchment area, Tummel and Garry watershed, River Tay catchment area, River Clyde catchment, River Don, Scourie and Rhiconich area, River Tweed and the Loch Awe catchment.

For trout anglers the principal points to note on fishing in a Protected area are:

1. You must obtain a permit prior to fishing as you render yourself liable to prosecution without one.
2. Using methods not prescribed on the permit is an offence liable to prosecution.
3. All the previously mentioned laws on river/loch trout angling are legally enforceable and can carry a significant penalty.

There is no doubt Protection Orders have had a beneficial effect on reducing illegal fishing, however, they remain a somewhat

Choose your weapons.

inept not to say controversial piece of legislation. There seems to be little legal impetus on the riparian owner to allow increased access on his waters. It is of course in his interests to do so, however he is not legally bound to work to conserve the indigenous fish stocks. In large catchment areas not all riparian owners deem it necessary to follow the spirit of the local PO, they simply use the additional legislation to benefit their existing trout stocks and give little or nothing in return. In 1998 Lord Sewel the then environment minister for Scotland took steps to rescind the River Tay PO on the grounds that the riparian owners were ignoring the parameters of the Order. In doing so he did not offer any better conservation process in its place – a quite extraordinary move in the light of severe wild stock depletion! However after some discussion about access for grayling angling that situation was resolved and it now looks as if the Tay PO will stay. (See also Chapter 11 The River

Tay.) Also in 1998 a largely independent review body was set up to report into the working of POs and made various recommendations on how they can be improved. One important point in the review was the emphasis on the need for holistic care of a watershed (see Chapter 32 Scotland's Trout Scene).

You can see even from this potted review of the current legislation covering wild trout that there is significant room for streamlining and improvement, particularly in better conserving the species in the long term. At the moment Protection Orders are the only means of cutting down over-exploitation of all wild fish species of which trout are a part. How much simpler it would have been in the first place, to bring brown trout into the legislation governing salmon and sea trout. And can someone please tell me, if sea trout and browns are exactly the same species, just why does the law not recognise that?

Chapter 3

Facets of Angling II

'A good fisherman is one who has learned to control his actions to a rising fish.'

Colonel Oatts

SKILL FACTORS

Following on from the ecological factors affecting our trout angling let us look at the skill factors involved. This chapter gives you a Glossary of essential tactics for trout on loch and river, general tackle requirements and various fly tying skills for loch or river.

Tactics

There is considerable detail given on a variety of specific river and loch techniques in the forthcoming chapters. However, to whet your appetite there follows a few general rules of thumb.

Lochs
- Traditional 'loch style' fishing is carried out from the boat or the shore normally using floating line and a team of wet flies (normally 2–4

flies in size 10 or 12). Adaptable fishers vary flies according to the conditions, switching to dry fly or teams of wets or nymphs as the trout demand.
- Those using teams of flies normally employ a longer rod of 10 to 12ft, with this they can work the top dropper successfully on floating line. Shorter rods and a single fly can be used to give a more delicate presentation particularly in calm weather.
- Floating lines are the essence of traditional loch style, intermediates are lesser used and sinking lines relatively infrequently. For depth, some local experts lengthen the nylon and slow the retrieve to make flies swim deeper whilst still working with a floating line.
- Wild loch trout fishing is normally conducted with 3–5lb nylon. In bright conditions with light winds rub the leader with mud or Fuller's Earth to avoid glitter.
- Space the droppers around 6ft apart so they look unrelated – I use a long leader and only one or two flies, sometimes a dry bushy fly on the surface and a sunk wet on the point, others prefer the traditional three fly cast.
- Though 'loch style' normally calls for wet flies, be versatile in your loch fishing. React according to how the fish are behaving. If trout are visibly moving on the surface use a single dry fly or a dry fly on the top dropper and wet underneath. If the loch looks inert try 'graduated' wet flies with a heavier pattern on the tail, e.g. a weighted nymph, an imitative pattern midway and a lightweight bushy dropper nearer the surface.

Altnaharra sea trout on the wet fly.

- Retrieves for traditional 'loch style' flies are normally medium to brisk paced so that the wet flies are drawn sub surface over the noses of trout quickly to stimulate aggression. Different paced retrieves, e.g. very slow for nymph or fast for Muddlers, are also used. Single dry flies require static, twitched or very slow retrieves – always retrieve suitable to your fly choice.
- Preliminary fly choice on an unfamiliar water should incorporate a black or black and red pattern, the two colours most effective in wild trout loch fishing.
- When the trout are being dour change your flies every 15 minutes or so, a new fly can bring new confidence to you and a new perspective for the trout.
- Dapping with long rod, floss line and large bushy pattern is sometimes used on lochs when there is a good wind blowing. Kingsmill Moore describes dapping as having its place, 'as a means whereby absolute novices can catch large trout, but it is, next to trolling, the dullest and least skilful of all methods.' I'm rather afraid I agree with him!
- Trolling can also sometimes catch large dour trout but ditto Kingsmill's comment above!
- Do not waste precious angling time over dead water. Always start your fishing over obvious trout holding areas first, e.g. from shallow to deep, off promontories, ledges, weed beds, skerries etc.
- When bank fishing and/or wading, fish down the bank as fast as you would drift in the boat.
- For best results from the bank fish your flies across wind and wave rather than with the wind directly behind. You show the trout more of the outline of the fly this way.
- In the boat or off the bank use bigger flies (8–12) in big winds, smaller (12–16) in light winds. Old wives' tales such as 'dark water/dark fly' and the converse also sometimes work.
- If you enjoy fly dressing remember loch patterns are in general more heavily dressed than river patterns but there are some flies which are equally useful in either environment.
- Classic patterns to tie for lochs include the Invicta series, Zulus and Soldier Palmer. Learn

these old 'fail safes' first as many modern day variants are derived from them. Others to tie include the Bumble series, particularly the Golden Olive Bumble plus the Bibio, Pennel, Kate McLaren, Wickham's, Greenwell's, Grouse and Claret and so on ad infinitum!

Rivers

- Traditionally river trouting in Scotland has leaned heavily toward the wet fly 'across and down' technique. However, there are times when upstream dry, wet or nymph fishing is equally successful. Auspicious river fishers do what the conditions and the fish dictate on the day.
- Rods for river trouting should obviously match the river height and the day's conditions. Anything from 8ft (low water summer conditions) to 10/11ft (high water early and late season conditions) is normally adequate.
- Floating lines are normally used but for depth, intermediate, sink tip or sinking line can be employed especially early in the season. Match the line density to where you think the trout are principally feeding. Note that sinking lines need different and sometimes quite arduous techniques in casting, you must 'roll' all that sunk line up on to the surface before lifting off and aerialising the line.
- Always start your river angling with a good recce first. Taking time to assess likely trout holding stations like little inflowing burns, weed beds, channels, riffles, edges of boulders and pots or backwaters pays dividends.

Young Shetland angler prepares for the loch.

Heads together on the River Clyde.

- If employing upstream tactics, fish the near bank first and then fan your casts out across. Starting with the far bank first only means you line any trout which are lying closer in.
- The ability to control the line retrieve is undoubtedly the key to successful upstream dry fly fishing. The angler must keep in constant contact with the fly and has to bring back line according to the speed of the current.
- For wet fly 'across and down' river angling, teams of flies can be used (usually not more than three flies). As with loch trouting space the droppers well apart so that they look unrelated. Often a weighted nymph on the point helps to control line speed and gets the flies down quicker.
- When wet fly/across and down fishing, the retrieve of the fly is kept to a minimum and the flies allowed to travel naturally down with the current. The exception to this is when sea trout are known to be present. Catching the tidal silver trout with a medium to brisk retrieve is often much more effective (see Chapter 6 on River Conon).
- Control of line is critical when wet fly angling and you may need to extend your forearm to 'follow' the line as it travels down and around

boulders and weed. Trout are often missed with too much slack so keep contact with your flies at all times (see Chapter 7 on River Don).
- Preliminary fly choice for unfamiliar rivers where there is no local guidance available should incorporate something along the lines of Olive patterns, Partridge and Orange, Black Gnats, Hare's Ears and March Browns. Use wet/nymph forms when no fish are visible, change to dry during surface activity.
- Most upstream fishers whether dry or nymph, employ only one fly or two, so as not to spook the trout.
- When 'downstream' fishing cover each section of water carefully before moving down with two or three steps.
- When upstream dry fly fishing try to place the fly delicately ahead of the rising fish and let it drift down. Some anglers cast slightly to the side of the trout to avoid spooking it with line.
- In fast streamy water a larger fly can sometimes be used, conversely in slower flows smaller more subtle flies are often in order but generally speaking river flies are smaller, say 12–22, whereas loch patterns fall into the 8 to 14 range.
- On unfamiliar waters choosing a fly with similar tones to the trout's immediate environment, i.e. the coloration of the river bed, will usually provide a good starting point. For example trout

lying over reddish brown stones often seem to favour reddish brown flies.

- For fly tyers classic river patterns to tie include the Snipe and Purple, Ginger Quill, Partridge and Orange, Hare's Ear nymph, Black Spider, March Brown, Black Gnat, Pheasant Tail Nymph, Dry Greenwell and Dry Wickham. Flies like the Adams, Deer Hair/Elk Hair Olives, Rough Olive, Stimulator, Red Tag and Red Sedge are also popular and are interchangeable between loch and river. Note: certain rivers can demand specific patterns in particular sizes (see Clyde Chapter 5 and Tummel Chapter 12).

A word on tackle for wild trout

Tackle makers make great distinctions between reservoir/loch tackle and the equipment needed for the river. Though undoubtedly some distinction needs to be made, do bear in mind this is a useful ploy in selling more equipment!

In general terms I recommend versatile equipment, especially rods which can fulfil

a number of roles. The 10ft carbon fibre rod I use on the lochs with WF floating line works just as well on a river when the conditions dictate a bit of power and distance is necessary. Equally, when finesse and fine art fishing are called for to delicately present tiny dry flies, I will not hesitate in using a much shorter rod of 8ft 6in and lighter line on either the shore of a very calm loch or on a small meandering river.

Whilst the environment where you are trout fishing does play an important part in your choice of tackle, the prevailing conditions dictate an awful lot more. Fish with the weather rather than at odds with it. Light delicate wind and wave need a lighter touch and vice versa. If you present your fly to a trout in a lifelike way so that it looks reasonably natural and does not scare him, then you are in with a chance. Trout are not super intelligent creatures but they are creatures of a strong inherited instinct for self preservation. If you are using a proverbial sledgehammer of a rod to crack a small fishy nut then believe me, the trout will be aware of you! Similarly, if you approach a big water on a wild day using naught but an 8ft wand and No. 4 line and a single size 22 dry, you are going to find it very hard going against a gale intent on blowing you over to Norway. Let common sense prevail and the weather conditions dictate your equipment choice as much as the venue itself, and you should not go far wrong.

Tying flies for loch and river

These days more and more trout anglers are wanting to make their own patterns and it is worthwhile highlighting some of the distinctions in fly design for loch or river.

Nowadays many anglers like to design their own flies.

River trout flies

Traditionally, river patterns have always been much sparser dressed than loch flies and generally fall into a more exact imitative category. Tyings are usually softer and less garish with grey, brown, black, dull orange, olive and yellow being the predominant colours. River trout flies are also tied in smaller sizes from 12 down to 22 and are designed principally to stimulate a feeding response rather than one of aggression. It follows therefore that when constructing a dry or wet fly for the river you should be thinking light and lifelike rather than anything too thick and clumsy. Weighted nymphs are the only exception to this rule but even here you have to make them natural-looking and fish them in a lifelike way to get a good response.

There is a long history of thinly dressed river patterns stretching back to W. C. Stewart (mid-1800s) and many of these are still in use today. 'Spiders' and some 'Clyde style' patterns are classic examples of river patterns which have stood the test

of time. Interestingly there appears to have been less of a steady development in the design of patterns for the Scottish river and today you fish with trout flies either over a century or less than a decade old! This is possibly because river trout fishing has never been easily accessible, especially on prime salmon beats, and therefore centres where trout river fly tying skills could be developed were much less common than in loch fishing. With only a few rivers on which wild trout expertise could be developed, our accepted national river patterns took on the overall mantle of 'Tweed flies', 'Tummel dressings' or flies tied in the 'Clyde style' no matter where they were used across the country. Thus at one time if you fished for trout on say the River Thurso you were almost expected to use flies originally constructed for the Tweed! Of course there are 'universal' river flies, the Snipe and Purple or the Partridge and Orange being two, but it so much nicer to have to hand local flies developed for specific regions. Unfortunately it seems that for the wild river trout across Scotland this has been a long time coming but we are slowly getting there.

When choosing river flies, it is interesting to look at what that doyen of Irish trout angling, Kingsmill Moore has to say. Kingsmill emphasised movement in the water as the essential prerequisite for good river fly tying. Making pretty patterns however realistic must never supersede how they actually behave/swim in the water. Trout first and foremost recognise their prey by the way it MOVES underwater (see also 'Loch trout flies' below). As an aside to this he also describes the old Border/Lowland dressings with single upright wing and short hackle as being flies which move with a bobbing motion when submerged in the river current more like a shrimp than any natural insect. This is an unusual theory and rather flies in the face of all the modern carefully constructed

Traditional loch patterns, as popular today as they were when first created.

of the many American designs. Our USA angling cousins are much more river trout orientated than us and have produced some cracking Elk Hair designs. Flies like the 'Stimulator' have now found a deserved place in many of our fly boxes so today there is overall a growing repertoire of river trout patterns.

Loch trout flies

Unlike river patterns, designs for traditional Scottish loch flies have been constantly evolving since the first Zulu or Soldier Palmer rolled off the vice. In general loch flies are tied in bigger sizes ranging from 8 to 14 with 10s and 12s normally the most commonly used. They run the whole gamut of design from beautifully imitative to broadly general representations of insects with some very 'other worldly' patterns thrown in for good measure. Loch fishing has always been relatively easy to access and therefore numerous centres of excellence exist across the country and many different fly tying skills have emerged.

Loch dressings tend to be much more bushy and colours of flies cover the whole spectrum. The colours black, red, brown and silver used to predominate in loch patterns but nowadays there are all sorts of shades used from hot orange to bright magenta. In general they are designed to attract the trout's attention and/or stimulate aggression but do remember they still have to do this in a 'user friendly' non-threatening way. Flies which have gone overboard with the dressing move awkwardly in the water. Overdressed, unwieldy patterns are more likely to frighten the fish rather than attract them so be lifelike in your tyings and if in doubt about a pattern do what I do and look at its properties in the aquarium first. By popping your new creation on the water surface of a fish tank and looking at it from below you will see a rough outline of what the trout initially sees. The results of this

'shrimp' patterns we see today, still debate is what fly tying is all about.

Today there is a growing band of very skilled river trout anglers and to their credit they have designed newer and often better patterns, still in the traditional mould but in my opinion, much more flexible. The 'modern' Scottish flies of Robert Sharp or Paul Buchanan (mentioned in the Chapters on the Clyde and the Tay respectively) are exceptionally versatile patterns combining old concepts with some more practical materials. Versatility is the key to these fly tyers' work and I have used a range of their tyings both on rivers and lochs and found them just as effective whatever the venue. Alternatively you can try out some

Typical loch selection.

will often surprise you as dry flies are but pin prick points on the surface while wet flies create more of a large shadow. If you are trying out a wet pattern you should then sink it on some nylon and tweak it through the water in short bursts. The first time you do this you often see traces of air bubbles from the hackles of the fly, however the more soaked the fly becomes the more the hackles simply pulse in the water. If the hackles of your creation are poorly tied or too stiff, the fly does not take on a life-like appearance and will simply frighten the trout.

On the modern fly tying scene numerous 'variants' of original patterns now exist. Sometimes these work to enhance the original pattern quite considerably, however on occasion the new variant seems to lose sight of the original concept altogether. I often think that if God had wanted the Soldier Palmer to be dressed up in fluorescent pants with twinkle around its neck he would have made it that way in the first place! Use variants sparingly and keep to the original theme as much as possible. If you need examples of exceptionally good tyings for lochs follow the styles of Kingsmill Moore who was way ahead of his time regarding theories of how trout perceive our artificial flies. His ideas on how flies trap light and air are just as applicable today as they were in 1960 when he first developed them. A more modern 'great' in loch fly tying is Stan Headley of Orkney. Stan's flies rate amongst the finest I have ever seen for loch work, he too seems to have gained inspiration from Kingsmill. As an aside to this I have been lucky enough to fish quite regularly with his father Ed Headley and I am indebted to him for ably conveying a considerable amount of information on trout in general and about Orkney fishings in particular (see also Chapter 29 on The Orkney Isles).

Whether you design flies for river or loch do bear in mind the first principles of trout fly tying. One, it should not appear a threat to the fish and two, it should move in or on the water in an exciting lifelike way. Now go and experiment!

Part Two

THE WILD TROUT RIVERS

There are 10 top quality Scottish trout rivers listed and though some of these contain other fish like salmon or grayling I have concentrated purely on aspects of their brown and/or sea trout fishing. Except for the chapters devoted to the Conon and Blackwater, River and Loch Ken and River and Loch Ness, each stream has an entire chapter given over to its charms . . . Enjoy.

Feeder stream, Northern Highlands.

River Ness.

Chapter 4

The River Annan

'Time spent in such surroundings is necessarily enjoyable, and the memory of it will be happy.'

R. C. Bridgett

OS Map Nos. – 85 and 78.

Nearest town/villages: – Annan, Lockerbie, Ecclefechan, Johnstonebridge, Moffat.

Accessibility of fishing: – Good. Permits are available from local estates, hotels, the Annan and District Angling Club and the upper stretches are accessed through the Upper Annandale Angling Association. The Hoddom Estate beat has day tickets available for visiting anglers. The local tourist board provides a very helpful comprehensive guide to 'Fishing in Dumfries and Galloway' with contact details and telephone numbers.

Best times: – For the resident browns, April, May and June are usually considered the better months. The sea trout are generally caught in numbers from June onwards.

General: – The Annan is a very picturesque border river, perhaps more famous for its sea trout than its browns, yet it holds good stocks of both. Ten-foot rods with matching floating and/or intermediate lines normally suffice. At a pinch, sea trout flies and tackle will catch browns and vice versa but local favourites are listed. As it flows over rich farming country this river can become muddied in a heavy spate, however most of the time it runs clear and provides superb trout habitat. Wading is often necessary (chest or thigh waders) and a wading stick and light flotation jacket are recommended for safety. Day tickets for trout/sea trout on some of the beats will sometimes include salmon fishing, but in most cases prices are very reasonable considering the quality of fish on offer.

★

Anglers visiting the Scottish Borders for the first time might be tempted to pass by the *River Annan* in favour of the universally known charms of its bigger neighbours like the Tweed, Clyde or Nith. This would be a great mistake however, for the grand gentle pools and sparkling runs of the Annan and its smaller tributaries like Moffat Water and the River Milk (so named because of its tendency to go cloudy in spates) contain a delightful range of game fish. Salmon and sea trout frequent the bigger pools of the main system while brown trout and grayling are found along most of the Annan. At one time this river had a coarse fish, the chub, introduced into it and these occasionally proved a talking point amongst anglers who thought they had hooked the game fish of a lifetime! Today however it is thought that few of these weighty golden specimens still exist as it is understood they have been actively removed to a new home elsewhere.

To reach the Annan from Glasgow takes little more than an hour or so along the busy M74 yet once you leave the throb of traffic, you enter a tranquil green world far removed from the busy highway. The main stem of the river flows through rich agricultural lands with neat hedgerows, mature deciduous trees and gentle rolling hills. It's a real pleasure to fish in this beautiful border land where idyllic landscapes soften ragged edges and soothe the soul. The Annan has clear water, except in spate, and is of a neutral to slightly alkaline nature, running over a river base of rock, clay and gravel for most of its 30 miles or so. As with many lowland rivers there is a delightful mix of deep pools, fast runs, slow bends, riffles and glides with the emphasis on meandering gently through agriculture rather than crashing down a high hillside.

The brown trout here, which average about 12oz to 1lb, are exceptionally pretty little fish with a richly speckled golden hue. Amongst the 'little uns', some cracking big trout of 3lb plus also lurk so be prepared, especially in the deeper slower pools. Annan sea trout range from the smaller bar of silver to the larger slightly darker 'greyback' coming in at 4–5lb. Though it is understood some stock additions have been made in parts of the lower river, all the trout generally retain that essential wild character with good natural spawning tributaries in the Kinnel and Moffat Water. There's a goodly length of fishing as trout can technically be caught all along the river right from below its source near the unusual Devil's Beef Tub (a startlingly deep, almost circular natural valley) above Moffat, to its exit into the Solway Firth at Newbie near the town of Annan.

With such charming pastoral landscapes surrounding it, it is little wonder the natural feeding is very good and, with plenty of river weed growth, a broad spectrum of invertebrate life is found. Caddis and hatched sedge, March Browns, Yellow Sallies, stoneflies and a wide range of olives large and small are present along with (I am told) the possible occasional appearance of mayfly. I mention mayfly with caution, for anglers on some border rivers had in the past a habit of calling any large winged insect a 'mayfly' (the Americans do the same!) when in fact they were simply large stoneflies or big olives. As I have not personally seen Annan mayfly I reserve judgement though I did note the clay-like deposits here are very similar to the marl deposits of Caithness from which many mayfly nymphs do indeed emerge.

For daytime fishing for brown trout, the best times are generally earlier in the season (April and May) while dusk or early morn are preferred in the summer months. A very general rule of thumb for the trout fisher would be to angle the early half of the season in the upper Annandale section around Johnstonebridge and then, once the hefty spates have subsided, move more into the mid and lower sections (normally by mid May). Tactics for the browns are traditional in the sense it is either upstream dry or across and down wet. Those who fish the Annan frequently tend to favour more dry than wet fly and certainly the bigger trout in the 1lb plus range tend to succumb more to this method. The dry flies in common use here tend to be small (12–16) and range from the delicate traditional Olive and Greenwell's varieties to the more robust modern tyings like the American designed 'Stimulator' a great general 'sedgey' pattern, or the small CDC Midge recommended by Scottish Internationalist Paul Buchanan (see also River Tay).

On my last visit to the Annan at the popular Hoddom Estate beat near Ecclefechan, I met up with river bailiff Dick Graham and local angler John Lyon. John showed me some unusual exquisitely dressed flies which he uses frequently during a good surface hatch. The first of these was the Parachute Olive also known locally as Clark's Special, and the second a Red Spinner originally tied by the late Mr Beech of Peebles (both sizes 14–18). Looking at these flies with their delightfully simple yet subtle design they looked so much more natural than the heavily dressed loch style patterns contained in

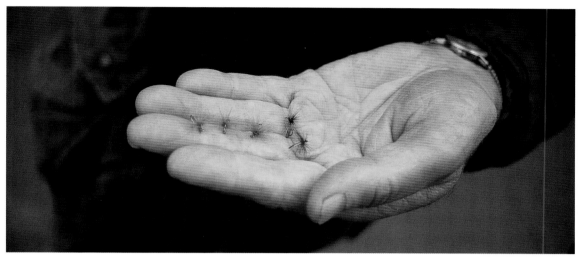

Simple but subtle – dry flies for the Annan.

my box. Indeed, you could see clearly how the old tradition of river anglers scoffing at the comparatively heavyweight flies and tactics of the loch fisher came about. What the old detractors rarely acknowledged in the past however, was the inter-change-ability of some patterns and skills for each type of fishing. Happily that blinkered view is slowly changing but it has taken an inordinate amount of time!

John Lyon finds natural imitations the most versatile for upstream floating line work, particularly the simple Parachute Olive which has versatile shades of spent spinners drifting down on the current. While the dry flies are fished in the tradi-tional way, John did tell me that the fly he casts tends to be more 'square' rather than directly upstream. Certainly this method tends to lead to more reliable hooking of the lightning fast Annan trout. The method of fishing upstream dry on the Annan at an 'angle' rather than standing directly below the fish and casting up, is mentioned in renowned Clyde angler Robert Sharp's book *Let's Fish Again.* Sharp enjoyed many excursions to the Annan, so it may be something of an established tactic for these challenging waters. If utilising across and down wet fly

fishing, a range of patterns can be fished on floating, intermediate or sink tip and Partridge and Orange or Snipe and Purple (size 12–16) are perennial favourites here as are Cinnamon and Gold or any of the wet versions of March Browns.

If you are intent on chasing the sea trout, these migratory fish arrive in the system in some numbers from late May on with a peak of fishing normally occurring in July. There are prime sea trout beats all along the system but Hoddom down through Lockerbie and towards the town of Annan are probably the most fished-for migratory trout. The Hoddom beat, which river bailiff Dick Graham has fished for most of his lifetime, contains some exceptionally good sea trout as well as browns and Dick advised me that these tend to demand night time 'gloaming' fishing with flies fished across and down in the traditional way. The Brown Turkey is a top fly for Annan sea trout but traditional patterns like Teal Blue and Silver, Mallard and Silver (with blue hackle) or Woodcock and Mixed also do well. Good sea trout in the 2.5lb to 5lb range are caught frequently and if 'specialist' night sea trout fishing is your penchant, do give the Annan a go. Incidentally the Hoddom beat also holds some very large browns sometimes caught on salmon flies or big sea trout lures. These biggies (up to 5lb or so) are more than likely the male partners of the female migratory trout which have gone to sea. The male trout have chosen to stay on and protect their territories in the deep pools rather than follow the ladies downstream and when the females return, the males will simply latch on to the crowd again hoping to find a mate.

Annan sea trout are cracking fish demanding much of your angling skill. One hint from Tony King, another Annan expert and REFFIS guide on this lovely river, is not to start your evening fishing too hard too early. Tony says you can unsettle fish, especially in any smaller pools and a pause every now and again allows fish to calm down. Tony also advises being adaptable in your approach, playing night sea trout fishing very much by ear. In common with most other rivers a lot of success will depend on localised conditions, whether the water is high or low, what the air temperature is and the time of the local tides. Annan sea trout are no different than any other in reacting to these factors, and time spent in prior observation pays much more than rushing headlong into the fishing. Sea trout can also be caught during the day especially if the weather is grey and windy, however night is nearly always the most productive time.

In the past few years the Annan has enjoyed a higher public profile with the holding of the National Sea Trout Festival celebrating all aspects of that wonderful fish. This has brought increased numbers of anglers to the river, however there is still space for all. Be assured, when fishing here, you are following in the footsteps of many like minded enthusiasts from as far back as Stoddart's time for this stream has a lengthy angling reputation. The keen trout angler is well served, being able to fish in what, in places, more resembles a lush chalk stream habitat. With good stocks of resident browns and their sea going cousins on offer, the demands of the discerning are easily met.

Annan in full flow.

Chapter 5

The River Clyde

'There is often a rise of fish just after a change of wind, light, or weather.'

G. W. Maunsell

OS Map Nos. – 64, 72, 71 and 78
Nearest town/village(s): – Glasgow, Coatbridge, Motherwell, Lanark, Carstairs, Biggar, Abington, Crawford.
Accessibility of fishing: – Very good. Numerous permit outlets in shops, hotels, Post Offices etc. all along the Clyde. Various tackle shops in Glasgow also sell day tickets. Three ACs exist; the United Clyde Angling Protective Association Ltd (UCAPA) have the most water with three long sections of river (upper, middle and lower) from Daer Reservoir down towards Motherwell. Lamington and District AC also issue permits as do Hozier AC.

Best times: – The trout fishing gets underway by April and stays reasonably good right through until September. May and June are usually the most productive months for trout.
General: – The Clyde has seen fluctuating fortunes, especially in its industrialised reaches near the city of Glasgow where it became heavily polluted for a time. The trout of the Upper Clyde, away from the main centres of population, still remain of challenging quality. Because of angling pressure, widespread restocking is undertaken by the local AC. A Protection Order introduced in 1994 now covers much of the Clyde making it an offence to fish without a permit. Strong support from local police and angling organisations has brought about a reduction in the amount of illegal set line angling to the benefit of the resident fish and their fishermen. Apart from trout, the river also contains grayling, pike, perch and roach and efforts are being made to reintroduce migratory stocks of salmon and sea trout. Using a 10ft rod with floating, sink tip or intermediate line, 3–4lb nylon and a traditional selection of river patterns usually does the business.

★

The angling history of the *Clyde* is rich and varied. Over the last century a significant number of past 'master' anglers have been linked to the Clyde and this river also has associations with some unique tackle and

'Fish fair an' free, an' spare the wee anes.'

Great expectations – River Clyde.

fly tying techniques. W. C. Stewart in the acclaimed book *The Practical Angler* (first published 1857 and revised many times since) mentions the Clyde as containing 'large, well shaped, and in general, red fleshed trout' which he puts down to the fertility of the Clyde valley giving 'superior feeding' for the fish. He also pointed out that the fish were 'generally not numerous' owing to the lack of favourable spawning in the lower reaches and also the presence of pike which devoured the trout fry. Webster circa 1887 recounts using his 'loop rod' here and Henry Lamond in *Days and Ways of a Scottish Angler* circa 1932, gives a glowing account of Clyde fishing with a wonderful description of angling upstream between the village of Crawford and the Daer reservoir. He talks of grand pools in the Elvanfoot area holding a 'race of 5lb trout' and of trout 'swimming about over the golden bottom' in the upper springs of the 'majestic Clyde'. As Lamond approached the upper part of the river near Daer, he describes the 'immense lone-liness of this great basin in the hills'. Atmospheric stuff indeed!

Though much road development has taken place since the early pioneers walked and fished the high stretches of the river, its character of green valleys and windswept hills largely remains. It's strange to think the north-flowing Clyde actually has its source in the same area as the mighty Tweed and the sinuous Annan (in the hills above Moffat), yet it flows out in a completely different direction. There is a funny little rhyme worth repeating about this;

> 'Annan, Tweed an' Clyde,
>   A' rise out o' ae hillside;
>   Tweed ran, Annan wan,
>   Clyde fell, an' brak its neck
>   O'er Cora Linn.'

To complement its excellent trout angling, a whole trend of fishing techniques have grown up around the Clyde. Fly dressings, originally unique to the river, have now become universally established as river trout patterns. These flies, tied 'Clyde style', are generally very sparsely dressed and follow W. C. Stewart's declaration on the 'necessity of avoiding bulky flies'. They are rather similar to the lightly dressed Tummel flies (see River Tummel Chapter 12), however the older varieties of Clyde wets set themselves apart from others by their distinctive upright wings tied in at a steep angle to a short body. The head hackle was tied in sparse above the wing (rather than the more usual method of tying the hackle below the wing) and this gave the flies a very upright bold appearance.

Quite why this rather stark-looking design was developed in this particular way is lost in the mists of time, however in conversation with expert fly tyer Geoffrey Bucknall he surmised it might have been to use the fly's extra wind resistance to help propel them and the old, very light horsehair lines onto the water. The original Clyde anglers of the 1800s used up to a dozen flies, sometimes known as a 'strap', which were tied directly into a length of gut and then attached to a cleverly tapered horsehair line. This unusual 'no dropper' fly attachment has all but died out now but I do remember in the 60s my father remarking about having met some elder statesman on the river who still used 'a string of flies all knotted into the gut'. The odd upright wing design of 'Clyde style' may have been deliberate to allow the wind to blow the flies out to alight naturally on the water as if they were a natural hatch. On the other hand the original gaunt upwinged patterns of the Clyde may simply have been to imitate the multiple and profuse hatches of upwinged flies still found on this river!

Though it may be true that some past fly designs have been overtaken by more fashionable constructions of modern wet flies, there is still a very significant place for 'Clyde style' tyings on any lowland river where a more subtle and delicate pattern is required. The flies mentioned by the late Robert C. Sharp* in his book *Let's Fish Again* published by his widow in 1985, are now accepted standards for most lowland wild trout river fishing. Sharp took the important step of recording generations of important 'Clyde style' fly designs like the Sand Fly, Yellow May and the Dark Spring Olive, some of which stem from the early 1900s or perhaps even earlier. He mentions some flies as his own variants while others were dressings passed on to him by other esteemed Clyde anglers of the day.

Downstream wet on the Clyde near Abington.

Happily, the 'Bert Sharp Fly Tying Club' still thrives today keeping his memory and those wonderful tyings alive and active. These experts are ensuring that old traditions are worked to their fullest potential and I have listed a couple of the most versatile patterns at the end of the chapter.

Incidentally unusual fly dressings were not the only curious tackle feature of the Clyde. D. Webster, a noted Clyde angler, wrote in the late 1800s of using his 'loop rod' with a 'strap' attached on the river. This tackle appears to have been used more like a dapping rod with the hair line attached by loops directly to the top of the rod. The whole caboodle of line, trailing gut and numerous flies was then cast upstream. Needless to say Webster's method did not stand the test of time! The fly line Webster used was made of twisted horsehair strands from the tail of a grey or white stallion and the whole thing could be tapered down to one lone strand which acted as the fly leader. This is almost certainly the first version of today's tapered leaders. These old hair lines were more like dapping floss and casting with them must have needed to be wind assisted. Wherefore now monofilament!

Willie Miller fishing the upstream dry fly.

Most of my childhood was spent living on the northern outskirts of Glasgow and the River Clyde was an old 'weil kent' friend. Not that we spent much time actually fishing in it as the mid-1900s saw it reach a peak in pollution near the main city centre stretches. It was more a question of passing it quickly by on shopping expeditions, with a clothes peg handy for your nose! My Dad did occasionally visit the Upper Clyde on the old A74, however road communications in the 50s and 60s were very much slower than today. Such an outing involved a difficult day of travelling across city traffic, out through suburbs and down towards Border country. This tortuous trek never went down well with any of us and consequently the quicker escape north to the Trossachs waters had much more appeal. All that was long ago however and nowadays the Clyde is vastly more accessible from Glasgow. Visiting and local anglers can zoom up or down the M74 to their favourite pools in less than an hour. Lovely golden trout are their quarry and these can be caught along most of the river's 50-mile length. Grayling and various coarse fish (pike, perch or roach) are also available in the slacker water of the

lower reaches of the more industrialised Clyde valley. This productive trouting water provides good mixed trout habitat of slow flats, deep pools and fast runs. Its base is of gravel, sand and rock and the water in the upper stretches is generally clear and untainted by much run off, except during spates when the river muddies up with earth run off from the surrounding fields.

The available natural feeding provides a broad spectrum of insect and invertebrate life with stonefly, March Browns, iron blues, caddis and sedges, Yellow Sallies, olives, sand fly and Diptera all present. In early season those fat stonefly nymphs known as 'Gadgers' (ugly bottom-hugging crawlers which look like tiny scorpions) are popular with the trout and some anglers will switch over to fishing these as bait if the conditions demand it.

The brown trout of the Clyde have always had a reputation for being remarkably fastidious at times and, even though today they are mainly 'stocked' rather than wild spawned fish, this reputation remains intact. The UCAPA have restocked the river periodically over many years with locally indigenous fish and 'imported' Leven strains, and today it is still the practice to bring trout from outside sources to supplement the indigenous stocks. There is a healthy mix of trout sizes in the river and anything from ½lb to 1lb 8oz are taken quite frequently with the odd much larger trout also caught. Despite the stock additions, this is not a 'beginner's river' by any stretch of the imagination. It is said that if you can catch trout on the Clyde you can do so anywhere because you must work for your fish, especially as the days lengthen and the sun shines into the translucent depths. Most of the angling is done by wading and thigh waders with studs are recommended as it is slippery in places. Some will use chest waders, however in the upper parts of the river these are not considered absolutely essential.

Tactics involve quite a traditional approach in that in early season you tend to fish wet and/or nymph and then progress to dry if the trout start to rise a little more freely. Ten-foot rods and floating line normally suffice though some anglers prefer sink tip lines if they feel the fly needs to be fished deeper. Locals will tell you that when fishing the Clyde, the time of day is probably more critical than choosing a particular pattern. Early on you should think about the warmest part of the day, say 11am to 4pm until about May and then spread out your fishing more to utilise the beginning or end of the day. Dusk fishing can be highly productive in high summer and upstream dry fly really comes into its own then.

The fruitful stretches of water around Abington in Lanarkshire are a good place to start your exploration as here the river runs narrower with plenty of variation between deep pools and fast runs. It was in this land of green rolling hills that I met up with local expert Willie Miller to rediscover the Clyde in all its early season Easter glory. It is always a delight to fish with someone who knows his river intimately, so much more interesting to share knowledge and ideas than muddling along on your own. We began at the pools below the memorial to Matthew McKendrick who together with William Robertson of Glasgow founded the UCAPA in 1887. The inscription on this dedicated stone 'Fish fair an' free, an' spare the wee anes' rather embodies the atmosphere of the place, for this stretch of the Clyde is open and remarkably tranquil once you get away from the busy M74. Willie is an expert dry fly exponent and while he plied his rod upstream I wandered down, fishing wets in the time honoured way. A cold downstream wind was something of a deterrent (to both of us as it turned out) yet for a moment the sun came out around 2pm and a dense flotilla of March Browns sped down river, their speckled brown wings acting as sails in the sunshine. Suddenly the Clyde came alive, with trout rising in determined splashy unison. It may have been too brief a hatch to bring a bountiful catch, yet it showed what the river is capable of, even in the coldest early season. For the record Willie used a floating line with a selection of flies like the Dark Spring Olive, the Sandfly (a fly unique to the Clyde, see below) and the Beacon Beige. I too stuck with floating line, experimenting with wet patterns commonly used on the river like Teal and Black, Blae and Harelug and a Greenwell or two.

For me the joy of fishing the Clyde again after an absence of thirty years or more was immense. This is a taxing and enigmatic river, capable of stretching your capabilities to the limit. Get out there and enjoy some Clyde style . . .

★

*Two versatile Clyde patterns of universal use for wild river trout from Robert Sharp's book, Let's Fish Again.

1. The Sandfly (size 14–16)

Body – black thread and sparsely dubbed mole
Hackle – black hen
Wing – speckled brown partridge
The natural sand fly (also known as the gravel bed fly) is common to the Clyde but this imitation is a great attractor of trout anywhere. Tie it sparse but straggly rather than overly neat.

2. The Yellow May Dun (size 14)

Body – stripped quill from dyed yellow ostrich herl
Tail – yellow cock hackle fibres
Hackle – yellow cock hackle.
This imitates the natural hatch of 'Yellow Sallies' common to the Clyde below the town of Lanark. If you introduce more subtle blends of yellow and olive you have a brilliant mayfly imitation (see also Harry Davidson's tying of the Wet May) mentioned in the chapter on the lochs of West Caithness.

Chapter 6

The Rivers Conon and Blackwater

'Like the stars, one river differeth from another in glory, but every river has its own charm and individuality.'

Henry Nicoll

OS Map No. – 26
Nearest town/village: – Dingwall. Depending on where you fish, Contin, Strathpeffer and Maryburgh are also easily accessible.
Accessibility of fishing: – Good. Permits for the Dingwall AC tidal stretch of the Conon are available from Sports and Model Shop, Dingwall. Permits for the Upper Blackwater are available from Loch Achonachie AC at the Marybank Post Office. To fish for wild trout on either river you must obtain a 'salmon/sea trout'

River Conon.

permit, however in real terms this is inexpensive. Note: on the Conon, visiting anglers can fish any weekday, Saturdays are reserved for local AC members only. No Sunday fishing on either river.
Best times: – For brown trout April to June. For sea trout on the Conon, July onwards.
General: – Traditional wet fly fishing is normally required, some scope for dry fly during sedge/olive hatch. Not a lot of arduous walking involved but the banks are very overgrown in places. No chest wading allowed as the river height fluctuates with Hydro discharges. Thigh waders with studs suffice.

★

The River Blackwater flows into the River Conon at Moy Bridge near Marybank in the heart of lovely Strathconon and both these streams provide excellent yet slightly differing wild trout sport. The local area is pleasantly wooded and agricultural and the good adjoining road systems mean you can reach the highland capital of Inverness in 20 minutes or so. Ease of access does not detract from the charms of these rivers and both are well worth a visit.

To take the upper reaches of the *Blackwater* first, this tumbling stream flows down from Loch Garve via Loch na Croic, over the Rogie Falls, on past Contin to its confluence with the Conon. The Achonachie AC fishings stretch from little Loch Croic to just above the Rogie Falls (a series of waterfalls which are spectacular in high water). Access is by a rather complicated series of forest tracks on the opposite side of the river from the busy A835 Gairloch road. The AC beat is pleasantly wooded and offers a complete and tranquil escape from the tourist hordes who haunt the walks around the waterfall and fish pass. Your surroundings are birch, bracken and pine and the river flows around bends, down over boulders and through small pools with reasonable but not excessive force. This is an interesting section of river for though it all looks very natural, a lot of its pools and banking have been man-made. All credit to the club for its efforts, for the end result maintains the intrinsic appeal of a wild river. Though there are some casting spaces between tree and fern, the undergrowth is still pretty lush so beware of catching the back cast at a vital moment. Roll or even Spey casting is a distinct advantage as the prickly gorse in particular is a real killer! For respite, the club have provided a secluded fishing hut which makes it the ideal venue for a days' trouting in some style.

The water is moderately tinted with a light tea stain and the bottom is wobbly rock and covered with an extremely slippery brown algae. This environment favours the midge family (and in summer particularly the biting ones!) but there are also some small caddis/sedge fly, olives and needle fly present with plenty of nymph activity in the water. Huge dragon-flies 2–3 inches long, also flit along the bank and, as I have only found dragonflies present in a more peaty/acidic environment, I judge this river also to be of an acidic character. The AC stretch of the river has very much a mountain stream feel to it for, though the forest crowds around, the Strathconon hills are still visible behind, forming a pleasing tranquil backdrop.

The trout are burnished gold with black and red spots and dark backs, and they have a reasonable spread of sizes varying

from about 6oz to ¾lb with the occasional 1lb plus fish being caught. Large trout up to 5lb or so are sometimes taken in the early half of the season and there is a possibility that these are mature male sea trout which have lingered after their spawning. While the females of the sea trout clan run up the river to spawn and then return quickly to the sea, the big males like to stay on in the fresh water, sometimes all year. As river residents, they stoutly defend their territories and thus it is quite possible that the angler who hooks a fat trout in the Blackwater in the Spring has actually contacted one of those big male sea trout.

This is very much a traditional wet fly river where 'across and down' fishing with little retrieving is normally more success-ful. You can cover most runs and pools adequately with a 10ft rod and floating line. Intermediate or sink tip lines are sometimes used in high water conditions but as this is very much a spate river, most

Quiet pools on the Blackwater.

of the time they are not necessary. Four pound nylon will suffice for the trout; only the salmon fishers use higher density. Even though I fished it in the height of summer with quite profuse terrestrial insects present, dry fly did not seem to have much appeal though admittedly the sun was extremely hot and bright, making the fish very hook shy. The principal food for the trout seems to come from below the water surface rather than on it and I found any winged dark coloured fly very successful in size 12s. I had great sport with a fly with jungle cock cheeks generously given to me by a past acquaintance. This fly (in size 10/12) turned out to be the 'Kingsmill' developed by one of my great heroes Kingsmill Moore and on my visit constantly proved the most useful on the trout of the Blackwater when fished on the point fly. It is worthwhile reiterating KM's dressing here for the 'Kingsmill' as it works exceptionally well as a beetle or nymph imitation:

Tail – GP topping
Body – black ostrich herl
Rib – oval silver
Hackle – black cock or hen
Wing – rook secondary 'rolled to keep solid, tied long, low and narrow'
Sides – small jungle cock 'not too white in the enamel'
Topping – GP topping 'taken hard up against the top edge of the wing, and long enough to intersect the topping at the tail'

Kingsmill Moore explains that the shape and design of this fly suggests the light trapping qualities of shiny wing cases almost like a halo around the fly. Whatever the explanation, it's a great fly on darker more peaty coloured waters.

In terms of trout angling the Blackwater is not perhaps the most demanding river I have researched, though casting amongst the vegetation is something of an art in itself. Nevertheless there are definite pluses in its fighting wild trout, the intense feeling of complete peace and isolation and that fishing hut is a masterstroke!

Though just a few miles down the road, the *River Conon* has a quite different feel to it. Here the Dingwall AC stretch broadens out to meander through an unusual SSSI (Site of Special Scientific Interest – a protected nature area) complete with hazel woods, wild raspberries, Himalayan Balsam and some most unusual tall, yellow flowered plants which the locals know as 'cone flowers'. In places the banks are fairly overgrown but unlike the Blackwater, once you are wading you can usually escape being hooked on the backcast. The water is tidal and the fish population includes resident brown trout, sea trout, salmon and grilse and also the occasional slob trout. The river beat lies between the two small villages of Maryburgh and Conon Bridge and is crossed by two quite busy roads yet it is tranquil enough and the class of trout fishing makes up for any traffic noise.

There are several easily accessed pools and these include the Morrison pool (more favoured by salmon anglers) and the Anchor and End pools generally fished more for their sea/slob and brown trout. If you have timed your weekday visit to coincide with the sea trout runs of July onward then you are in for some excellent sport. To make the best of the silver greyhounds of the sea which average about a pound but are caught up to 2–3lb, watch the tide timetables and fish two hours prior to high tide and two hours directly after. Choose either a grey breezy day or fish at night in the gloaming, and wade quietly and carefully on the rock and gravel bottom. There is some algae present on the stones but apart from making things slippery underfoot, it provides succour to caddis and snail. The natural feeding is quite profuse in this rich area and olive, midge and black sedge are present in some quantity.

A cast for the sea trout of the Conon.

A 9ft 6in to 10ft rod, floating line and traditional patterns is generally all that is required for trout on the Conon AC beat though locals use 6lb to 8lb BS nylon in case they contact a leviathan. You would be wise to employ a couple of old faithful size 10s like the Teal Blue and Silver (or alternatively the Dunkeld) on the point and a Black Zulu or Kate McLaren on the bob. Alternatively if you like using local flies you could use the 'Conon Lure' which has a gold or silver body and brown feather streamer wings tied on a tandem hook. Whatever your method, work down the pool casting 'across and down' in traditional fashion. Instead of allowing the fly to naturally swing round, I found the best results were obtained with a medium to fast retrieve. These Conon trout like something to chase and, if you do intercept a shoal of sea trout nosing in to taste the freshwater, you are in for a real treat. The fish hit the fly like express trains, leaping and crashing in the pools and to avoid spooking the whole shoal it is a wise move to lead the fighting trout into the side as quickly as possible. The club have a strict 10in return rule and a voluntary 12in return and in common courtesy I would advise following the latter and only take what the table requires, two larger or three medium sized trout are quite enough.

When specifically after the sea trout note that the river can give the impression of feast or famine as the shoal cruises slowly past you upstream on the flow of the tide and then drops slowly back on the ebb. Thus you might fish a pool hard for a while with absolutely nothing showing then suddenly, within the space of 15 minutes or so, you start picking up a lot of fish. I found the larger trout almost invariably took the deeper fished point fly quietly but firmly (the TBS was particularly effective) whereas the smaller finnock/sea trout of 1lb or less took the top dropper so hard they gave the initial impression of being mighty fish! It was interesting to see that when gutted, my sea trout and the one slob trout I had caught, had all fed only lightly in the freshwater. Apart from one large black beetle in one of the trout, there were only traces of well digested shrimp present in very small quantities. This might suggest that they were using this patrol into fresh water to explore the stream of their birth but that they were not yet physically ready to run upstream. The ocean was still their home and they were just having a little wander to prospect on things to come.

The Dingwall AC have worked hard to maintain trout numbers, releasing a quarter of a million sea trout fry of 1in into the feeder burns in 1993. I am sure that they now reap the benefits of this fry addition as some of these fish are now coming back as well fed mature adults having gone to sea as smolts. The fact that there are no fish farms sited in the vicinity of the main sea trout runs is also indicative of their high survival rates. Even if you do not contact official 'sea trout' those interesting 'half

casts' the slob trout make for just as spectacular sport as do the browns. The slobs (such a silly name for a bold game fish) have partly silver and partly brown trout markings and spend most of their time haunting the rich estuary feeding instead of speeding well out to sea with the rest of the shoal. They take the traditional wet flies just as readily as do the sea trout, perhaps the only slight difference is their behaviour once hooked. They tend to bore deep and away from the shore whereas the sea trout leap spectacularly but they are just as good a prize with some reaching large sizes.

On one of my visits to the Conon it rewarded me with a spectacular almost dream-like few hours of daytime trout fishing. In the beginning I had two hours when I caught nothing, but then the sudden transformation from dead water to a water truly alive with fish was fantastic. A shoal of silver beauties had crept in on the tide and for a time I got lost in an intense angling world, held rapt in riverine paradise. Truly magical and I cannot recommend it too highly . . .

Silver beauties from the Conon.

Chapter 7

The River Don

'The afternoon knows what the morning never suspected.'
Swedish Proverb

OS Map Nos. 37 and 38
Nearest town/village(s): – Aberdeen, Kintore, Inverurie, Kemnay, Alford, Monymusk, Strathdon.
Accessibility of fishing: – Good. Permit outlets exist through the various estate offices dotted along the Don. Local ACs, hotels and tackle shops both in Aberdeen and Inverurie also supply tickets. River Don Brown Trout Improvement Association oversee workings of the Don Protection Order.
Best times: – April, May and June are generally considered best for larger browns so try to make this river your early rather than mid-season venue. After Spring the trout seem to fan out more along the system, apparently disappearing until gathering for the next spawning. Consequently it is less fished in summer but it is still worthwhile having a look on the off chance.

General: – The Don has a big reputation as a trout stream often being rated the finest in Scotland. It provides classic dry fly water but do not be deterred from nymph or wet fly fishing when it is called for, good results come to those most willing to experiment. A 9–10ft rod, small patterns 14–22 with floating line are usual. Some wading with chest or thigh waders is normally required; tread carefully and take a wading stick for safety as there are some sudden deep pots and large slippery boulders underfoot. The Don PO covers most of the catchment area and permits must be obtained prior to fishing. Trout fishers should give way to salmon anglers.

★

The Don flows through some of the loveliest parts of the lower Grampian hills

Early days on the Don.

deterring the bus party anglers and allowing proper management plans to flourish.

On first viewing, the Don shows a delightful variation of clear water glides, gentle bends and fast rocky stretches. The base is of boulders, gravel, and sandy grit with a reasonable weed growth including Ranaculus as similarly found on the Tweed. The intense fertility of habitat coupled with the gin clarity of water (most of the time you see straight to the bottom) makes for ideal if demanding trout conditions. The water quality is neutral to alkaline in nature and unlike its lowland river counterparts, the Don does not tend to suffer many prolonged dirty spates. Yes, in high water it can be a little coloured but in general terms the river remains consistently clear in all but the very worst of conditions. The speed of flow in the Don is not as fast as say the Tummel or the Tay but this allows weed growth to establish itself more quickly to the benefit of all local organisms. It is interesting that historically the migratory fish of the Don had a hard time with pollution from the paper mills near the mouth of the river. However after a purge on polluters during the 1980s the river has seen quite a turn around in fortune. Migratory fish are again increasing in number making for healthy populations of all game fish throughout the system.

The natural feeding here is exceptionally rich with profuse varieties of olive, sedge, midge and stonefly present. March Browns and Iron Blues can cascade down, caenis dance, minnows flit and shrimp and caddis adorn the bottom, making this river a provider of some of the trout's most succulent larder. It is of little surprise therefore that Don trout grow sleek and fat on the bounty and generally they are of the order of ¾ to 1lb with some considerably larger taken each year. The colours of these fish are a joy to behold with yellow gold, silver and butter cream all enhanced by a liberal sprinkling of black and red spots. Indeed they look rather like Leven trout

with a delightful mix of green fields, rolling hills, deciduous woodlands and wispy hedgerows softening the view. Everywhere reeks of prosperous farming country and this richness provides an ideal backdrop to some fabulous brown trout angling. The river rises from a confluence of streams near Cock Bridge (Scots may be familiar with this area because of the notorious Cock Bridge to Tomintoul road, so often announced on radio as being blocked by winter snows). From there it flows a meandering 60 miles or so down to Aberdeen and the North Sea. Almost all the river provides a fantastic haven for wildlife and your angling efforts are just as likely to be surveyed by ospreys and merlins as they are by dippers and wagtails. Apart from its exceptional brown trout the Don also has a reasonable head of salmon and sea trout present. The river has an ongoing Protection Order (granted in 1991) which has generally assisted in the conservation of all native fish species, and why not, they are after all, 'East coast' river fish! The Don has a good natural stock of native browns though it is understood some Association waters add supplementary stock to their stretches to meet heavy angling demand. The spawning is adequate with plenty of small tributaries and burns especially in the upper parts of the river. Catch sampling surveys carried out by Brian Shields of the Game Conservancy in the early 1990s indicated a spread of fish sizes with the heavier fished lower river producing smaller younger trout, and the lesser fished upper river beats producing older heavier fish. Surveys also showed that it appeared at that time to take twice as long to catch a trout on the lower river as it did on the upper reaches. Size isn't everything it seems! Some habitat degradation was also indicated in some lower spawning reaches and various restoration projects have been undertaken including a recent one on the Blackburn tributary with assistance from the Wild Trout Society and Dr David Summers of the Game Conservancy Trust.

When fishing the Don for trout do not expect these canny well fed fish to give themselves up easily. Of all the trout rivers of Scotland this one can at times be super demanding of your skills and patience. A lot of the time the fish stay out of sight to concentrate on feeding on sub-surface nymph, caddis or shrimp and may only rise solidly when there is a sustained profuse surface hatch. Even when there is a rise on you will normally require a considerable degree of angling proficiency and delicacy of touch, on a par with say the Tweed or the Tummel. Local advice centres around fishing when the hatch is definitely on rather than simply fishing the water blind. Hatches in April and May tend to be intermittent during the warmer part of the day say from noon until about 5pm or so. It's not a cut and dried business however and David McDonald who fishes the Don regularly, gave me expert advice

David McDonald fishing the 'dead drift'.

on the best tactics for this beautiful but challenging water. It seems you need to fish much more on the 'dead drift' here, i.e. avoid unnecessary tweaking or retrieving of flies which is fish scary in the extreme. Also your presentation of fly has to be spot on if you are going to have any chance of attracting a trout. The fish have a lush bounty to choose from and they are constantly making split second decisions on what to take and what to reject. Given anything suspicious short shrift becomes second nature to them!

Most trout angling is done on the floating line and either upstream dry or across and down wet are employed with rods of 9½ to 10ft the most commonly used. When trout are rising freely David told me it's sometimes a good idea to cast straight to them rather than try and be too clever with the traditional upstream, drift the fly down approach. Too much nylon and knots are highly visible in this crystalline water and spook more fish than they catch, at least they did with me! Control of the fly line and flies is critical in this glittering stream. Because the base of the river is a scatter of treacherous boulders, the speed of flow varies considerably across the stream and this makes it difficult to be in command of the line as it drifts down. Little kinks and bellies constantly appear in the cast and too much slack can mean those swift trout are on and off before you know it.

On the Don it is not simply a case of watching the last foot or so of fly line for any sudden draw, you continually have to make frequent adjustments to keep in touch with your flies. David was a seasoned expert at this and watching his skilful working of flies over trout lies was a joy to behold. His technique was very much to extend his arm forward to follow the line as it drifted. This allowed him to make quicker alterations to fly line movement and, once the cast just reached the first quarter of the dangle, he lifted off again. This technique differs from the more traditional one of fishing out the whole curve of the line and it calls for much more casting effort. It does however give much greater line control and hooking ability so it is worth trying it out if proceedings are proving tough.

I would also add that to avoid frustrating tangles with the lush undergrowth and trees behind where you are fishing, you should adopt a more strategic casting of the line to the side rather than shooting it high in the air in the normal overhead fashion. I spent the first couple of hours of a recent fishing visit more attached to various tree branches than to fish. It seems my back cast had worked itself higher and higher during a spell of nasty gales on my local waters. Virtual 'steeple' casts are often essential to avoid the fly hitting you in the ear or the back of the neck in a big wind from behind, but I do not recommend

them for the Don! An ability to roll or Spey cast is an additional advantage on the more overgrown banks but equally there are beats with little or no tree cover so it is not 100% essential.

Apart from some adroit casting it is also necessary to be highly flexible in your choice of patterns. Though there are standards in common use on the Don like the Greenwell's, Snipe and Purple, Hare Lug, Partridge and Orange or GRHE, you will need to switch sizes from small to very small almost in the blink of a fish's eye! Size 14 down to size 22 are recommended with a size 16 often doing the most damage. Don trout are both fastidious and shy and you need the gentlest of touches. Big baskets are not frequent and even when the trout are really showing well, many anglers practise catch and release on the wild fish. Given the degree of challenge involved I would also recommend sensible restraint; these wonderful fish deserve your fullest attention and command your deepest respect.

The Don has benefited from being carefully managed and monitored for a lengthy period and is now reaping the benefits of this forward-looking approach. Projects are on-going to research the trout populations in detail including surveys of nursery stock and an analysis of catch returns from anglers to try and determine if stocks are declining, staying roughly the same or improving. Management have acted in tandem with the Improvement Association and the results are there for all to see.

Many anglers return year after year, held spellbound in the charms of the Don. In my mind's eye I forever hold a picture of a sudden flash of silver and burnished gold rolling over my fly just as a tiny burst of sunlight casts shadows through the lime trees to reflect on sparkling waters. In an instant I tighten, but in my anxiety I miss him. That Don trout has me captivated and urges my swift return . . .

Chapter 8

The River Ken and Loch Ken

'It was the trout, not himself, who had broken the rules.'
W. A. Adamson

OS Map Nos. 77 and 84.
Nearest town/villages: – Castle Douglas, Cross Michael, New Galloway, Dalry, Carsphairn.
Accessibility of fishing: – Very good. Permits for the river from Carsphairn PO, Ken Bridge Hotel and New Galloway AA. Tickets for the loch (which also contains a wide variety of coarse fish) from New Galloway AA, local bailiffs and the local Marina.
Best times: – Early on in the season is better for the browns. April is often a month when some of the biggest trout are caught.
General: – This green scenic area is probably more well known for its coarse fishing than its wild trout, however the trout of the Ken are very unusual and are well worthy of your attention. The fish have been the subject of some genetic studies which have highlighted a fascinating past. Traditional trout tackle usually does the business, the river is not very wide and a 10ft rod will normally suffice.

★

The *River Ken* and the sprawling 13 miles or so of *Loch Ken* lie roughly north/south across the centre of rural Kirkcudbrightshire. These waters near the small town of Castle Douglas form a major attraction in the Galloway Forest Park providing a tranquil backdrop to a green land of gently rolling hills and fertile fields. Here and there the course of loch and stream is interrupted by small dams and power stations as together with Loch Ken, this system has been harnessed to generate electricity for the surrounding Border area. Both the loch and the river play host to a wide cross-section of coarse fish with pike, roach and perch all on offer. Be assured however that there are some very special trout also residing in Loch Ken, genetically linked to those of the inflowing River Ken and the outflowing River Dee.

The Galloway Forest Park is a popular tourist destination and consequently the waters see some heavy visitor pressure in the high season and not just from the coarse or game angler. In fact in some areas of the loch I would say fisherman are in the minority when compared with other recreational user groups. Nationally, demand for water sports has risen quite dramatically in recent years and Loch Ken has become a haven for all kinds of aquatic pastimes. This is now a major outdoor destination frequented by everyone from jet skiers to power boaters and from bird watchers to canoeists. It appears the loch has sometimes struggled to keep abreast of public demand for its facilities for though there is a council led voluntary scheme in place on the loch which requires craft registration and the observance of wildlife restriction zones, the environmental pressures from all water users are growing. Acrimony between recreational groups is sometimes aired with 'birders' representatives berating canoeists for disturbing nesting birds, wildlife enthusiasts cursing anglers for leaving waste nylon or lead weights behind, anglers objecting to jet skiers disturbing the peace,

Galloway Forest Park.

power boat aficionados bemoaning speed restrictions and so on ad infinitum!

With such apparent ecological disturbance plus awkward fluctuations in water height on the river from hydro discharges, you may be beginning to wonder just why I selected these Border waters over say, the better known Nith or the Esk. The reason is simple. The trout populations of the River and Loch Ken are quite unique in nature with a number of characteristics not thought to be commonly found elsewhere. This makes them well worth the effort of investigating. However, I would suggest you begin your quest for these lovely trout by the river rather than at the loch where a high proportion of the fish caught are pike! Life on the River Ken is altogether quieter, beginning as it does high in the hills above Carsphairn and meandering down through open moor, dense forest and rich agriculture before it joins the main loch.

The *River Ken* (also known as the Water of Ken) is a lovely clear stream flowing over a base of rock, boulders, gravel and some clay/mud deposits. It lies roughly on a geological split between acidic western soils and the neutral to rich soils more commonly found in the east. The general fertility of the surrounding landscape, particularly along the eastern fringes of the watershed, encourages a wide range of invertebrate life including freshwater shrimp and all the usual insect groups like olive, sedge, midge and Diptera are to be found. Fishing here is relatively simple with little wading required or advised because of sudden water height fluctuations. Up near Carsphairn, the river is comparatively narrow and easily covered with a 9ft rod and floating line. It is only from around Dalry down that a longer rod and a switch between floater and intermediate may sometimes be needed, especially in high water. The best times to fish the River Ken are normally early and late in the season for the bigger specimens which come in at anything between 1½lb to 4lb plus. Bait fishers do particularly well at these times but in the warmer summer months dry fly is also exceptionally productive with all sizes of trout being taken.

Local fly fishers usually use traditional upstream dry or downstream wet with tactics altogether very similar to those used on the Annan or the Clyde. Popular dries include the Elk Hair Sedge range, Adams and the dry March Brown in size 12 to 18 and good wets include Snipe and Purple, Partridge and Orange, Greenwell's, and most dark spider patterns. Weighted Nymphs are often used on the tail fly in high water, for example Olive Nymphs, Pheasant Tail Nymph or Hare's Ear and sometimes a 'goldhead' or a bead is attached at the top of the traditional tying – I prefer a tiny twist of copper wire if extra weight is needed, it depends on how purist you want to be! Larger trout are also taken with Mepps spinners or bait as all methods are practised here but I recommend fly as it's less damaging to fish you may wish to return.

Sadly, in common with some other lowland

Loch Ken system.

rivers, the fly experts on the Ken seem to be more thin on the ground than they used to be. It seems the slightly worrying trend today is for the old masters not to be replaced by up and coming youngsters. Modern youth either fish only for rainbow trout or demand faster moving water sports like jet skiing! This effectively means inherited skills may be lost for all time but at least on the Ken this effect is being balanced with some important trout research into the trout population which will expand our overall knowledge of Scotland's trout. The research is being supervised by Andy Ferguson and his team from Queens University, Belfast with assistance from a number of local enthusiasts including accomplished artist and brown trout enthusiast Robin Ade. It is believed that the genetic studies of trout on the Ken, together with similar projects across Scotland, will highlight unique and perhaps potentially fragile populations of truly native fish. Once the data is linked up with other ongoing research, we should be able to take vital steps toward better long term conservation of species *Salmo trutta*.

It is important to remember that when the lochs and rivers of Scotland were colonised by trout after the last Ice Age, each water would have its own genetically distinct strain of trout specifically adapted to survive within that environment. As we saw in Chapter 1, Scottish native trout

originally divided up between East coast trout with Leven characteristics and West coast trout with ferox qualities. Over time some of the more 'migratory' Leven trout (which more resemble sea trout) swam around the coast to meet and interbreed with West coast strains. Ferox however did not move far from their ancient homes, indeed some ancestral strains of trout remain largely genetically intact to this day. It was only when the Victorians began their rampage of restocking that ancient ancestral strains saw real interference with millions of extra 'alien' fish tipped into their homes – a practice which still continues today.

In further discussion with Robin Ade he told me the research on the Ken has centred around showing genetically distinct strains of trout within its lengthy system. The native trout in the upper reaches of this river are around 60 per cent pure ancestral fish with genes dating back thousands of years. They exhibit characteristics predominantly of the West coast 'ferox' strain and the trout bear a distinctive pale emerald sheen over their long bodies and big heads. Robin has made detailed studies of the native trout of the Ken/Dee system and refers, as others do, to the Ken trout as the 'long green ones', exceptionally sporting fish which tend to feed mainly from near the bottom.

Interestingly, because of the hydro dams in the river, the Ken 'ferox' strain are as much river dwellers as they are inhabitants of the loch. Their big heads and mouths mean they can consume larger items of food than is the norm for trout of their body-weight. Apart from other fish fry they will happily consume frogs and toads, big snails and any other juicy bit of protein that comes their way either in the loch or the river. This makes them distinctly different from the native East coast 'Leven' trout which have their smaller heads, free rising fly devouring characteristics and pelagic open water lifestyle. Ken trout can still rise on the surface during a big hatch but in general they tend to prefer to stay out of sight attacking their prey beneath the ripple. Robin has also observed that the native Ken trout have a well developed ridge above their eye, whereas stockie browns or browns with Leven characteristics have hardly any noticeable eye ridge when you run a finger over it. This unusual quality is a useful yet simple way of checking whether your catch could possibly bear any relation to the ancient strains.

Though results of the trout genetic studies are still to be published by Belfast University, preliminary findings indicate that there could be two or possibly more distinctive races of trout in the Ken, the 'long green ones' and the 'yellow bellies', which seem to enjoy different spawning sites. Their genetic make up will usually compel them to reside in particular parts of the loch or river and spawn with their own 'kind' rather than with any introduced trout. Interestingly, few of the Ken trout seem to go on to exhibit the migratory seagoing characteristics of the East coast strains, indicating a pretty pure race of trout exists here.

Despite their apparent uniqueness, the trout of the Ken do suffer the odd interloper for, from time to time, riparian owners make additions to the river with stockie browns. Fortunately these embellishments to stock tend to fail to thrive, are caught quickly by anglers, or spread out along the system, often ending up amongst the predatory pike of the big loch. It is rather questionable why this stocking policy needs to be pursued at all, especially when there are excellent native trout proven to be present. Back to the old 'restocking cures all ills' ethos I fear! At least on the Ken there is usually enough space for the introduced trout to drift off to find their own territory. In smaller waters too many stocked trout competing over small spaces leads to some pretty stressed fish. Competition for room can actually lead to more stress related illnesses in fish than competition over food. (See also the research being undertaken on Carron Valley in Chapter 25 on Loch Talla.)

Robin also made the excellent point that we trout enthusiasts should stop referring to our pure ancestral strains of trout as 'wild' and start referring to them as *native trout*. This is because the recognised ancestral strains now surfacing through research are the pristine popula-tions of Scottish trout with genes dating back thousands of years. They differ considerably from introduced trout which have interbred with the native fish to produce more second or third generations of 'wild' trout. He makes the plea, which I echo wholeheartedly, that native Scottish trout are the ones we should be looking to conserve urgently. He also adds that though stocked rainbow ponds are something of a cultural disaster, especially when youngsters fail to even recognise that a Scottish trout is not one with purple flanks and ragged fins, at least rainbows do not interbreed with our native trout unlike the stockie browns. (See also Chapter 32, Scotland's Trout Scene)

When you fish for secretive trout on the pretty stretches of the River Ken think hard on what has been said and how in the future, our native trout can be best conserved. Trout angling is surely not just the catching of fish, it is the conserving of them for future generations and there is much work still to be done . . .

Chapter 9

The River (and Loch) Ness

'I have little doubt that the immense depths of Loch Ness contain trout as large, if not larger, than are to be found in any other loch in Scotland.'

Charles St John

OS Map Nos. – 26 and 34.

Nearest town/village(s): – Inverness, Drumnadrochit, Invermoriston, Fort Augustus.

Accessibility of fishing: – Good. Inverness AC control permits for the town river stretches; salmon, sea trout and browns are included on a single day ticket. Permits from Grahams Tackle shop, Tourist Information Centre and other outlets. For Loch Ness try Inchnacardoch Hotel at Fort Augustus; Glenmoriston Estate office, Dochfour Estate and the Foyers Hotel.

Best times: – On both river and loch, the trout season 'proper' normally comes good from May on and is productive right up to September. Sea trout come into the estuary reaches at Inverness from about June onwards.

General: – The Ness system is principally known for its salmon fishing, however the river and parts of the main loch also offer exceptionally good trout habitat. Though some locals may be slightly dismissive of fishing for wild Ness trout, there are some really top class fish on offer throughout this lengthy system. Traditional wet and dry fly tactics use a 10ft rod and floating or intermediate line. Take care when wading, the Ness river is an extremely powerful and fast flowing watershed, and the big loch is mighty deep in places! Most permit issuers require you to purchase a 'salmon' ticket even though you might only want to angle for trout, but this is not terribly expensive and with browns of up to 2lb plus being caught the ticket offers good value for money. Trout fishers should give way to salmon anglers.

★

As you pass through the traffic bedlam of busy Inverness it is hard to imagine that some exceptionally fine brown trout fishing is lying just under your nose. With its clear streamy flow and golden gravelly banks, the *River Ness* provides some excellent trout holding water and angling here makes an interesting diversion while in the Highland capital. Admittedly this 'city fishing' is not going to be everyone's cup of tea but, if you don't mind being overlooked by passing cars, tourists, joggers and dog walkers, do give it a go, there are some fine trout to compensate for the built-up surroundings. The Inverness AC

Well-marked trout from the Ness system.

stretch runs for just over three miles (both banks) and though the river is over 100 yards wide in some places there are some interesting features, particularly islands and weirs, to break up any apparent monotony. The most productive areas from the trout fishers' standpoint are the stretches near the islands across from Bught Park while those also after sea trout (usually present from June on) can find productive water at the estuary mouth.

The clear racy waters of the River Ness hold some plump but cautious trout with anything in the ¾lb to 2lb plus range being caught with regularity. The natural feeding is remarkably good with olive, midge and sedge hatches all occurring with high frequency. Once you move up from the road bridges in the town centre, the river becomes much more tree lined and this extra vegetation harbours a plentiful number of insects. Fishing technique tends to revolve around clear water tactics and smaller flies (size 14–16) are normally employed. Depending on the time of year and what is hatching, use a Silver Sedge, March Brown, Pennel and/or Olive quill with confidence. Dry fly can also be productive with little Elk Hair Sedges highly useful on balmy summers' evenings. If sea trout are present then you can add a Teal Blue and Silver, Silver Invicta and Dunkeld to the list.

Note that in parts of the AC beat, a degree of casting skill is essential in order to reach the trout without hooking trees on the back cast and an ability to roll or Spey cast is a distinct advantage. Some stretches have dense undergrowth extending right down the bank and when the water levels are high it is impossible to wade out far enough away from the shore to allow a full back cast. Wading must be done cautiously as the Ness can look deceptively quiet and tame, the flow of water is top speed and one silly moment can see you floating off apace downstream. I must admit to very vigilant wading here; the thought of a load of Japanese tourists taking pictures of me as I drifted down under the bridges and out to sea is a supreme deterrent to any recklessness!

Fishing the river on warm dull days with a smirl of rain is usually best but many locals also prefer to fish on late summer evenings when a sedge hatch should come on and the hubbub of the city has died down a bit. The trout respond well to either across and down or upstream fishing and are often quite close to the bank feeding in the swirls and eddies off to the side of the fast main current. A degree of stealth and casting accuracy is required to get them to rise but when they do they fight extremely well, being strong deep golden specimens used to competing for food in very fast water.

Tactics for the sea-going trout are very similar to those used on the River Conon, with fishing two hours prior to high tide and two hours after being the most common. Teams of two or three of the aforementioned traditional wet flies fished across the flow and then retrieved quite quickly should do the business and if a shoal of finnock do come in then you are in for a real treat. The sea trout are not perhaps as common as they used to be and finnock under a pound should be returned. Silver trout in the 1lb to 1lb 8oz class are usually taken around the 'Friars Shott' a lower section of the river but large slob trout also inhabit the estuary mouth. Some of these grow to substantial sizes (3lb plus) and these add further spice to your fishing.

Trout fishing on the River Ness basically needs self confidence in a) your ability to cast amidst trees, tourists and other obstacles, b) wade fast water and c) the knowledge that there are good trout there even in the midst of a city and your skills are enough to get them out!

Turning now to the long deep ribbon of *Loch Ness* (the name Ness seems to be an English corruption of the Gaelic 'Loch an

The grandeur of Loch Ness hemmed in by the Great Glen.

Eas' – loch of waterfalls), there can be few casual visitors who have not passed this 22-mile water by and given it at least one cursory glance. More than likely they are hoping for a glimpse of 'Nessie', the supposed monster of its deeps. Whether you believe in the tales of her presence or like me, believe it little more than a good marketing ploy, considerable myth and legend surrounds Loch Ness and its fishy inhabitants. The water's immense depths hemmed in on either side by the steep hills of the Great Glen, further add to the mysterious nature of the venue and on a wild day the visiting angler may well feel intimidated by the scale of this great loch.

It is vitally important therefore that you concentrate on fishing the more likely trout holding territories. The shallower bays at Fort Augustus, Invermoriston, Drumnadrochit, Foyers and Dochfour are productive as are any of the river/stream mouths which flow into the loch. As long as you keep quite tight to the shore and out of the busy navigation lanes (remember Loch Ness is part of the Caledonian Canal) you should be covering fish. Avoid the more bald wave lashed sections of shoreline unless there is an obvious burn in view. The constant wind and wave action does not allow aquatic plants to take root nor associated invertebrate colonies to flourish. Consequently trout make their principal homes around the more sheltered areas, rarely if ever venturing out into the cold sterile deeps.

The water of Loch Ness ranges from gin clear at the very edge to a dark peaty colour in the central water column. Profuse suspended mid-water sediments make it look dour and unyielding and these sediments make it almost impossible to see anything beyond the depth of a few

Salmon angler on the River Ness.

feet down, hence Nessie spotters have a hard time of it! The old *Bathymetrical Survey of Freshwater Lochs of Scotland* notes that on one survey they found 'a quantity of pollen from flowers' suspended in the loch and that the motion of the particles indicated that 'different layers of water were moving in different directions'. This shows that while the loch can look reasonably calm, there are still a considerable number of turbulent sub-surface currents at work, a situation still common today.

It is said that you will rarely see trout rise freely on this vast loch; even in flat calms very few tell-tale rings can be seen. However this does not mean there are few trout present, rather it emphasises the need to carefully plan your angling campaign around being in the right place at the right time. Try and fish later in the evening (in summer you should start after 9.00pm) when the sun is off the water and the sedges come to life. Alternatively you can fish during the day in May when the first abundant midge/olive hatches stir the trout into action. Natural feeding, particularly cased caddis, is better than expected in the small shallow inlets and the trout grow to a good size, often averaging 1lb plus and a fair proportion are in the 2lb plus class. Ness trout are exquisitely speckled specimens, butter brown and gold and they rank amongst some of the finest I have caught. In this I echo the words of Philip Geen who fished the big loch in the very early 1900s and declared the trout to be 'the prettiest and most plucky that I know of anywhere'. Interestingly Geen also remarks on the 'abundance of trout of several species which grow to a great size'. Presumably he was referring to there being ferox present in this immense water, possibly in different strains. Certainly Geen had a trout of 19lb, stuffed and mounted by a local Inverness taxidermist. This large specimen, caught by a friend, he described as being of absolutely 'perfect shape and colouring'.

My introduction to the trout of Ness came rather unexpectedly when I fished for a hastily arranged evening with local anglers Charles and Lawrence Court of Fort Augustus. Like many disbelievers I rather doubted the presence of such quality trout in Ness amidst the toothy pike and monster eels. Yet my fears were quickly dispelled that August evening when the sedges fluttered out and the trout rose determinedly. The hatch did not last for more than about an hour but the action was spectacular with hefty browns charging down both the natural and our imitations. Equally intriguing was the flight of the many swallows above our heads. First they soared in the sky twittering expectantly and then as the sedges

hatched, they swooped low and fast across the water snapping up the flying insects with pin point accuracy. The birds' flight reminded me of an old rhyme about swallows flying high in fine weather and low in dull (better angling) conditions.

Tactics were traditional loch style with trusty 10ft rod, floating line and nylon of 5lb BS, a heavier density cast than normal as you never know what you might connect with! Though fly selection was nothing too out of the ordinary, locals seem to favour dark flies like the Claret Bumble or Bibio on the tail and a paler fly like the Silver Sedge or White Hackled Invicta on the bob. Fishing on in the dimming evening light the trout, like the sedges, seemed to emerge from nowhere. Smash and grab hits on our flies followed in dramatic fashion with rods well bent for the next hour or so. Though we returned all our trout, none weighed in at less than a pound and the largest was nearer the two pound mark, quite remarkable for a loch often dismissed as poor trout water!

Both the river and the loch of Ness offer the angler excellent trout in unusual and highly dramatic surroundings. Forward planning is required however, to make sure you get the best from your visit. Neither water is a venue for random fishing, you need to take time to select productive stretches amidst the featureless straights, and you must fish when natural insect hatches are at their height. I suspect particularly on the big loch, that considerable insect activity is required to draw the trout toward the surface and away from their normal diet of bottom fodder. As the loch is so exposed, massive hatches take time to build up and it can be difficult to encounter the loch trout at their best. This should not stop you from trying however and who knows, you may become a 'Nessian' just like me!

Chapter 10

The Upper River Spey

Badenoch Angling Association

*'The big trout lying above that rock will go on feeding for the next
half an hour; watch him and think how you can catch him . . .'*
                                                          John Inglis Hall

OS Map No. – 35
Nearest town/village(s): – Dalwhinnie,
Laggan, Newtonmore, Kingussie.
Accessibility of fishing: – Very good. Permits
from the Badenoch AA are easily obtained
from a wide variety of sources including
Laggan stores, Spey Tackle Kingussie,
Ashdown Stores Newtonmore and Ben
Alder restaurant at Dalwhinnie.
Best times: – April, May, June and
September. Note this part of the Spey can
become low without rain but is still
fishable in the pools.
General: – The river is covered by the
Upper Spey Protection Order and it is an
offence to fish without a permit. However,
permits are of very reasonable cost and
also cover various lochs in this area (see
Chapter 20). Traditional wet and dry fly.
The river is divided into beats so please
allow anglers to fish down and then on to
the next pool. Trout anglers should give
way to salmon fishers.

★

Mention the *River Spey* to any game angler
and almost immediately images are
conjured up of magnificent salmon and/or
silver sea trout. Further down the praise
scale come the brown trout as perversely
these are often overlooked in favour of the
bigger but much scarcer fish. This does not
mean they are a poor second however, far
from it, the sparkling waters of the Spey

hold some excellent browns well worthy
of your careful attention. I first came
across the trout pools of the Upper Spey
while on a reconnaissance trip of the nearby
River Truim so lyrically written about by
John Inglis Hall in his book *Fishing a
Highland Stream*. If you ever want to read
an atmospheric yet practical book on river
trout fishing get a copy of this tome, you
will love it! Though I found the Truim
somewhat changed from the heady, lightly
fished days of the 50s when Inglis Hall did
most of his fishing there, the trip was far
from wasted as I simply transferred the
skills so ably conveyed by him to its bigger
neighbour instead.

The amount of fishing available on the
permit for the Upper Spey is vast. Various
lochs and dams and some 15 miles of the
river are covered and the setting could not
be more beautiful with lush green fields,
heather braes and the grand hills of
Badenoch ever prominent. Technically
there are 15 river beats available to you on
any one day, however, the logistics of
fishing such a long stretch really mean you
need to concentrate on doing a smaller
area thoroughly, if not you will spend a lot
of time driving from A to B. The most
popular trout beats are around the main
villages of Newtonmore, Laggan and
Kingussie. Despite being quite busy at
times, parts of the Upper Spey seem lightly

fished, mainly due to being heavily overgrown. The man or woman who walks a mile or two away from the main centres of population does best and, occasionally carrying a machete may also help! My main forays on the river have taken place in low water summer conditions out on the leafy green beats around the Laggan area. This quiet backwater is as good a place as any to begin your Spey quest and its not as public as say the back of Newtonmore golf course or near the narrow and busy A86 road which runs alongside the river.

At one time the Upper Spey was fished regularly for salmon. Remains of old, long removed suspension bridges and walkways are still visible, however it is the trout you should concern yourself with now for these come in a nice range of sizes from about ½lb up to 2lb or so. The fish are heavily spotted with golden flanks and when caught fight exceptionally well for their size. Inglis Hall alludes to the trout of the Spey and Truim as having brilliant spots with 'a golden pink sheen to their skin'. This is apparently a characteristic coloration found particularly during the months of May and June, possibly something to do with protective mucous though we cannot be sure. Certainly I too have caught browns with this extraordinarily beautiful pinkish sheen in May elsewhere in the highlands. Whatever their markings, many trout I contacted on the Spey leapt and crashed around just like sea trout. Their behaviour gives rise to speculation that they are the male trout who have stayed behind to guard their territories while the females have gone off down river to the sea to become 'sea trout'. Whether 'sea' or 'brown' the Spey fish give a bold account of themselves and provide testing sport.

Depending on your exact beat you will either find meandering slow pools, fast runs or gentle glides and the river takes plenty of twists and turns, creating a good

Lesley Crawford fishing the Spey in low water.

variation of natural pools and ripples. Here and there are artificially raised banks presumably to deter flooding and these can make your casting a high and prominent affair. Try and keep as low a profile as possible but be warned you may find that a bit tricky in places. Also, depending on where you are, some sections of the river are heavily tree lined and careful back casts are called for if you want to avoid snags. Thankfully the upper river also has some long clear beats accessed over agricultural land so all in all it's a good mixture. The base of the river is a mix of sand and gravel and the banks are strewn with those characteristic smooth grey rocks and boulders so common to the Spey valley. Wading (if necessary) is reasonable depending on water height. The water is clear to a slight tea stain in spate conditions, and the natural feeding varies according to which section of river you visit. When I was plying my rod around the beats between Laggan and Newtonmore I found the natural feeding to be of the sedge/olive and midge variety. There is normally plenty of (highly slippery!) brown algae on the stones and this provides good cover for nymph and small caddis.

During bright days the trout mainly concentrate on this bottom fodder and can be hard to move with any surface fly tactics. When this happens you can try using a weighted nymph like a Cove's Pheasant Tail (size 12) on the point and a dark sparse fly like a Black Gnat or a Blae and Black or Pennel (size 12–18) on a top dropper. Simply cast your flies across or slightly upstream and then let the heavy nymph draw the dropper down. Picture the nymph bumbling along near the bottom and the dropper being tweaked along above it. Any suspect straightening of line however momentary must be met with a quick strike (a lift of the rod tip to see if it has met with tension will do) and, if the gods are smiling, you will have a lovely Spey trout on. In any conditions, techniques with nymphs are excellent if you have the patience for it, however I must admit I prefer to cast to rising fish. This is not to infer that dry fly is 'better' than wet and thereby join the ranks of the silly snobbery of yesteryear, seeing and stalking my quarry just makes river fishing that much more exciting! It's all a bit hit and miss when you cannot see the occasional rise. Plops and splashes add hope and encouragement to your fishing, without them it can get a bit dour – it is as simple as that.

Fishing dry fly on a dull warm day with the odd smirl of rain or alternatively into the evening until dark, will mean you are more likely to encounter good sedge and/or olive hatches and as if by magic, you will suddenly see some of the larger browns start to rise. Now is the time to experiment with single upstream dries like a dry Greenwell's, dry March Brown, dry Medium Olive or an Adams (size 12 to 18). Alternatively, you can employ my favourite combination of a wet fly on the tail and a dry on the dropper. In mid-summer when I tried the Spey, the trout were showing a definite preference for small dark or black flies and I found a wet Pennel on the point and any of the darker aforementioned dry flies worked admirably. There is always a debate about whether trout actually see colour in flies or whether it's just the outline they are after, scientists now tell us it's a bit of both. Like many anglers I have pondered on this and one useful rule of thumb I have found is to have one fly on your cast which is coloured similar to the bottom of the river/loch. For some reason trout seem to see best the flies which we would think the most inconspicuous, probably because of light refraction. Thus I have found that on rivers with a greenish algae base, greenish tinged flies like the Greenwell's or Grouse and Green do well and in rivers with dark brown algae, dark brown flies are better. Conversely in clear rivers with a pale rock base, paler flies like a Wickham's Fancy often do best, in sandy shingle-based rivers gold/yellow flies do well, and in dark peaty waters black patterns often excel. These are only a rough guides and by no means etched in tablets of stone, however from hard won experience I have found fly patterns which match the colours of the trout's immediate environment do seem to work best.

Equipment requirements for the Upper Spey trout revolve around a 9ft 6in to 10ft 6in rod (the massive salmon rods of the lower Spey are normally not required on this narrower stretch), floating and intermediate lines, 4–6lb nylon and a selection of the above flies plus a few of your own favourites. Thigh waders are really all that's necessary and here and there you can get by in wellies. A wading stick is a boon as the slimy algae can upend you

A trout to hand – River Spey.

even with studs on! Most trout can be easily beached or slipped back unharmed but if you are adamant that you will catch that elusive two-pounder, take a light landing net along if you must. 'Spey casts' and the like are not really used much, except to avoid trees or high banks behind and you should concentrate your delicate casts at the necks and tails of pools, in the fast streamy runs and below any overhanging undergrowth. Here and there the pools are very deep and slow and though I am sure a few specimen trout lie in the centre of them, most sport seems to come in the faster flowing water. The necks and tails of pools are productive as are the streamy runs. Any junctions of inflowing burns with the main river also surrender trout and look out for the odd 'biggie' mixed in among the half pounders. Fish for the Spey trout like Inglis Hall did for the trout of the Truim. Be canny with as light a touch as you can muster, try upstream dry whenever possible and for best results, keep your reflection and profile well out of the trout's view.

Do not confuse the Upper Spey with the huge salmon pools of the beats below Grantown. It's a lot smaller and less threatening with many neat bends and curves, shady pools and sudden races; excellent trout water in fact. The atmosphere is tranquil, the trout wild and free spirited and there's a vast amount of inexpensive river fishing at your disposal. All you need to do now is get out there and enjoy it . . .

Chapter 11

The River Tay

'It is always a privilege to participate in a sport centred and protected by great anglers of the past, and try and ensure that similar pleasure shall be available to anglers of the future.'
W. A. Adamson

OS Map Nos. – 52 and 53.
Nearest town/village(s): – Perth, Dunkeld, Aberfeldy, Kenmore.
County/District: – Perthshire.
Accessibility of trout fishing: – Good, the river has a huge reputation as a salmon river but the trout are also an excellent if rather well kept secret. Trout permit outlets (over 40 at the last count) are strung along the Tay in the form of hotels, tackle shops, riparian owners, camp sites, post offices, shops etc.

Best times: – Normally early and late season trouting is more productive. April and May can be particularly good if water levels are not too intimidating.
General: – The Tay is deep and fast flowing and great care should be taken when wading. Wear a flotation vest and use a wading stick when venturing any distance from the bank. All the Tay and its tributaries are covered by a Protection Order and you must obtain a permit prior to fishing. Trout fishing permits on the Tay are inexpensive and it is not normally required to purchase a (more costly) dual purpose salmon/trout permit. Provided you get yourself a ticket and stick to the trout beats outlined on it there should not normally be any problem with access to fish for trout. If there is then you should report it to your permit supplier and the PO Liaison Officer for the Tay. Remember trout anglers should always give way to salmon anglers.

★

The Silvery *Tay*, the Mighty Tay . . . whichever way you describe this water, it is one heck of a river! Right from its source at Loch Tay with the Rivers Dochart and Lochy beyond, this powerful stream develops a wide rapid flow, rushing down through Aberfeldy, Dunkeld, Perth to spill out to sea in the Firth of Tay. During this race to the ocean, its waters are increasing in volume all the time with feeder rivers

Harry Davidson selects a fly for the Tay.

like the Lyon, Tummel, Isla, Braan and Almond further adding their weight. It is said this river holds the largest volume of water in the UK and few would argue with that. Despite passing through the built-up centre of the Fair City of Perth, most of the surroundings are agricultural rather than industrialised and delightful trees and green fields line much of the Tay's banks.

Not many Scottish rivers capture the angling imagination in quite such a way as this magnificent stream. From its record breaking salmon caught by the redoubtable Miss Ballantine to its quaint opening ceremony in January when muffled up anglers assemble to try their hand for a 'Springer', and from the headline grabbing fights first to introduce a Protection Order in 1986 and then in 1998 to keep it, the Tay is never far away from public attention. The river has been ardently fished for generations and though it is a salmon river par excellence, the wild trout population also provide top quality sport.

When you approach the Tay for the first time, you cannot help but be struck by the clarity and force of its water gliding and tumbling over a base of clean rocks and gravel. This habitat provides excellent spawning and with a constant supply of clean well oxygenated water, superb golden trout of a pound or more flourish here. Many much larger trout from 3lb plus are also present but they can be difficult to tempt. For the more cautious or the less experienced angler, the bigger fish are only accessible in low water as they tend to lie in the central channels. They are a long wade out, a long way to cast and even if you do hit a likely spot, there is no automatic guarantee of a rise! Still for all that, Tay trout are of excellent quality and some really spectacular fish are caught each year.

As far as can be ascertained there has been little or no restocking of brown trout

Approaching the Tay for the first time, you will be impressed by its clarity and force.

on the Tay system and the 'Tay strain' of brownies seems largely unadulterated. The brown trout are particularly interesting as they show some strong tendencies to migrate. As far back as 1969 D. H. Mills had shown by experiment that some river trout will migrate long distances downstream throughout the year, and today on the Tay this behavioural pattern is still much in evidence. It is quite possible to fish a stretch of this river in April and then again revisit the same spot in July to find those plentiful free rising trout seem to have all but disappeared. Though the conditions and available feeding will undoubtedly play a part in this, there seems definite evidence on the Tay that the resident browns move up or down stream almost at will. Presumably they are following a particularly lush food source and/or following some deeply ingrained gene which compels them to do so. Either way anglers should beware of this migratory tendency which can occasionally frustrate their best fishing efforts. Even if it doesn't, remember this fish behaviour as a useful excuse for the empty creel!

The river supports a host of lush invertebrates for the trout to consume. Scottish International river trout expert Paul

Be ready to alter your tactics according to the conditions.

Buchanan who fishes here frequently, advises me that the trout forage on a wide range of goodies. Early in the season the trout like to feed close to the river floor, gobbling up the prolific stonefly larvae present then. Stoneflies (known locally as 'Gadgers') are vitally important in the first half of the year as the other food groups have not yet become established in any number. For any real success early on Paul advises fishing heavy/weighted nymphs with Gold Head Hare's Ear or Czech Nymphs (sometimes tied with tungsten wire to make them heavier) usually being the most productive patterns in size 10/12. These must be employed deep and slow to get down to those Gadger-consuming trout and a sunk line or sink tip is normally used. Some really good trout are caught in this way but it does take perseverance in

those cold Spring conditions. (See also Chapter 12 on River Tummel.)

Paul also told me that most branches of the olive insect family are common on the Tay with all stages from nymphs to spinners being taken by the fish. Dark olives and March Browns are eagerly snatched when they appear early on and, once things warm up a bit, Paul said his fishing tactics will encompass a more traditional team of wet flies on intermediate or slow sink line. Often he will continue with a weighted nymph on the point with say a Partridge and Orange mid dropper (this fly Paul thinks makes the ideal representation of any olive spinner awash in the current) and a Silver March Brown on the point. He did make the adroit comment that flexibility is the key and, should the trout switch to surface feeding during a hatch which they can do even very early in the season, then you should be just as ready to switch line density and flies to match. Dry fly can be highly productive in those early sporadic hatches when the trout make their first forays to the surface. You have to be ready to alter tactics accordingly.

Numerous sedges appear on the river from late May onwards particularly the marbled sedges, and the successful angler makes more and more use of the dry fly on floating line. Bushy dry flies size 10/12 do well on the Tay with a well dressed Greenwell's or dry March Brown very productive. Those elk hair or deer hair sedges also take a lot of beating when the trout are actively feeding. As the season progresses early morning and late evening fishing produce the best results. For some peaceful, away from it all trouting Paul recommends the stretches above Dunkeld and also at Birnam. Aberfeldy can also be good but it can be heavily fished in the tourist season. The tree lined banks need a bit of care here and there as regards your casting, other than that enjoy the fun and the challenge of this river and its superb

Anglers on the Tay share the water with many other users.

trout. Its sheer scale can be a little off-putting but if you concentrate your efforts around the more productive trout stretches you should be rewarded.

While the quality of Tay trout has never been in dispute, access to fish for them has and I feel I cannot leave this grand river without some comment on its oft misquoted and sometimes controversial Protection Order. First introduced in 1986 after some appalling over-fishing by so-called 'anglers' using set lines usually in 'bus party' groups, the Order has been the subject of much prolonged debate. It has been felt by some fishermen, bona fide or otherwise, that the spirit of increased access to fishings has not always been upheld on the Tay. In some cases, even when fly fishers have purchased trout or grayling day tickets, they have been denied access by over zealous bailiffs and keepers intent on preserving 'salmon' water for their guests. The genuine trout

fly anglers' complaints, which appear quite justifiable, have either been ignored or worse, been lumped together with the less scrupulous category of angling visitor who has no intention of buying a day ticket and wants to continue to use multiple rods and set lines. Let's get one thing straight – there is a wealth of difference between the bonafide fly fisher and the callous fish-monger, but it appears not all parties involved with the Tay have acknowledged this important fact. It may simply be crossed wires but I can find sympathy with the well intentioned trout fly fisher who, having paid for a permit, finds himself classed as a passing thug and is denied access.

The PO situation came to a head in 1998 when Lord Sewel the Scottish Environment Minister suddenly announced he was going to rescind the Tay Order as the riparian owners, he claimed, were not following the rules of the Order. In doing so he offered no better method of trout conservation in its place and frankly seemed to invite a return to the state of near anarchy that existed prior to the PO being instigated. Worse still this sudden step appeared to have been politically prompted not by the genuine fly fisher, but by a small but vociferous confrontational group (SCAPA) who wish all trout fishing in Scotland to be any method, free of charge. Just why a senior government minister chose to listen to a tiny group of militants instead of paying heed to the more reasoned argument of the majority who believe that the Tay Order, despite its occasional shortcomings, works reasonably well as a conservation measure, is not clear.

Thankfully, after a flood of objections and a panning in the more angling friendly sections of the press, Lord Sewel had a change of heart on his conceivably daft idea and the Tay PO has stayed in place. The saga did not end there however for it is reputed that the need to rescind the Order

The Tay passes through the centre of the Fair City of Perth.

was prompted by grayling anglers being denied access to certain parts of the river. Of the trout/grayling populations on the Tay, grayling form around 10 per cent and trout the other 90 per cent. When you think of this as an appeal from a minority group, however authentic their complaints, cleverly manipulated to suit the radical aims of SCAPA, the whole affair takes on an even stranger look. It would seem that organisations like SCAPA are much more adept at influencing the media than we the more restrained silent majority, and in that we have much to learn from them.

In the year 2000 the Tay will still be providing us with superb trout. Though there is some work to be done on both sides of the fishing fence in terms of access to fish, progress has to be made. Entrenched arguments attain little in the long term recognition of the real worth of brown trout fly fishing. However I am optimistic that, with a bit of give and take, we should get there . . .

Chapter 12

The River Tummel

'You will of course, use dry fly if you have luck to find them taking flies on the surface.'

W. S. Jackson

OS Map No. – 52
Nearest town/village: – Pitlochry
County/District: – Perthshire
Accessibility of trout fishing: – Good. Very reasonably priced trout permits can be had from Pitlochry AC, Mitchells Tackle Shop, Pitlochry. Approx. five miles of river are available.
Best times: – Fishes best during the day from April to early June, thereafter evening fishing is usually more productive.
General: – Most methods, e.g. dry fly, wet fly or nymph are successful according to the time of year. Chest waders and wading stick are required for high water. Trout fishers must give way to salmon anglers.

★

The *River Tummel* lies in central Perthshire, an area renowned for salmon, sea trout and brown trout. It starts life flowing out of Loch Tummel, through Faskally and from there speeds down through the lush green Tummel valley to its junction with the mighty river Tay. It is one of the fastest flowing rivers in Scotland and presents the angler with some exceptionally challenging trout angling. It has had a long and illustrious history of game fishing with the local Pitlochry AC being established over a century ago in 1884. Since then many trout anglers have come to sample the demanding Tummel. Indeed just recently it has been the venue for the (catch and release) World Eliminator River Championships so its reputation as an exceptional brown trout venue is well established.

Despite its close proximity to the A9 trunk road (you literally fish some of the pools with traffic coursing overhead!) this magnificent river is a delight to fish. There are a number of access points on both banks and fishing is undertaken by wading unless you hit low water conditions when wellies may suffice. The river is surrounded by fields, trees and shrubs but there are gaps here and there for the backcast and vague paths along the waters' edge to assist the anglers' progress. Wide pools, deep channels and many fast riffles are the principal characteristics of the Tummel and these provide a superb mixed habitat for the trout. The bottom is mainly of shingle and stone with plenty of boulders and pots to provide depth variation. Although the water looks dark and peaty as it races to tip its contents into the Tay, the Tummel is actually a rich, clear, alkaline stream providing excellent natural feeding. The trout here enjoy a superb diet of shrimp, snail and caddis direct from the river base and when hatches do occur, they rise well to prolific olive (in particular large Dark Olive) and sedge. Although there is little or no rooted plant life within the stream, the profuse algae which collects on the stones nurtures the invertebrate life and in turn the trout grow sleek and fat.

There is a good range of fish sizes present (always a good indicator of fish quality) and growth rates for these well marked indigenous trout are very good. By the time they are around three years of age, they weigh a healthy 1lb plus and at five to six years they come in at around 2½lb plus. Occasionally mature indigenous trout latch on to feeding on other smaller fish 'à la ferox' and can attain weights of 5lb plus. Catches of brownies weighing between 1lb and 3lb occur quite frequently on the Tummel so its status as a great trout stream is well deserved. Pitlochry AC supplement the natural stock with Tummel trout reared in a local hatchery under the guidance of Dr Andy Walker, fisheries biologist, ex Scottish Internationalist and long time member of the local Pitlochry Angling Club. Young fish are planted out as fingerlings into inflowing burns and effectively supplement the numbers of naturally spawned trout. The little trout linger in the burn offshoots for up to two years before entering the main system. The club is careful to introduce only indigenous trout so that the top quality Tummel strain remains more or less intact. This thoughtful long term stock management of wild trout is to be commended, especially in the light of today's obsession with stocking 'outsider' strains sometimes in unrealistically heavy sizes. Artificially fed fish can never naturalise unlike introduced fry or finger-lings, and large stockies therefore gain the reputation of being stocked at 9.00 am and out again by 10 past! Tummel trout show no such doubtful characteristics and, with their dark burnished gold flanks and black and red speckles, they make for wild river trout at their very best.

While researching the Tummel, I was greatly assisted by Andy Walker and I am indebted to Andy for providing a fund of pertinent expert, regional information. It seems that to get the best of daytime fishing on the Tummel you should visit from about mid April to early June when the trout are actively feeding in daylight.

Bottom dwelling invertebrates like shrimp, caddis, stonefly nymph and snail are high on the trout's menu at this time and most anglers seek out the trout on wet fly patterns which vary from sparsely dressed Spider/Tummel flies to weighted nymphs with opportunities also for the March Brown, Black Gnat, GRHE, Snipe and Purple and Partridge and Orange (size 12–16). Andy also advised that using a wee double version on the point wet fly takes the flies that bit deeper in high water conditions. A rod of around 9ft 6in to 10ft 6in is normally used with a 5/6 floating DT line and 4lb nylon. Wet flies are normally worked across and down in teams of two or three but there are no hard and fast rules on this, for example upstream nymphing is also commonly practised. Once Spring really arrives on the Tummel (unfortunately this is unpredictable as it can be anytime from early April to late May!) the many local varieties of olives begin to hatch and flies like the Olive Quill and the Greenwell's (size 10 to 16) do well fished dry or wet according to fish activity.

In summer conditions with lower water height and much higher air temperatures, best results call for an upstream dry and you must concentrate your efforts around the evenings from say 8.00 pm to whenever it is too dark to see! With the sedge hatch prolific in the summer months the witching hours for the bigger Tummel trout, i.e. those over say 1lb 6oz seem to lie between 9.00 pm and 11.00 pm. My last visit here was on a warm July evening and, with the water level low but the trout visibly rising, Andy recommended a short 8ft 6in rod and a 4/5 floating line. Upstream dry fly to rising fish is 'de rigueur' for summer conditions and Andy's choice of fly for the evening rise was from a versatile assortment of dries mainly constructed with buoyant elk hair (size 12). These he fished singly on a short line making as little water disturbance as possible. The tactics for the Tummel summer rise are

The Tummel is one of the fastest flowing rivers in Scotland.

very much to delicately stalk a trout, cast slightly upstream of it and then keep a solid control of the fly as it drifts back in the swift flow. Keeping in touch with the fly is the most important aspect of this technique and be warned, the speedy waters of the Tummel do not make control of your fly overly easy. However, with the trout heading and tailing well in the dimming evening air it makes for exciting, exacting fishing even if it is not entirely suited to the more novice casters amongst us.

As we fished the conversation was as ever, wide ranging and for my part most thought provoking. With the Tummel being the venue for the World Championship Eliminator in river fishing, local anglers get the chance to absorb the techniques of some of the world's best river anglers. Andy told me of a comparatively new tactic known as the 'Rolled Nymph'

method used during the Championships. With this style, anglers use weighted nymphs (tungsten is sometimes used) which they flick upstream and then bump and trickle back along the bottom towards themselves. The rod tip is kept high so as to avoid snags and also to enable the angler to watch for any takes on the nylon itself rather than the fly line. Although not a fan himself, Andy declared the method very effective in difficult daytime conditions. However, peripatetic anglers should not worry too much about any lack of such specialist skills for, given the right weather, the Tummel can see a huge variety of successful tactics. Traditional wet fly fished across and down is favoured just as much the upstream dry and 'loch' patterns like the Black Pennel, Red Sedge, Invicta and others are just as commonly used as the more select river patterns.

Amateur fly tyers will find of interest the special 'Tummel flies' developed of old to cope with the extremely fast flowing

Andy Walker at home on the Tummel.

could not dress the most dainty and masterly trout flies . . .' Lawrie goes on to describe the original Tummel fly as *'representing great skill and judgement in the art of trout fly dressing'* and ponders just why the dressing had to be so sparse. He mused that thin 'spider' dressings of flies are normally used for clear bright waters whereas the waters of the Tummel are somewhat brownish in nature. He then concluded that the thin wisps of Tummel flies were instead designed to sink down fast in the very speedy current. Nowadays we would use weighted nymph patterns to drop down to where the trout are feeding but in earlier times the theory of 'bare hooks' sinking faster than heavy dressed patterns (which might trap air), did seem quite successful. Interestingly Lawrie thought that as long as a fly was correct in form and coloration and was fished at the proper depth so that it was noticed, *'trout will see what they wish to see'.* Food for thought in today's obsessive world of fly construction where ever more glitzy materials are piled atop of the hook.

Personally I found dry fly by far the most exciting method to use on Tummel trout especially when they began to show well in the fading evening light. They are game and bonny fighters and a dry Wickham's Fancy or Red Sedge (14–18) cast just upstream of the rise almost always produces a response though they are lightning fast and a full connection cannot always be made. As the shafts of sunlight fade, the hubbub of traffic drops away and the splashes of large trout eager for the hatch can be heard. Gulls and swallows skim up and down the water to snatch the airborne insects and though the sounds of the city remain with you, the river takes on an air of intense but serene activity. As the night draws its cloak around you the Tummel holds you to rapt attention. This is a river to inspire the travelling trout fisher and I wait impatiently for my next visit . . .

water. These are still used by some of the local anglers today, however, before you rush out to buy some take note: they are so finely dressed they look little more than a bare hook and a turn of sparse hackle! The local tackle shop Mitchells of Pitlochry who also issue the permits for the river, told me they do not stock Tummel flies as anglers complain there is so little to them they are not getting their money's worth! The best description I have read on Tummel flies comes from W. H. Lawrie's book *Scottish Trout Flies.* He stated that *'The austerity of dressing of the Tummel fly . . . constitutes the most conclusive refutation of a widely held assumption that our forefathers*

Chapter 13

The River Tweed

'You would attain to the divine perfection, and yet not turn your back upon the world.'

Longfellow

OS Map Nos. – 72, 73 and 74.

Nearest town/village(s): – Tweedsmuir, Peebles, Selkirk, Galashiels, Melrose, Kelso, Coldstream, Berwick on Tweed.

Accessibility of fishing: – Good. Fishings are let mainly through estates and/or their agents. Tackle shops will supply day tickets at Kelso, Melrose, Peebles and Galashiels. The leaflet 'Fishing in the Scottish Borders' published by the Scottish Borders Tourist Board is an exceptionally useful guide to the Tweed fishings (and others) in this lovely area. Keep one in the tackle bag at all times!

Best times: – May, June and July are considered better for the browns, sea trout are best late in the season especially in the upper reaches of the river.

General: – The Tweed may be synonymous with great salmon fishing but the trout are well looked after under the auspices of the Tweed Foundation and its Fish Conservancy Centre, one of the few river management groups in Scotland to monitor and maintain ALL local stocks of freshwater fish rather than just the migratory ones. This is a big demanding river and most of the fishing is by wading. Take at least a 10ft rod especially for early fishing and a selection of lines (floating to sinking), fine nylon and traditional flies. Later on in the season you can get by with lighter tackle, especially in the upper reaches. Wading is required on some beats, thigh or chest waders are the norm. Take a wading stick for safety. A Protection Order is in force and you must obtain a ticket prior to fishing but there are numerous permit providers strung along the system.

★

The *Tweed* and its inflows represent 92 miles of trout heaven. Starting as it does in the hills of Upper Tweeddale, the river tumbles, races and glides swiftly down its lengthy course deepening and widening all the time until finally tipping its clear waters into the ocean at Berwick Upon Tweed. The main river is fed by tributaries like the Teviot, the Ettrick, the Leader and the Whiteadder and the whole system positively reeks of fish. The abundance of rust red well-tilled fields, lush pasture, green rolling hills and gentle woodland gives you just a hint of the fertility of the land surrounding this enigmatic river. Yes, the famous Tweed is a highly productive salmon and sea trout stream, but if you want a well-managed, well-cared for trout habitat, this has got to be it!

Few river systems in Scotland see their trout populations as well monitored as those of the Tweed. Fish management has been in place here since the 1857 when the River Tweed Commissioners, drawn from representatives of owners of fisheries, angling clubs, local authorities and others, took it upon themselves to work toward 'the general preservation and increase of the salmon , trout and other freshwater fish in the River Tweed and its tributaries'. The Tweed Foundation, formed in 1983, assumed an active research and management

Neidpath Castle near Peebles on the River Tweed.

role under the guidance of Dr Ron Campbell, eminent fisheries biologist, and this organisation has gone from strength to strength.

The Tweed fisheries management plan takes full account of the importance of brown trout populations and in particular the monitoring of stocks of wild trout in terms of juvenile recruitment, general abundance, distribution, fish sizes, numbers in spawning burns and so on. This work is long term and relies heavily on co-operation with angling associations both in operating trout traps for survey purposes during spawning time and with individual anglers making detailed catch returns. Local fishers are issued with a 'Brown Trout Fishing Diary' which records in comprehensive detail their degree of fishing effort, the numbers of trout caught, numbers returned, if the trout were marked with a dot/tag or number, what size they were, the places visited, methods of angling, river height and colour, the weather and the numbers of other anglers seen that day. The diaries provide information essential to the making of future decisions about any need for stocking, and habitat improvement.

Modern day log books make interesting comparisons with the fishing records of old. This river, like the Clyde, has a huge history of trout angling and over time a considerable amount of background information has been amassed. Since the dawning of the nineteenth century anglers have expounded the prolific catches of trout made on the Tweed and its tributaries. In 1810 John Younger refers to 'my grandfather in the olden time, killed 36 dozen of trout in one day'. Stoddart in 1866 refers to '57lb of common trout' being caught on the Teviot 'between 11.00 am and 5.00 pm'. This classifying of trout catches in terms of weight or numbers is somewhat misleading and has led to some popular misconceptions about the Tweed. Remember our fishing forebears caught and killed everything from tiny trout of 3oz or less to mature fish and therefore when Wanless wrote in 1937 that in the good old days the Border rivers must have 'swarmed with tiddlers' and that these probably formed the bulk of the huge catches made by the 'great ones', he was probably right.

While there is no doubt that the Tweed system with its copious amount of natural spawning, still produces a lot of trout, the 'average' size sometimes appears to be quite small when compared with anglers' expectations. Generally it is only when you angle in the deeper slower pools from Kelso down towards the sea that you begin to pick up what is today considered to be a more desirable size of trout in the pound range. This does not detract from the angling in any way, indeed it is a sign of a healthy and diverse wild trout population, it is simply to point out that angling perceptions of what is a takeable trout are always changing and evolving. As well as copious small trout the Tweed also produces some very large fish. *The Field* in October 1897 records a 'large yellow trout' caught in the Teviot at 7lb 4oz, 27½in long and 13½in 'in greatest girth'. It was a heavily spotted trout with black and red spots, apparently not in very good condition and was said at that time to be 'the largest trout ever taken from any of the rivers in the Kelso district'. The Marquis of Granby reporting this in 1898 makes the caustic aside that perhaps the trout was out of condition because of the time of year (spawning time) and adds 'those Tweed fishermen are past praying for!' Much more recently (1990s) a trout of 6lb was found dead on the banks of the Tweed, so big ones do indeed exist.

In the 1990s, to cope with public demand for angling an amount of trout restocking is done in busy access points to the Tweed.

The fertile Tweed valley sustains a healthy and diverse trout population.

It is interesting that policies over re-stocking have changed markedly in recent times, with the old practice of introducing fry into feeder burns being stopped because of fears that this practice was largely wasting resources. Surveys of the spawning burns showed many wild trout fry already present and simply placing more fish among the native ones was thought to be causing more harm than good in terms of competition for space and food. Today blue dot marked stocked trout

The viaduct at Leaderfoot dwarfs two Tweed anglers.

analogy about the wild fish being like wolves and the stockies being like poodles. Out in the big bad world, who is going to survive, the wolf or the pampered poodle! Anglers are encouraged to put back any fish not marked with a blue dot as these are technically the wild stock and should be allowed to go on to spawn naturally. Before 1972 a number of angling clubs maintained their own hatcheries in water-works close to the river. In these they grew on native Tweed trout to supplement existing stocks, however, since government reorganisations these hatcheries have closed and the river relies solely on natural spawning and to a much lesser extent, its 'put and take' stock.

It is tremendously important that the Tweed strain of trout continues to flourish as it is totally 'one of a kind'. This river has the highest rate of trout/salmon hybrids in Europe. Tweed trout have a 20 per cent salmon gene which is most unusual and is put down to the close proximity of the natural spawning redds of both trout/sea trout and salmon. The sea trout of this river can grow as large as the salmon and some brown trout err more on the size of a grilse, perhaps reaching 6lb or more. The mixing of genes tends to create a more mobile trout population and it is well documented that there is a substantial in–river migration. The Tweed Foundation Review of 1992 commented that the trout population here is 'very dynamic' both in distribution and structure and that genetic forces 'may be dominant' in encouraging this migration.

Preservation and improvement of spawning habitat forms an important part of the overall management plan and there is significant work being undertaken on habitat improvement for the benefit of both fish and wildlife. The Tweed Foundation in co-operation with Scottish Natural Heritage, Borders FWAG and the EC Agricultural Guidance and Guarantee Fund has worked tirelessly on the Tweed

are added (as big as 10–12in) on busy town waters and this makes their stretch largely 'put and take'. This may seem a rather heretical move, but in actual fact this supplementary stocking allows anglers' demands for bigger trout to be met whilst taking pressure off the native trout. Genetic strains of Tweed trout still appear to remain largely intact as the stocked fish appear to be unable to spawn successfully in the wild. Ron Campbell made the great

Salmon and trout anglers on the Tweed enjoy tremendous quality of fishing.

River Heritage Project. This is aimed at the restoration, protection and improvement of the natural heritage (including wildlife habitats, woodlands and fish stocks). Already various smaller spawning streams have been restored/rescued from over-grazing and general degradation and the results are there for all to see.

Fishing tactics for the Tweed centre

around the heavily traditional and there is a place for all fly methods here. The water is clear and of an alkaline pH with a base of gravel, rock and plenty of weed including much beloved Ranaculus. All the major insect hatches of insects are here in profusion; olives, March Browns, iron blues, duns and spinners, sedges and so on ad infinitum! This is for the most part a Scottish 'chalkstream' and light tackle and a light touch are the norm for trout here. A 10ft rod with matching floating or intermediate line (5–7) and 3–4lb nylon is quite adequate for most conditions. In low water you can get away with shorter rods and lighter lines but you must play it by ear on the day. Crystalline water and easily spooked trout demand your most considered casting attention and good presentation and a dull breezy day helps considerably. If you are after the truly wild (rather than the more biddable stocked trout) you must go on the river away from the main popular areas like the town waters of say Peebles or Galashiels. Remember that with the wild/native trout you will be contacting are sometimes smaller than the stocked fish (though there are larger trout present) but in my opinion these are just as sporting and I know you will gently return them anyway.

Early in the season a range of wets like the Cinnamon & Gold, March Brown, Black Spider, Wet Greenwell's or the Snipe & Purple (size 12/14) are normally employed either on floating or intermediate line. Incidentally the Greenwell's Glory, one of the most famous trout flies of Scotland, was tied here in 1854 for use on the Tweed. Canon Greenwell commissioned James Wright of Sprouston, Roxburghshire to tie a copy of a natural insect he had found on the water and a local schoolmaster who viewed Wright's fly christened it the 'Greenwell's Glory'. It's funny how things come about! This

versatile pattern has stood the test of time and is still highly popular for river or loch trouting. Nymphs like the stonefly nymph or the Pheasant Tail are also productive in general wet fly angling especially when fished as the tail fly to the other droppers.

As the season warms up wet fly anglers will use the aforementioned flies plus Woodcock and Hare's Ear and Partridge & Orange amongst others. With prevailing summery conditions fishers often prefer dry fly on the Tweed and the Grey Hen & Rusty is popular as are the Dry Greenwell, Iron Blues, Dry Sedges and so on (size 12–16). Fishing in the late evening is often more productive on bright sunny days and experienced local fisherman and Tweed Foundation Trustee, E. W. Hunter of Anglers Choice told me that sometimes the old custom of using a 'strap o night flies' is still used. These are bigger heavier dressed flies in 8/10s such as Invicta or Cinnamon & Gold, which create a disturbance across the water. Local anglers used them to fish for trout and sea trout 'from the grey dark to the black dark' though this practice seems to be less popular now. Different generation of anglers wanting different things perhaps?

It must be remembered that in many ways the Tweed is a 'recovered river' rather than a pristine stream as the old woollen mills and heavy industry dotted along its banks at one time produced some pretty grim pollution. Thanks to the exceptional work of the Tweed Commissioners and the excellent Tweed Foundation, the river and its fish populations now thrive. As Dr Ron Campbell put it *The River Tweed Commissioners are the only "Fisheries Board" in Scotland charged with the general preservation and enhancement of trout and other freshwater fish (like grayling) as well as salmon and sea trout'*. Visit this river for yourself and see why other Scottish waters should be following its example . . .

Part Three

THE WILD TROUT LOCHS

Although one or two top quality lochs mentioned here may have other fish present such as char or salmon, all the lochs are recorded from a wild trout fisher's perspective. Apart from one or two noted exceptions like Loch Awe, the waters are listed in small groups or by areas. Scotland has some 35,000 lochs in total and it is an impossible task to list them individually. Most chapters are therefore designed to give you an insight into a distinctive trout loch region. I also believe in the old adage that if the trout are not behaving you don't change the fly, you change the loch! . . . Enjoy.

Loch Calder, Caithness.

Loch Hope, Altnaharra.

Chapter 14

Altnaharra Waters

'The object of a wet fly fisher is to present imitation flies in the water at depths in ways and places where trout may be expecting to find natural insects . . .'

W. A. Adamson

OS Map Nos. – 9, 10 and 16.
Nearest village(s): – Altnaharra, Tongue, Lairg.
Accessibility of fishing: – Good. Altnaharra Hotel guests have priority but space for brown trout angling can usually be found for the bona fide visiting angler. Permits for Loch Loyal and Hakel can also be had from Tongue and District AC, c/o Ben Loyal Hotel, Tongue.
Best times: – From May on for browns. Sea trout run into Hope and Naver from late June onward. September can also be an excellent month all round.
General: – Altnaharra has long been associated with Loch Hope and its sea trout, however the surrounding trout lochs are also worthy of a visit. Traditional loch style reigns supreme here though there is some scope for other techniques including dry fly and dapping.

★

Altnaharra is a place of extremes. It has an extremely long history of good fishing in the midst of an exceptionally dramatic wilderness, battered by extremely volatile weather! – Legions of game anglers have descended upon the environs of Altnaharra in search of the fabulous trout, sea trout and salmon which can be caught there. As far back as the 1870s, the lochs of this untamed, lonely area were being revered across Scotland. Watson Lyall's *Sportsman's Guides*, those monthly 'anglers' bibles' published during the Victorian era, make numerous references to Hope and Naver as places of great sport with excellent bags of trout and salmon. The Guides also allude to Loch Meadie, Loch Hallium and Loch Loyal all containing 'splendid trout' with numerous ferox also being caught in the latter.

By the middle of the twentieth century, Altnaharra had become further enshrined in the annuls of angling history when its fishings were brought to the fore courtesy of the late Charles McLaren. McLaren, then proprietor of the Altnaharra Hotel, wrote that classic practical angling tome, *The Art of Sea Trout Fishing*. This book centres around his lengthy experiences of sea trout angling in the Kinlochewe and Altnaharra areas. The book became something of a standard reference for sea trout fishers and linked Altnaharra to top quality fishing forevermore. It is interesting that the McLaren family is also connected with Loch Maree. Charles McLaren's father was a proprietor there in the early 1900s and Charles grew up fishing for the trout and salmon of Kinlochewe before moving to Altnaharra.

The Altnaharra lochs of principal concern to the wild trout aficionado lie scattered across exposed heather moor tucked below the massive Munros of Klibreck and Hope. The waters have settings of bleak and rugged grandeur and they can take a real savaging from the elements. Altnaharra is one of the few places in Scotland to record a temperature of minus 20°C in winter (it lies in a 'frost hollow') and plus 28°C in summer, so you can expect the unexpected! However, catch this area of central Sutherland in one of its more benign moods and oh what trout you can enjoy, it's just a question of being there at the right time. Though Loch Hope is undoubtedly the jewel in the Altnaharra crown let me take you first on a tour of some of its other wild trout waters for they are by no means lesser neighbours and can demand just as much skill and patience.

Loch Loyal is one of my perennial favourites and I have fished it frequently over the last fifteen years or so. It slices a deep North/South valley between Ben Loyal and Ben Stuminadh and because of its long sweeping shape it can, at times, be intimidating and windswept. Its waters are dark and often stained with peat run-off and the loch is over 200ft deep in its centre. Interestingly Loyal is composed of two deep basins separated by shallows roughly 2.5 miles up from the south end. Boats will often congregate there to pick off trout lying in this area. Going afloat is recommended if you wish to fish the far shore away from the adjacent Tongue/Altnaharra road, however do use these craft with some caution. From experience I can tell you of a few near capsizes here when the gales have got up with a vengeance. Also be warned of the 'Dragons Teeth' at the southern end. These are serrated boulders which lie under the surface and are only fully visible in low water. It is easy to run aground on these and damage engine, boat or both.

These cautions aside, Loyal is a real delight to fish and can produce many a heart-stopping fishy experience. You can bank fish in the early season on Loyal for superb trout in the pound class on quite horrendous days when most sane anglers would be toasting their toes by the fire. In summer you can use tiny dry flies in flat calms and catch game little half-pounders

while fending off ferocious midge attacks. Just occasionally sea trout of 3lb or so will crop up amongst the smaller fish so be prepared. In Autumn it is possible to have the boat towed around by a salmon or possibly a ferox, those gargantuan fish rarely show themselves so it is hard to tell. This is a loch which constantly produces new surprises. Like any Highland loch it is also capable of dour days but, if you are prepared to travel around its differing bays, you can usually meet up with a few obliging fish.

Tackle for Loyal should be long rod and floating line, dapping rods can also do well in late June and July. Flies are broadly traditional 'wets', Watson Lyall prescribed using 'gaudy flies' in the late 1800s and this still holds true today. Kingfisher Butcher, Zulu, Silver Invicta and Dunkeld excel and Kate McLaren or Claret Bumble are good on the top dropper during midge hatches. The natural feeding on exposed Loyal is not overly rich (midge, olive and sedge) and the southern end tends to fish better owing to its shallow food harbouring bays. Other good areas are where extra food is being brought down into the water for example around the burns and drains which lace its shoreline. Though Loyal is daunting on a wild day, it often produces much better fish in rough conditions than when it lies quiet and still. It fishes best from April to July and then again in mid September. Late season fishing is particularly dramatic here with the autumn colours of gold and purple drenching the moors and the great stags of Ben Loyal roar their rutting calls across the loch.

Snuggled below the Queen of the Scottish Mountains Ben Loyal, is the enigmatic *Loch Hakel* which has to rank as one of the most scenic lochs in the north of Scotland. Despite being rather plagued by worm fishing it is still a select wild trout venue and is one of my most loved waters. The trout are grand fighting, golden specimens complete with black and red speckles and hues of burnished gold. Though there are some big boys hiding away amongst the little fellows (my best from here was just under 3lb), the 'average' trout is about half a pound or so but they are absolute beauties whatever their size. The feeding is rich and by late June the loch dances with mayfly while shrimp, snail and caddis litter the loch floor. The water is gin clear over a gravel and rock base with reasonable patches of weed here and there. Long skerries lead out into the loch and the edges of the islands also harbour some fine trout holds. This is a great place for dry fly when the fish are rising freely and boat or bank fishing is productive. Loch style prevails here and June and July are excellent on this loch. Good all round imitations to have on your cast include the Olive Bumble, Silver Sedge, Zulu, Pennel and Soldier Palmer. For best results on Hakel use a 9–10ft rod, floater and 4lb nylon.

Nearby *Loch Meadie* makes an ideal starting point for trout anglers new to Altnaharra. Boat and bank fishing is easy here and the trout are numerous if some-what small. The loch lies on the high exposed part of the Altnaharra/Hope road in a peat and sandstone environment. Its better fishing areas lie around the islands and the weed beds but fish can rise all over. Given its copious natural spawning it is likely that Meadie is not fished hard enough. The 'Sportsman's Guides' of old mention the trout of this loch as being 'very fine, of one or two to the pound'. Today's averages are much smaller so it looks as if there are too many fish competing for too little food. The water is peaty to clear depending on rainfall and the natural feeding similar to Loyal. A light outfit, 9–10ft rod and floating line of say 5/6 is ideal. A 4lb nylon line is all that is required and with a few old favourites like the Pennel, Zulu, Soldier Palmer or Invicta (10/12s). Go and have fun with the spirited golden occupants of this loch. Just

Loch Hakel reflects Ben Loyal, Queen of the Scottish mountains.

occasionally a bigger trout does take hold, so be prepared.

Once you have worked up a fishing appetite on Meadie try *Loch Naver* lying below the majestic bulk of Ben Kilbreck. Naver is much lesser fished than its famed sister Hope and this is somewhat remiss for, on its day, it can produce excellent browns and sea trout as well as salmon. Fly and trolling are productive here and the loch shows an interesting range of fish habitats. The northern end has numerous browns lingering in its shallows, the middle sections of the loch are productive for sea trout particularly around the burn mouths and the southern bay sees more salmon being caught. I like this idea of being able

Adrift on Loch Naver.

to hone slightly differing angling skills all within the one water and always enjoy darkly mysterious Naver. Boats are exclusively used here and traditional methods with 10–11ft rods, floating or intermediate line and 6–8lb nylon are favoured. A higher density of nylon is used as you never know quite what you might make contact with in this big deep loch. The trout of Naver principally go for either dark flies (Kates and Bumbles) or lure-type patterns such as the Dunkeld or the Teal Blue and Silver. The browns can be on the small side but there are some ferox sized ones lurking in the depths too. The sea trout are classic strong fish in the 1.8oz to 3lb plus mould. You will not get many of these but nevertheless they are there from late June onward. As an all round fishery Naver is often underrated probably because it takes too long a time to get to know it well. Most visitors to the area have but a short while to fish and Naver is a loch which does not give up her charms easily. The sea trout in particular rarely show on the surface, giving the

loch the appearance of being 'dead' water. Persevere however and she does grow on you!

Of all Altnaharra waters, enigmatic *Loch Hope* undoubtedly has the biggest reputation. Despite the loss of wild stocks further west, the sea trout of Hope continue to flourish. With no fish farms in the vicinity of its short river adjoining the sea, Hope's fish stocks have generally held up well. The trout are particularly fascinating because, though they are all technically *Salmo trutta*, they split into very obvious classes of fish. In Hope, the native browns usually remain quite small dark specimens of half a pound or less and these are genetically some of the oldest undiluted strains of trout in Scotland. Amidst these little trout of burnished gold also lie some hefty ferox which occasionally give the angler a mighty shock by taking his fly. Alongside the browns are goodly numbers of finnock, small silvery sea going trout of around a pound, which have made the journey down from the big loch to the ocean and back up again, probably all within the space of a year. The silvery and brown trout make for great sport but the crème de la crème of trout is found in the loch from July onward. These are the bigger mature sea trout which have grown fat on oceanic feeding and are now returning to spawn. Interestingly these larger sea trout very rarely run to double figure sizes, comprehensive records at Altnaharra from the 1900s on, show the bulk of mature trout being caught fall into the 2lb to 7lb class. There are of course exceptions to this rule including one from the past at 18lb but the quality of trout is magnificent and size is definitely not everything here. As we enter the new millennium current records show plentiful sea trout in Hope and unfortunately this cannot be said for many other fisheries further West. Apart from benefiting from no fish farms in the immediate area, I believe Hope has a huge advantage over other lochs in the form of its numerous spawning burns. Over thirty inflowing streams of various size rush down into the loch itself and at the head of the loch and the Strathmore River and its tributaries also provide excellent spawning facilities. Natural spawning is prolific and numbers are usually maintained at high levels.

There is no bank fishing on Hope and boat fishing is divided by beats. For this loch I would recommend gaining good local advice from a knowledgeable ghillie. The sea trout enter the loch at the north end via the Hope river and then follow defined routes around the loch. Without an initial introduction to these underwater paths, the casual visitor to Hope may find its six miles of indented shoreline a daunting prospect. Best tactics revolve around wet fly and this big windy loch cries out for traditional loch style from the boat. Dapping is also practised here but in truth, unless the trout are showing themselves very freely on the surface, I believe this method is not as productive as searching different depths with a team of wets. 'Dapping's for those who canny cast' is how I once heard it rather cruelly described!

Concentrate your efforts around where the fish 'nose' the inflowing freshwater from the burns and streams and linger in and around the shallower bays and off the various promontories. While it is generally thought that sea trout do not feed once back in fresh water, the mature sea trout of Hope often show copious amounts of food in their stomachs. I have caught sea trout in this loch full of flat winged flies like Heather fly and Oak fly, leading to the suppositions that either the migratory Hope trout convert quickly back to freshwater habits, or they are simply prolific, greedy feeders making the most of big hatches.

The best approach to tempt them involves a long rod 10–12ft, floating or intermediate line and 8lb nylon (these trout are very strong and occasionally there's a salmon amongst them). Frequent visitors to Hope often use size 8 flies with a lure-like fly on the tail, e.g. a Dunkeld or TBS and a top dropper of the Kate or Zulu variety. A mid fly may also be added for good measure, say an Invicta or Pennel, but this is a gale-battered loch and the more droppers you have the more likely you are to end up fankled and cursing. Fish your flies on a medium to fast retrieve and dibble the top dropper the last few feet before recasting. By using lures on point and black bushy flies on the dropper you are following well established techniques. It is said the point fly looks like a small fish chasing its prey and the big trout simply cuts in and snatches the dropper away, but whatever the reason, many trout fall to this ploy. It seems the ability to compete and chase down prey is particularly strong in Hope trout!

I love the rugged wildness of Altnaharra and its exciting expansive lochs – in fact if you see a small bespectacled woman muffled up in waterproofs hunched intently in the boat or pacing the bank in search of trout then give her a wave – it's probably me . . .

Chapter 15

Loch Arkaig and Loch Garry

*'You may pass over the heads of hundreds of large trout when they
are lying at rest and not hungry, and you will not catch one.'*
Charles St John

OS Map Nos. – 33, 34 and 41.
Nearest town/village(s): – Invergarry, Spean Bridge, Bunarkaig, Fort William.
County/district: – Lochaber and Inverness-shire.
Accessibility of fishing: – Good. Ardochy House Hotel and Tomdoun Hotel supply permits for Garry. Arkaig permits are available from Rod and Gun Tackle Shop and the West Highland Estate Office both in Fort William, also from various hotels in Spean Bridge and Fort William. If you go straight to Arkaig then the local forestry office within the collection of houses at the foot of the loch also does day tickets.
Best times: – Usually early and late for ferox sized specimens. Try May, June and early July for the 'normal' sized trout. These are large expanses of water and a degree of steady warmth is required to get things moving amongst those trout which do rise on the surface.
General: – Though these lochs initially look quite similar in appearance their trout populations have developed different behavioural characteristics. Fly and spinning

A cast on Garry.

on both lochs but Arkaig has a Protection Order in force and a permit must be obtained prior to starting your angling.

★

I have selected these two lochs, lying roughly 15 miles apart deep in the Lochaber and Glengarry hills, for two reasons. Firstly the waters provide a good comparison between the productivity of a loch which has been impounded by dams (Garry) and one which has naturally maintained water heights (Arkaig). Secondly they serve to illustrate typical approaches to brown trout management used on some of Scotland's large deep water lochs today. This is not to heap criticism on either of these particular waters, rather it is to show how the quality of trout angling on lochs which appear so wild and untouched, can be dramatically altered by man-made external influences.

Lets start with the tale of *Loch Arkaig* first. This is a deep narrow loch some 12 miles in length stretching from the 'Rough Bounds' of Knoydart in the West to the 'Dark Mile' in the East. To reach the loch from the Fort William/Loch Lochy side you must drive along the rather sinister winding road known as the 'Mile Dorche' (Dark Mile) which runs from Clunes out to the head of the loch. Scottish history buffs may well be aware that this is part of the route used by Bonnie Prince Charlie on his flight from Culloden and that it's a road steeped in mystery and legend. Angling buffs on the other hand usually cannot wait to reach the other end, for Loch Arkaig has a long established reputation for producing some very large wild trout.

This loch is a popular haunt with 'Ferox Man', that eccentric individualist who spends hours/days nay weeks hunched over an echo sounder in pursuit of this mighty but elusive trout. Amidst the loch's quite plentiful stock of ½ to ¾lb golden well speckled specimens lie some excellent ferox with trout in the 10lb plus range quite common. These massive trout which

Ferox!

ferox expert Ron Greer describes as being like large dull coloured sea trout, not only feed on their siblings, they also make inroads into the shoals of char which inhabit this water. Pike too are found here but fortunately not in too overwhelming a number. Trout recruitment is reasonable on Arkaig with natural spawning adequate in the numerous small burns running down into the loch. Dr Jon Watt, fisheries biologist with the Lochaber Fisheries Trust has done some electrofishing surveys of the Arkaig burns and has found that they hold adequate stocks of wild trout fry and parr to supplement the main loch. To his knowledge no restocking of Arkaig has ever taken place from outside sources and by and large the trout population appears to remain genetically intact.

Interestingly there seems to be a clear distinction between the 'normal' smaller brown trout and the ferox in Arkaig as there is in many other of Scotland's bigger waters like Awe or Ericht (see separate chapters). The lesser trout seem to stay forever small within relatively defined territories of the loch whereas the bigger fish grow much faster and rove over considerable distances. This points to two

Loch Arkaig.

separate strains of indigenous trout. In consequence your approach to fishing for them varies from traditional 'loch style' fly angling to using the ferox hunter's outfit of echo sounder, dead bait and stubby spinning rods capable of containing the great power these massive trout generate.

When fly fishing on Arkaig you want to concentrate your main efforts as far from the maddening crowd as possible. Surprisingly for a dead-end, no through road this area can get quite busy and I would urge you to take to the Western hills for some more peaceful bank angling. There are a number of small bays here and streams flow in from Glen Dessary and Glen Pean. Wading is reasonable over rock and gravel but for greater flexibility you can fish Arkaig by boat, though do note you must bring your own craft for surprisingly there are no boats for hire on the loch. One

can only presume too much vandalism has occurred here in the past as it does on many other highland lochs. Loss or damage of boats taken illegally is a constant headache for the fishery manager. Tactics are as traditional as the mighty hills surrounding Arkaig and you should have on your cast, amongst others, a Zulu, Clan Chief and Silver Invicta. If trout are visibly active on the surface use floating line loch style, otherwise try an intermediate or sink tip. The trout rise like rockets depending on what time of year you are fishing, late May and June seems best for the smaller specimens, April and September for the big boys.

Arkaig's waters are neutral to slightly acidic and range from clear to faintly peaty stained according to run off from the surrounding landscape. The natural feeding is principally midge, small sedge and olive but it is quite adequate in sustaining the 'smaller' trout population. Parts of the bank are afforested particularly the eastern reaches, however as you travel further west the loch opens out in all its majestic grandeur. Unlike many of its sister lochs, Arkaig has not been dammed and impounded for electricity-generating schemes and as a direct consequence the trout population and its food supply have remained more or less stable. Not that the loch has escaped scot-free of problems as, from the 60s to the 80s, this water saw ever more pressing demands made on it from anglers using multiple set lines. The numerous camp sites along the bank did little to enhance trout conservation and by 1990 public perception was that stocks were being decimated, particularly along the easily accessed roadside shore. As a direct result of this over-exploitation a Protection Order was introduced. Like Loch Awe in Argyll, Loch Arkaig has benefited from the PO in that it has cut down the amount of illegal set line angling and allowed some trout populations to re-establish themselves closer to shore.

Though trolling and spinning still go on, indeed they are a permitted method on the day ticket, the destructive 'ten rods strung along the bank artists' have somewhat declined in number.

Further resource exploitation took place on Arkaig when smolt cages were introduced at the Eastern end of the loch. Now, if you choose to fly fish in that area, you can be plagued by little escapees, however the remainder of the loch does not seem to be as affected. Some anglers, usually trolling or spinning, deliberately fish near the cages as a number of the loch's Arctic char population have taken to feeding voraciously on the fish farm waste. Some unusually large char of 7lb or more have been caught in the vicinity of the farm which shows the char's willingness to adapt its diet according to food availability. Despite its past problems with over fishing, Arkaig remains a place for drama filled trout angling amidst grand hills and heck, take along a glass case just in case.

Nearby *Loch Garry* needs similar tactics and equipment but considerably more perseverance. Garry is linked by tunnel to the even bigger Loch Quoich above it and it forms part of a massive hydroelectric scheme which runs down to the power station at Invergarry. This is utilisation of water resources on a truly massive scale, and anglers' fortunes have fluctuated on Loch Garry almost as much as its water heights.

Initially, after the post war impound-ment of Garry, a dramatic feast of natural feeding became available to the resident trout and growth rates proved spectacular. The loch always held a reasonable head of ferox and Arctic char, however with the sudden raising of water levels by over 20ft, all the indigenous fish populations enjoyed an absolute bonanza of feeding. Bill Currie wrote in the late 60s/early 70s that Loch Garry seemed to have 'risen to a new peak of trouting' with the connecting Loch of Inchlaggan which

Loch Arkaig has benefited from a Protection Order.

forms part of Loch Garry, then producing bags of free rising trout in the pound range. Much larger trout also came regularly to the fly fisher with a record ferox of 18lb 4oz caught on the fly, a Black Pennel I believe, in 1965.

After the feast, the famine was bound to arrive, however, though the quality of angling fluctuated, good fly-caught trout still came from the upper parts of Garry and Inchlaggan in particular until the early 80s. Since then the overall picture has altered for all time, I believe principally because pike introduced in the late 1970s began to multiply and overrun the loch. Apparently pike were placed in the loch in an attempt to diversify the fish species and provide coarse angling as well as game fishing. To introduce pike into any fresh-water system already containing high quality salmonids seems to me to be little short of crass environmental vandalism. However there we are, the damage was indiscriminately done and game anglers paid a heavy price. Over the next thirty years the pike population has established itself throughout the Garry system and prime trout water has evolved from the relatively free rising to the incredibly dour. It is my belief that pike are now the 'number one' species in Garry and though large ferox trout are still taken, the overall range of trout sizes in the loch (from fry to smolt to adult) has now declined to unacceptably low levels. It is now rare to catch a young trout of say ¾lb, though some char of this size upward can still be caught late in the season. Sadly it is either a leviathan trout of 3lb plus capable of competing with the pike for food, or little or nothing to the fly.

This unsatisfactory situation has not been helped by the poor availability of natural spawning in Garry, with many of the little inflowing burns containing hard bedrock rather than suitable amounts of good gravel. The survival of any trout parr that do make it past the egg stage is further hindered by their growing sites being alternately dried out or flooded as water levels rise and fall in the main loch area. Add to these problems the lack of protection afforded to the remaining trout with unregulated methods of fishing and forestry developments which tip their acid run-off into already slightly acidic water and the whole picture is disturbing. Unfortunately, all community attempts to improve the trout fishing and thereby generate further much needed local rev-enue have so far floundered. To angle for Loch Garry trout now almost certainly means using a spinning rod and trolling a Rapala, Toby or live bait. With the 'average' size of trout coming in at 4lb and

char up to 8lb or so Garry is still fished but few anglers seem to use a fly rod now, more's the pity.

Some still persist with fly fishing (myself included) for the natural feeding is actually quite reasonable with caddis, midge, hatched sedge and olive prevalent. However it is rather soul destroying not seeing any trout rising to the natural hatch, however prolific. Evening angling is some-times more productive but can still be hard work on floating, intermediate or sinking line. Try a massive Muddler on the top dropper to create surface disturbance and perhaps a Dunkeld or Ace of Spades lure on the point and you never know, you might get lucky. And, if you do manage a 'big un' please photograph him and put him back, not to do so these days almost verges on the criminal offence!

I am always very reluctant to state that any wild trout angling is in a state of decline. Public perception can make fools of us all, especially if you go and look at so called 'poor' or 'dour' trout lochs in winter and find numerous fat trout busy spawning in the burns. It is easy to declare 'the fishing is not what it was' but highly difficult to prove it. Looking at Garry and Arkaig they have both had a fair share of negatives. Yet while Arkaig has rallied somewhat with local partnerships and the introduction of a Protection Order, Garry's decline has gone on largely unchecked. Fluctuating water levels from hydro schemes, poor spawning facilities, unregulated fishing and the unnecessary introduction of a voracious predator, the pike, have all contributed to the once magnificent loch's present state. There's even a fish farm there in the middle of it though with so many pike I doubt whether escapees get a chance to plague the angler! Such environmental influences are man-made and the ecological effects are there for all to see. I shall leave you to make up your own mind about how you wish Scotland's wild trout habitats to be developed in the future . . .

Chapter 16

The Lochs of Assynt

'Of the lake are the mystery, old romance and the larger air.'
Hamish Stuart

OS Map No. – 15
Nearest town/village: – Lochinver
County/district: – Assynt district of Sutherland.
Accessibility of fishing: – Very good. Trout Fishing Permits from Assynt Angling Club and Assynt Crofters' Trust via Lochinver Tourist office, Stoer and Drumbeg POs, Ardglas Guest house and most local hotels.
Best times: – Generally May through to September though a mild April is also productive.
General: – Traditional wet fly country but dry flies effective when trout are rising well. Copious limestone in the vicinity leading to exceptional feeding on certain lochs. Profuse mayfly on a good number of waters. A fair amount of hard rough walking is involved for some of the more remote waters. Boats available on some lochs but bank fishing is often as productive.

★

The lands of Assynt exercise a compelling, magnetic appeal over the many anglers who visit them. The scenery in this region of Sutherland is some of the most spectacular in the North of Scotland. With strange lunar-like hills like Quinag, Suilven and Canisp rising directly up from sea level it's something of a hill walker's paradise, but for the fisherman it's probably the next best thing to heaven on earth. The principal community in this dramatic area is Lochinver and most of the many trout fishings here can be accessed from outlets in this pretty seaboard village. Assynt angling aficionados are drawn here as much by the stunning landscapes as by the size of trout for there can be few finer places on God's earth in which to catch fish. If you like long walks in very remote surroundings and are reasonably physically fit then this is the place for you.

There is a huge amount of top quality trout fishing available (several hundred lochs and lochans) and there are endless opportunities to enjoy angling in a vast unspoilt environment. Assynt waters range from small lochans speckled with lily pads to long miles of ferox and char water like Loch Assynt. Despite this land's obviously wild appeal, many of the lochs of Assynt hold some remarkably well fed brown trout. The casual visitor must be forgiven for assuming that this area of bleak moor and rugged hill, so often rain swept and gale lashed, can produce only tiddlers and a few ferox monsters. In actual fact there is an excellent range of fish sizes and the reason for this apparent contradiction lies within the land itself. Great strips of limestone curl their way around the parish of Assynt particularly in the Inchnadamph area and the whole area is deceptively fertile. Many of the lochs are crystal clear and the natural feeding for the trout bears more resemblance to an English chalkstream than a barren Highland landscape. Shrimp, mayfly, caddis, damsel fly, midge and sedge are found in abundance in Assynt and as a consequence of this rich larder the trout grow to surprisingly plump proportions. The fish range from ½lb to 2lb plus depending on your chosen water and a number of lochs also contain the mighty ferox and the mysterious Arctic char.

I have been an ardent fan of Assynt for well over twenty years spurred on by the writings of early 'pioneering' anglers like McDonald Robertson or Carron Wellington. Though they seemed less concerned with the natural feeding in Assynt and more with some very large bags of trout, they wrote in atmospheric terms of the beauty of the area and also offered some useful hints on the angling. Their practical advice centred around traditional wet patterns like the Peter Ross, Butchers or Alexandra which McDonald Robertson said should be 'cast on a delicate line at rapid intervals' very much in the modern 'loch style' vein. Wellington used similar standard wet fly tactics or a mix of dry fly on the dropper and wet on the point and he seems to have had endless success with a fly he called a 'Shaggy Whaup'. As far as I can ascertain the name of this old fly refers to dressing its wing/hackle with curlew feathers as 'whaup' is an old name for this particular bird. Whatever the exact pattern was remains something of a mystery. Wellington is coy on giving the precise dressing, but I suspect it resembled any bushy, well palmered fly with a brownish hue. A Bumble or Kate McLaren would be a good alternative to the mysterious Shaggy Whaup though if you know what the original dressing was, do drop me a line! Wellington also declared that he thought the trout *'not so fastidious about their choice of diet as they are about the time and manner in which it is presented to them'* which still has a ring of truth about it today.

Happily the brown trout fishing has altered surprisingly little in quality since those early days of exploration and this is still very much *the* venue for traditional 'loch style' angling for freshwater brownies. It is almost as if the mountains frown upon anything new fangled – this is an ancient land used to the old ways and the mighty hills seem to strongly disapprove of pink Baby Dolls and luminescent Christmas Trees! For best results therefore you should equip yourself with the simple armoury of your forebears and a 10ft rod, floating line (I prefer WF for the gales) and 4lb nylon should suffice. Add a range of old trusty favourites like the Soldier Palmer, Black Pennel, Invicta, Bumbles, Greenwell's, Bibio and Zulu in size 10/12 and you are ready for action.

Where to start in Assynt can be a delightful problem but exploring the lochs to the North of Lochinver in the dramatic *Baddidarach* and *Stoer* areas (lochs now largely falling under the auspices of the Assynt Crofters' Trust), is always worthwhile. Some of the waters here, especially those away from the road, hold very fine

Fraser Campbell works the top dropper 'loch style' in Assynt.

Lands of Assynt.

trout which are occasionally tempted to rise to a big dark fly on a warm July evening. Be warned however that these brown beauties are not easily fooled and you can gain a false impression of size from some lochs by being constantly pestered by their much smaller immature brethren. I once spent a long warm dreamy day walking the lochans in the Baddidarach area encountering many trout in the 4–6oz range. As the heat of the day subsided one last cast in the dusk light suddenly left me shocked and open mouthed when what looked like an enormous torpedo sucked down the fly, arched its back and shot down into the depths of weed taking my fly and dignity with it – 4lb at least, maybe more, so be prepared!

For further drama wander among some of the lochs the Inchnadamph side, for here the limestone seams are particularly rich. On a recent visit I fished *Lochs Awe* and *Ailsh*, ably assisted by the highly knowledgeable REFFIS instructor Fraser Campbell then of the Inver Lodge Hotel, and the trout were to prove quite magnificent. What a joy it is to fish limestone lochs which do not require the patience of a saint in order to raise a local brownie! Trout should come thick and fast to traditional flies like the Kate McLaren, Olive Bumble and Greenwell's with modern variants like

the Doobry or Clan Chief also useful. Fraser also had additional 'never fail me' flies, most of which were familiar traditional patterns apart from an American fly known as the Renegade. This fly in size 10/12 resembles a Knotted Midge and I give the dressing as follows: – Gold Tag, white rear hackle, peacock herl body, front hackle of red game. There should be no merging of the hackles when tying so that the fly retains a striking appearance. The Renegade seems very effective fished wet throughout the seasons at Assynt, so give it a go.

All the flies we used were fished in traditional 'loch style' fashion in teams of two or three and these were cast out from the boat, allowed to sink momentarily and then brought back briskly through the waves. Prior to lifting off the top dropper was danced across the surface and this proved a great trout attractor. It is worth noting that the edges of the prominent wind lanes on the lochs are exceptionally productive. Some wind lanes were of the streaked foam variety but there were also those more unusual wavy lines of water which look rather like clear oil slicks. Most of the more 'oily' wind lanes found on Assynt lochs, and for that matter throughout Scotland, normally contain water of a different temperature to the immediate surrounds. The naturally occurring 'slicks' are formed when the wind changes direction

Quinag in the setting sun - Assynt.

and strips of (warmer) water are left on the surface. These concentrate trout fodder like daphnia, nymph shucks and spent flies and the trout near to them have an absolute field day (see also Chapter 2 on loch water phenomena).

Fraser Campbell's expertise in working the top dropper in true 'loch style' fashion was a pleasure to behold. None of that pussyfooting around with figure of eight retrieves here. He simply cast out a medium length of line and then after a brisk retrieve, dibbled the top dropper over the waves. His fishing forefathers would have been proud of this approach! It was interesting that the trout on my May visit seemed definitely to prefer flies with a greenish tinge. Whether this was simply to do with the natural hatch being mainly green drake and spurwing or whether they were just not intimidated by this apparently familiar colour I cannot say. However, apart from the late hours of dusk when black flies did better, green patterns were the order of the day with Olive Bumble and Greenwell's accounting for the majority of trout. Both bank and boat fishing are very productive in Assynt, and most waters fly fish better in the shallower bays than out over the deeps.

Hefty ferox trout also lurk in the icy depths where they hunt down the abundant Arctic char of this region, however you need a huge amount of patience to tempt them. Echo sounders and trolling are the normal method for these monster trout though just occasionally a bank fly fisher hooks a big one from the shore and all is forgiven. Interestingly another of the lochs we attempted looked to contain an abundance of 'baby' ferox for virtually all the trout caught had deep orange bellies, heavy black ringed spots and that give-away green/blue sheen on the gill covers. This loch is linked to the sea by a river and it was interesting to speculate whether these were distant relatives of the 'migratory' ferox found in the likes of the River Ken in the borders. How nice it would be to tag some of the larger wild trout and see where they wandered, for I bet they travel many a mile between sections of the river and the loch.

The ferocious fighting abilities of all the Assynt trout, ferox or otherwise, make for some memorable, heart stopping moments and is probably the principal reason anglers love the area. That and the fact that once you leave the road, 'civilisation' is largely excluded from this remote wild land. It is easy to see how many fly fishers constantly return to this wonderful region so full of wild trout, stern mountains, red deer and soaring eagles. I, like many, am forever caught up in its spell . . .

'Baby' ferox - pure perfection.

Chapter 17

Loch Awe

'Expectation throbs pleasantly within the angler when he is making preparations for his expedition to any loch, and when that loch happens to be one of the largest in the country . . . the great possibilities but increase the joys of anticipation.'

R. C. Bridgett

OS Maps Nos. – 50 and 55.
*Nearest village*s: – Oban, Lochgilphead, Dalmally, Loch Awe village, Ford, Cladich, Port Sonachan, Ardbrecknish, Kilchrenan, Dalavich.
Accessibility of fishing: – Excellent. Numerous local permit outlets including hotels, shops, petrol stations and boat hirers. Various tackle shops in central Scotland also supply advance tickets.
Best times: – Awe is a noted early season venue, it usually fishes best from March to June and then again in September.
General: – Traditional flies fished loch style from the boat work well but a wide range of methods are also allowed including bait, spin and troll. Boats are recommended to give much more freedom to travel over this vast expanse of water but wear a life-jacket, Awe can be a dangerously windy place. Bank fishing is fair but there can be a contrast of fishing styles experienced on the shore. Also there are small bank fishing exclusion zones, normally private gardens or similar, see maps provided with permit. Note: Loch Awe is covered by a Protection Order and it is illegal to fish without permission.

★

Of all the bigger Scottish lochs, *Loch Awe* is rated one of the finest. Its idyllic setting and fabulous brown trout (many of which grow to leviathan proportions) have made it an ever-popular angling venue for well over 150 years. Its fishing challenges are renowned and to gain a fuller perspective, it is worthwhile looking back over some of this loch's long illustrious past. In many ways, the development of Loch Awe mirrors the overall progress of Scottish loch trout angling, particularly as practised near the main centres of conurbation. Numerous angling icons past and present have fished here and their pithy comments portray Awe as an enigmatic, demanding water full of exciting hidden surprises.

In days gone by, Loch Awe was hugely productive and way back in 1857 the venerable Augustus Grimble found that 'it was an everyday occurrence for two rods to get from 3 to 8 dozen fine trout of herring size' per day. The esteemed Francis Francis also wrote of Awe in glowing terms and in 1874 referred to its trout as 'tough antagonists, among the gamest I have ever handled'. Somewhat obtusely however, he also refers to the 'ferox being not nearly so plentiful as formerly in Loch Awe' and claimed that the Awe ferox 'do not as a rule run large – under 6lb'. No sooner had Francis written this when records from the Taychreggan Hotel showed huge bags of salmon and trout in 1885, including a record ferox of 39.5lb being caught in the loch. I wonder if he was made to eat his words! Dry fly doyen R. C. Bridgett c 1924, wrote of Awe as a loch of 'enormous bays wherein must

Loch Awe trout.

roam veritable monarchs of the deep' and that the water was 'well stocked with sporting fish of fine quality'. Pioneering angler McDonald Robertson reported in the 1940s that Loch Awe held monster trout normally caught by trolling but occasionally taken on the fly and colourfully describes a 'Tussle with a Salmo-Ferox' . . . and so the glorious tales rolled on.

It seems that over its first 100 years or so of recorded angling history, Loch Awe and its fish populations remained little altered in real terms. Apart from the introduction of added competition in the form of pike around the 1830s, the resident trout, salmon, perch and two types of Arctic char saw little overall change to their environment. However from the post war era on, semi industrial developments occurred around Awe and these brought about some degree of change in the native fish habitat. Blanket afforestation around the loch partly disrupted the natural spawning streams used by the native brown trout and also the 'barrage' hydroelectric scheme of the 1950s drastically reduced the numbers of migratory salmon running

into the loch. The introduction of a freshwater rainbow trout farm in the 1970s (still operating today) also meant unwanted 'escapee' competitors increasingly invaded indigenous trout territories. Overfishing became a real problem during the 1980s when increased leisure time meant this already popular loch came under heavy angling pressure from all quarters, legitimate or otherwise. By the early 1990s the indigenous trout stocks looked under significant threat and a Protection Order was introduced in 1992 complete with bailiff system. This order, still in place today, has had a very beneficial effect in cutting down the amount of illegal set line angling on the loch (see Chapter 2, legalities of fishing). The Awe Fisheries Trust was also set up in the 1990s and a resident fisheries biologist is employed working full time on research into Loch Awe fish populations.

Today, despite a degree of fluctuating fortune, the loch has regained a degree of stability. The halcyon days of Grimble may not be there but for all that, picturesque Loch Awe still ranks as one of the most enduring of wild trout venues. The scenery is quite superb with its clear

Loch Awe nestles below the heights of Ben Cruachan.

waters cutting a glacial valley of over 25 miles across Argyllshire from Ford at the Western end, to Kilchurn and the gloomy Pass of Brander in the Eastern reaches. Though not particularly deep (around 300ft at maximum depth), Awe is the longest loch in Scotland and it certainly remains one of the most striking. The grand mountains of Ben Cruachan and the more distant Ben Lui gird its northern end, birch and pine swathe the lower hills and its lovely indented shoreline is sprinkled with ruined castles, ancestral seats and ancient burial grounds. Islands and crannogs dot the loch and wildlife of all kinds is abundant. Amongst other attractions, this is the place to occasionally see ospreys on the wing. Despite assorted commercial development along the banks, the whole area retains much of its original character and once afloat, a more peaceful setting in which to fish is hard to imagine.

For the angler, the native brown trout of Awe really put the icing on this scenic cake, being beautifully marked and of excellent fighting quality. Over time there has apparently been various attempts made to 'restock' Loch Awe, including the addition of Leven ova and fry by the local

Association in the early 1900s. Whether these stock additions impacted on the local trout population is unclear but the Awe strain of trout, diluted or undiluted, remains of consistently high quality. To a man those past pioneers of angling roundly declared the Awe trout as being excellent fighters, well marked and agile and the loch's trout today still carry these 'hallmarks' with pride. Awe trout are supremely athletic, butter coloured fish which tear away with your fly like trains. Despite the 'average' fly caught size wavering around the ½ to 1lb mark (remember averages are never an exact guide to quality), there are goodly trout up to 3lb caught regularly. And just occasionally much larger trout also fall to the fly including a recent 8lb 8oz fish entrapped on a Silver Invicta. Specimen hunters can also troll for the secretive ferox and Awe currently holds the current British record for rod caught brown trout at 25lb 5.7oz taken in 1996. Though I am not a fan of trolling, it was once archly described to me as being for the lazy and the desperate, I do see it has some advantage when the big loch goes into one of her more drastically fickle moods. Awe is no different from any Highland water in this respect and trolling can render a larger trout or two in impossible fly conditions when the trout have put their noses well down – enough said!

Loch Awe presents a huge variation of challenges and this is one of the few lochs where I do recommend using a boat rather than fishing from the shore. Twenty-five miles of loch is an awesome (sorry!) amount of water to cover and going afloat is really essential to achieve a visit to some of the more secluded bays. Anglers new to this water should equip themselves with a long rod of 10ft or more together with a number of different fly lines. Floating, intermediate and fast sink are all used here according to the day's cycle of events. Experienced local anglers favour intermediates especially in the early half of the season, but be prepared to change line density. I noticed a lot more spool changing going on here than on my northern 'floater' waters. The real excitement comes from fishing flies at different depths in the clear translucent depths – you never know quite what will take hold next!

There is comparatively rich feeding for trout and shrimp, snail, caddis, olive, sedge and heather moth all form part of the fishes' menu here. However, hatches on Awe tend to be sporadic rather than sustained and consequently a motley selection of flies are cast upon these waters. Popular traditional wet flies include the Kate McLaren, Clan Chief, Silver Invicta and Wickham's while the Mini Muddler is often strategically placed on the bob fly (all size 10/12). Teams of two or three flies are commonly used on intermediate line if the trout are not show-ing, but if they oblige by appearing on the surface, a floating line with perhaps a dry Sedge or Greenwell's will do the business. Most hackled flies do well here and two good old style imitations for Awe include one with an orange body, ginger hackle and pheasant tail wing and the other has a peacock herl body, black hackle and water hen wing. These are simple flies, so simple in fact they are without names being referred to as imitation 'Number 30 and 31 for Loch Awe' in the book *British Anglers' Manual*. As they have shrimp, sedge and midge connotations I am sure they would still work admirably well.

Because rainbow fish farm escapees sometimes interrupt the proceedings you will often find anglers using a wide variety of lures alongside the old patterns. Of the more sedate of these, the Dunkeld and the Ace of Spades will work for both the browns and the rainbows. Incidentally the rainbows of Awe are unwanted guests and should be killed. These are exceptionally greedy trout and gulp down much of the natural food meant for the indigenous species. Also, by providing extra competition amongst the resident fish, these American interlopers create additional stress on the native browns. That said, the escapees occasionally provide a bit of relief if the brown trout are playing exceptionally hard to get, so they do have a modicum of sporting use. It's interesting that after the rainbow trout farm was established on Awe, many anglers, my late father included, perceived a decline in the trout fishing. In truth it is difficult to establish whether the escapees are an extreme threat to the fishing or simply a nuisance to be tolerated. On the one hand it could be said that trout numbers had been declining well before the rainbow made its intrusion, on the other hand did the rainbow further hasten this decline? The fisheries biologist is still working on that one!

For the browns, the best time to visit Awe is usually in the early half of the season from March to June, thereafter the fishing can fluctuate between 'highs' and 'lows' before there is a late burst again in September. In the first half of the year the browns often linger very close to the edge and excellent bags are taken, whereas after

Awe from the West.

of these fish being recaptured. While some trout were caught only yards from their release point, some trout had travelled huge distances, being caught up to 8 miles away from their release point. This gives rise to speculation that some Awe trout have genetic imprints which make them travel from territory to territory while others do not. Equally one could follow Malloch's theory of the early 1900s that open water trout (like those of Loch Leven) travel through water 'at the rate of 2 miles an hour, their speed gradually increasing till July, when it reaches 3 miles an hour'. Malloch thought that trout of the Leven strain travelled around 6–18 inches under the surface usually heading upwind. Quite how he ascertained this is unclear! These ideas rather fly in the face of the convention which argues brown trout are territorial creatures, however it may help explain the results from Awe. Whatever the reason, common sense tells us that anglers should also move around and follow the fish!

All in all, Loch Awe has been something of a great 'survivor' for though there has been some past exploitation of this water, notably of its environmental and fish resources, the water and its trout have largely held on to their reputations. This is undoubtedly due to the fact that anglers and other water and land users have shown a willingness to co-operate on long term conservation issues. Of course there have been and always will be differences of opinion but by and large, interested parties have not lost sight of the central theme of maintaining Awe as one of the premier wild fisheries of Scotland. Tribute must be paid to the local Loch Awe Improvement Association, to the Awe Fisheries Trust and to the resident fisheries biologist for the continuing health of the wild trout within this wonderful water. They may not be caught in quite the colossal baskets of old, but in the modern age do we really need to be that greedy anyway?

June their roving habits seem to kick in and they can be found anywhere around the loch including over its deepest centre. Occasional limestone outcrops occur around the shorelines and the water has a neutral to slightly alkaline pH. Loch style fishing tight into the shore, around the shallow bays and in the lee of the islands is the most popular method of angling here but those who are prepared to travel around the loch do best. Sometimes the fish will be feeding well in one area yet be totally inactive in another, but that makes exploration that much more exciting. It also makes considerable sense in the light of recent tracking experiments carried out on the Awe browns. The fisheries biologist and his team, tagged and released around 160 indigenous trout back into the loch. Anglers were then asked to report on any

Chapter 18

Loch Calder and the Reay Lochs

A West Caithness Selection

'The wind on the heath, brother, two good things. . .

Borrow

OS Map Nos. – 11 and 12
Nearest town/villages: – Thurso, Reay, Halkirk.
Accessibility of fishing: – Very good. Permits and boats for Loch Calder are freely available from Harpers Tackle in Thurso and Mr Mackay, Calder Farm. Reay Lochs permits are also from Harpers.
Best times: – Normally from early season onward but May to mid August are considered the most productive.

General: – Caithness is predominantly a land of limestone and most of its angling waters are very fertile and alkaline in nature. Tackle along traditional lines is usually used, however there are excellent opportunities for dry fly and nymph according to the conditions. Shallow lochs of uniform depth like the Reay Lochs need thigh waders; wading on Calder must be exercised with care as there are unseen holes, ditches and soft mud patches. Long walks are sometimes required to reach shorelines not nearest the road but boats can be hired on the waters mentioned.

★

We moved from Aberdeen to the county of Caithness in 1984 and, as a fisher brought up on the ever busy shoulder to shoulder angling of the central belt, I could not believe the spacious quality and quantity of lochs available in this unusual wild land. Caithness is not only a region of vast rolling moor, stupendous sea cliffs, big skies, rich limestone seams and green agriculture, it is quite simply, a trout angler's paradise. What makes this county stand head and shoulders above the rest is its extraordinarily unique angling environment. To say this is a luxurious 'chalkstream' habitat full of unfettered trout, tucked away amid the wild Northern areas of Britain, is not an exaggeration, it is hard

Simply smashing! Jane Clarke with a 6lber from Loch Calder.

A trout to hand in the gloaming – Reay Lochs.

fact. Anglers who dismiss the Highlands as a land of peat bog where the only trout they are likely to catch are small half-starved specimens, should be compelled to spend a month in Caithness during the mayfly season!

Virtually all the trout angling lochs of this county are clear alkaline waters enriched from a variety of underlying limestone. This limestone is found in a number of forms including marl, a clay like mud which crofters of old extracted from lochs to use as a fertiliser, and shell sand deposits. At one time all of Caithness was covered by the sea to form an ancient sea loch called the 'Loch of Orcadie', and when the ocean retreated it left behind rich shell sand deposits still visible today. Indeed, any number of our shallow crystalline lochs, could technically be known as inland 'machair' lochs, Loch St Johns being a classic example of this phenomenon. In addition to the rich soil, the interior of Caithness is dotted with a host of natural springs known as Chalybeate Springs and these bubble up water enriched with minerals, which then finds its way down into all the watercourses. These springs are little discussed if ever, yet I feel they play an important role in maintaining and improving the natural water quality of the county.

Even though you might think me a little biased, in all truth you will find it difficult to match the overall environmental quality of the Caithness trout waters. Do not let that somewhat bleak grey aspect fool you, though admittedly in doing so, you simply follow the example of many who should know better. Even Volume XV of the Statistical Account of Scotland refers to Caithness as 'flat and uninteresting' and of 'dreary appearance'. Obviously not written by a trout angler!

The natural feeding is hugely diverse and of excellent quality. Shrimp, snail,caddis, sedges, sticklebacks, olives, numerous midge varieties, mayfly, stonefly, beetles, heather fly, damsel and dragon fly all exist here in profusion. With the diet of our trout being so rich and varied you would expect a fat trout on virtually every cast. However, there is one powerful variable which regulates our fly fishing and ensures most attempts at 'mass slaughter' do not happen and that is the volatile

Dreamy days on Calder.

Caithness weather. Caithness is so exposed (fishing on the edge of the world, is how it was once described) that variations in conditions, which occur rapidly and often, make for supremely challenging fishing. It is not so much that the wild trout are not there in abundance, it is more the swinging changes in the weather which dictates how your angling day will go. Gales, hail, boiling sunshine, mist, sleet, flat calm and thunder are all experienced here as elsewhere, sometimes all in one day, and the Caithness trout seem more highly attuned than most to these altering conditions. Consequently they go on and off the feed with great rapidity. While I am not making any excuses on catch rates do bear this in mind when fishing in this fabulous area. If all else fails you can always blame our weather!

Though Caithness is covered with famous trout lochs I want in this chapter to concentrate on a few of the waters of the western fringe of the county, lochs I know intimately well. To look first at my favourite learning ground – *Loch Calder*, this is a big loch, wild and daunting to some, but it is a superb teaching water which I treat as one of my oldest, wisest and most knowledgeable friends. It is here I have most contemplated the mysteries of the wild trout, observed nature at its finest and pondered on tactical nuances too numerous to mention. I have gleaned a huge amount on trout angling from wandering this loch's lonely banks, not least the vital tactic of treating each bay and shallow as a separate micro habitat rather than looking at the water as three long miles of empty shoreline. I feel I owe Calder a great debt of gratitude and though it is not perhaps classed as the county's 'premier' water (famed Loch Watten still lays claim to this honour) I write on it straight from the heart.

Spring fed Calder is the deepest loch in Caithness (about 90ft in its upper centre) and it lies over a sandstone basin just a couple of miles or so to the south of Thurso. It is thought the loch was originally two smaller separate waters but that when it was selected as a reservoir to supply water to Thurso, its levels were artificially raised to their current status. This theory is borne out by the significant ingress of water at the south west end (known locally as 'New Bay') and also the underwater strip of land which runs across the middle

Glorious Calder trout.

of the loch from West to East. Occasionally in very low water this shallow strip is just visible by its top growth of weed and it is a popular place for a drift or two, as is the New Bay which has flooded over rich agricultural land.

Calder is sparklingly clear and alkaline and has an abundant stock of wild indigenous trout of superb fighting quality. Though they vary slightly in coloration from dark orangy yellow to light pale gold, they are understood to be largely of the original indigenous strain. It is thought that stock additions have not been made here in the past and, given the loch's abundant natural spawning facilities, it would seem very unlikely. The natural feeding is rich and typifies the range of invertebrate life found in the county; shrimp, olive, stone-fly, sedge, midge and mayfly to name but a few. The trout range from a few ounces to ferox proportions and though the average is around ½lb there are many occasions when Calder produces a 'biggie' of anything from 1lb 8oz to 8lb plus, so be prepared! Also present are a good head of Arctic char and the ferox trout have a field day chasing and feeding on these deep water fish. These beautifully marked char are sometimes caught on the fly in May

and September. In the former month the char, which I often think resemble unusual goldfish, are caught while following the first nourishing daphnia blooms of the season, whereas in the latter half of the year they may be exploring the banks in preparation for spawning.

Not only does Calder provide abundant fish stocks, it provides water suited to any angling ability from complete beginner to the advanced specialist. It fishes well right from the word go and unlike its more shallow marl neighbours Calder's waters remain crystal clear throughout the season. Excellent trout in the 1lb plus range are caught close in from March to late June, thereafter a change seems to take place in the feeding habits of the larger trout. They seem almost to migrate out into deeper water, perhaps concentrating on the daphnia blooms, and their places in the shallows are taken up by the smaller trout of 4 to 8oz. This phenomenon is also observed on larger lochs like Loch Awe so it is not just a Caithness characteristic. I find bank fishing the most productive on Calder until around late July when a boat sometimes becomes more of an advantage. This is a wild windy loch however so do go afloat with caution.

Tackle errs on the traditional, 10–11ft

The setting sun on Loch Calder.

wild trout behaviour, lie to the south of the village of Reay and they are considered two of the more difficult and challenging lochs in this area. They lie 200ft above sea level and both are spring fed from a limestone base. Their alkaline waters, which rarely reach a depth of over 6ft, are gin clear in calm weather but after high winds can become silty, 'stirred' as the locals call it. To look from afar at these rather bleak stretches of water, lying on a high moor cluttered with nouveau forestry, you would be forgiven for assuming little if anything lurks within their depths. Indeed they are often inaccurately spoken about in disparaging terms by anglers who have never experienced anything of their true glory. Frequently the lochs appear quiet and lifeless simply because the loch's bottom feeding is so rich in shrimp, nymph and caddis that the trout rarely need to make any effort to rise. However the truth is that anglers have quietly fished these lochs for well over a century, references to them can be found in Watson Lyall's 'Sportsman's Guides' of the 1800s. Generations of fishers have enjoyed the profusion of mayfly, shrimp, stickleback, fat caddis, snail, midge, olive, heather fly and sedges found on these waters and the magnificent fish which rise to them. It simply takes a sustained and abundant surface hatch to bring the trout up to the surface and when those sleek powerful beauties do come on, then it's drama all the way.

The resident trout of the Reay Lochs fall into two interesting divisions. One population shows Leven characteristics with silvery flanks and athletic sporting ability. These trout with their longer bodies and small heads, show a definite tendency to rove pelagic style around the Upper Loch. They are much more akin to sea trout and I believe their origin could either date back to when the loch was part of the sea or (more likely) they are an introduced Leven strain put there in the early 1900s. The

rods, WF floating lines and 4lb nylon though there is scope to be adaptable and do try using the short rod/light line technique in flat calm, it can pay dividends. Popular flies on Calder do not stray much from the Soldier Palmer, Pennel, Bibio, Zulu, Ke He and Invicta mould (size 10–12) but there are occasions when a tiny fly like a Greenwell Spider (16) will do well. Success with small flies normally comes on hard bright relatively still days and I am sure the trout take this pattern as an imitation of a midge about to hatch. Whether in the boat or on the bank concentrate casting effort around where the shallows runs into the deep and fishing around Calder's many bays, promontories and weed beds is usually highly productive. There are days when nothing happens here (normally during oppressive thundery lows) but these are in the minority and if we don't meet there then I will see you on the slightly more demanding *Reay Lochs* . . .

These unusual shallow marl waters, on which I have spent many hours researching

The Wet May tied by Harry Davidson.

other class of trout more present in the Lower Loch, is the classic 'yellow belly' strain with deep orangy gold flanks and heavy black spotting. These trout seem highly territorial, rarely straying from their patch and tend to bottom feed except in June, July and August when the surface appearance of mayfly and/or Bibio will make them rise with some regularity. They are probably more related to the original strain of fish, a fact borne out by the occasional capture in their midst of 'Parr Marked' trout (trout with grey fingerprint markings along their lower flanks). Eminent natural historian Harvie Brown, made reference to trout with these markings being found in Caithness and Sutherland as far back as the 1870s, so they could be related to some of the oldest resident trout strains.

The natural spawning is also intriguing on these lochs for the Lower Loch trout appear to run up through the umbilical stream leading to the Upper Loch and then make their way around the loch to spawn on the Upper Loch's redds. Unfortunately the upper redds are not nearly as favourable as the gravel-based adjoining burn, yet the genetic influence seems so strong that very few trout are ever seen spawning in the better quality stream. Also the resident trout of both lochs will run to spawn at very defined times. The first wave will occur in late October whenever there has been sufficient rain to flush the Upper Loch stream and cover the redds. Then there will be pauses of up to two weeks when no trout will run followed by another sudden burst of spawning. This pattern of spawning interspersed with 'breaks' could mean different generations of trout run at different times or simply that the trout are having a rest before another effort on the redds. Certainly I have recorded the fabulous sight of wild trout spawning as early as 23 October and as late as 5 December.

The Reay Lochs are the home of dry fly on floating line, indeed they are so shallow that in low water wet flies will snag on the bottom, and some classic patterns to try here include the dry Mayfly, Grey Wulff, dry Red Sedge, dry March Brown, dry Black Sedge, dry Greenwell's (size 10–14) and so on. Harry Davidson's tying of the 'Wet May' in 10s or 12s is exceptionally useful during the prolonged mayfly hatch from June to August. Harry tied the fly in the 1970s to resemble a mayfly nymph fished wet, but it is equally useful when fished as dry either on the top dropper or as a single fly.

The Wet May (size 10/12/14)
Body – yellow floss
Rib – black thread (3 well spaced turns should suffice)
Hackle – badger (white with black centre) dyed yellow (ordinary yellow clothes dye will suffice, not too garish)
Tail – 3 strands of cock pheasant tied with a slight upturn.

This tying is a particularly good representation of the Caithness mayfly which can appears locally in two distinct types. We have both the brown bodied specimens with a faint grey lace wing and those with a more green/yellow segmented bodies and greenish wings. Harry's Wet May has connotations of both these varieties.

Having archetypal dry flies in the box is not always necessary however as a little

Mayfly are abundant throughout Caithness from June to August.

swipe of floatant on say a Bibio, dark Bumbles, Kate McLaren or Soldier Palmer will also do the business when the trout are rising on the surface. Though there is a boat, judicious wading is generally all that is required here and best times generally are from late April on when the first profuse black midge surface hatches get underway. Thereafter May sees increasing fish activity which reaches a peak when the mayfly will drift like sail boats down the loch from mid June to early August. Our sedge time also comes on song from mid June and the vastly underrated red legged heather fly (bibio) fall in late August/early September. Though of all the hatches the mayfly and the bibio are the most important, we occasionally see daddies, damsel and dragon fly here too. All in all appearances are very deceptive on the Reay Lochs for you could not have a more fertile environment if you wished for it.

Stalking trout with light line and long rod for example 10ft rod with no. 5 floater is particularly rewarding on warm breezy, grey days and invariably I will use a maximum of two flies on the cast for these difficult lochs. A single dry is the norm but a dry/wet fly combination sometimes works when the trout are playing hard to get, a frequent occurrence! Using say a dry Claret Bumble on the top and a slim line

Silver March Brown on the tail has worked for me in the past, particularly when the fish are on the newly bred young stickle-backs of early August. Another good tactic to use is the nymph (Cove's Pheasant Tail or similar) on the point and a natural imitation on the dropper. Fish this combination with a slowed retrieve and occasionally you will pick up one of these bottom hugging specimens.

Once surface feeding activity picks up you might also like to try a local fly devised by Melanie Brooks, daughter of expert fly tyer Pat Brooks of Harpers Tackle. The 'Brooks Bumble' has proved its worth around Caithness and as far afield as Argyll. It owes its origins to the most popular fish attracting colours of blue, black and red with a touch of teal. Shades of the Blue Zulu and the Camasunary Killer are also in there somewhere and this makes it excellent for sea trout. Fish it dry or wet on the top dropper in anything from a mild breeze to rough conditions and it will nearly always bring up a fish. It is at its most deadly when fished as a single semi static dry fly when the bibio, midge or mayfly are profuse.

'Brooks Bumble' size 10–12
Thread – red tying silk
Tail – pheasant tip dyed red
Butt – red floss
Body – red tying thread only with blue tinsel in centre to separate hackles
Body hackle – black hen hackle at top and base of fly. Can be wound along the hook and then separated in the centre with the blue tinsel
Head hackle – white hen or speckled teal tied long.

Loch Calder and the Reay Lochs are wild trout waters most dear to me. They may not gain the public accolades of Watten or St Johns but their trout are very special and I know them as the closest of well loved friends. I cannot give them a higher recommendation than that . . .

Chapter 19

Durness Lochs

'Let us suppose that rising fish are nowhere to be seen, a very common state of affairs . . .'

R. C. Bridgett

OS Map No. – 9
Nearest town/village(s): – Durness.
Accessibility of fishing: – Good but note that the trout fishing is normally reserved for guests of the Cape Wrath Hotel and all enquiries on the fishings must be made first through the hotel. Very occasional day visitor tickets can sometimes be had but these are not guaranteed.
Best times: – Usually May to September with a peak of excellent fishing around mid July.
General: – Boat and bank fishing on four 'top of the range' limestone lochs with numerous small hill lochs also available on the adjacent Cape Wrath peninsula. A complete gamut of fly fishing techniques are used here from tiny dry flies to nymphs and from wets to 'lures'. Flexible fishing tactics are essential. The four main waters are not really suited to beginners.

★

There is something uniquely compelling about approaching this area of North West Sutherland and its unusual lochs. To get there you must drive along miles of tortuous single track road frowned upon by dark mountain peaks and ringed by desolate peat bog. More often than not the wind howls and rain lashes the car. As you struggle to both navigate and keep spirits buoyant, you may begin to lose sight of your principal objective, those lovely Durness trout. Niggling doubts creep into your mind and you start to wonder why on earth you ever bothered to come this far

north then, suddenly, you turn a corner and emerge out into a different world. Stop for a moment and look down on this green fertile strip of land, dotted with whitewashed cottages each separated by long lines of white and grey stone walls. Sheep graze the lush grasses, sea birds wheel above the incoming tide of the 'Kyle' and the whole atmosphere is one of a tranquil oasis perched at the seaward end of a remote wild land. In the midst of all this verdant country lie four aquamarine blue pools, fantasy lochs which most trout fishers would kill for, and now you quickly forget the grim weather and the difficult drive. You have arrived at paradise.

While limestone outcrops exist in many places in the Highlands, for example most of Caithness is actually limestone based, they are never more noticeable than when you approach Cape Wrath and Durness. This semi peninsula of land is very special and so are its waters of Croispol, Borralie, Lanlish and Caladail. Initially these lochs look rather similar, however each has its own highly individualistic charms. *Borralie* is the deepest with a plunging chasm in its centre down to about 130ft or so. Eminent natural historian Harvie Brown recorded in the mid 1800s that there was an underground water filled passage linking Borralie to Croispol, quite possible given the 'soft' limestone rocks which surround them. Certainly the trout in both these waters are very similar with green backs,

Loch Caladail.

silver flanks and exquisite black asterix markings. They grow exceptionally fast especially in Borralie where an 'average' weight would be 1lb 8oz and trout of 4lb plus are commonplace. When the fish are caught they fight like demons and so closely do they resemble sea trout it is often impossible to distinguish whether it's a 'sea' or a 'brown' trout. As well as exquisite trout as long as your arm, Borralie holds a good long standing population of char which were noted way back in Statistical Accounts of the 1700s as 'Tar Deargan' (or 'Tarragan') which translates as 'Red Bellies'. Note the phonetic pronunciation of the Gaelic 'Tar Deargan' is 'char jeergun' or thereabouts, and it is highly likely the 'Arctic char' we describe today got their title from an English corruption of the original Gaelic name. As well as char, Borralie also provides a good habitat for a unique population of crayfish, one of the few lochs in Scotland to do so.

Loch Croispol is today noted for exceptionally good quality silvery trout of around 1lb plus. However it is interesting to see Malloch's *Life History . . . of the Salmon* (1909) contains photographs of trout of 3lb to 5lb caught from 'Loch Crosophuill' in the early 1900s (note this spelling is nearer the old Gaelic name). I will not speculate as to whether the average size has dropped in Croispol for it is quite possible the biggies are still there but are difficult to rise to the fly. Also in real terms this loch is slightly less fished than its neighbours and therefore more fish could be present and competing for the same amount of food. There is also the possibility that the large trout shown were not caught in Croispol at all but perhaps in Borralie or Caladail for the Victorian southerners were sometimes not too hot on their geography or their Gaelic pronunciation! Further confirmation of this comes in Malloch's book when he describes a 9lb trout from 'Loch Durness' (no such water!) as having such rich colour 'the spots on the sides become joined together'. This beautiful trout probably came from Lanlish but whatever its origin it shows clearly the illustrious past of the limestone lochs.

Close by Croispol and Borralie lie the enigmatic lochs of *Lanlish* and *Caladail* and these are just as spectacular. The trout in these waters grow equally large with leviathans up to 6lb plus appearing every now and again. They tend to assume a more mixed variety of colours from deep orange gold ferox shades to pale silver. Rest assured that whatever their colour they are the same magnificent quality. Both little Lanlish and limpid Caladail are shallower than Borralie and Croispol but with equally clear water and bases of shell sand, gravel and pale limestones. Though records show that there has been supplementary stocking done on all the lochs in the past, particularly in the post war era when the hotel was known as Keoldale Lodge, it is thought the genetic strain for each of the principal Durness lochs remains more or less intact. Today the hotel maintains its own hatchery and continues occasionally to stock the lochs on integral lines putting Borralie fry back into Borralie and Caladail stock back in Caladail and so on. Borralie and Lanlish have very little in the way of natural spawning facilities whereas Caladail and Croispol have a couple of obvious burns apiece. Some supplementary stocking is deemed relatively essential on the former pair of lochs owing to visitor pressure. While the necessity for stock additions at Durness is sometimes debated, some will say it is the extreme richness of the bottom feeding that makes the lochs appear dour with few fish in them when in actual fact the natural populations are probably self sustaining. I can say in all certainty that no harm has been done by any restocking at Durness. The fish are of the same supreme quality they have always been.

The first time I ever went to fish the 'limestone lochs' I assumed I was looking at sea water, such is their intense clarity. Those translucent waters simply scream well fed trout at you, making you want to rush headlong to their shores and thrash them to a foam! In fact many visiting anglers do this on their initial excursions to Durness and then come away feeling they could have done an awful lot better. The lochs demand a truly adaptable angling approach, the trout switch from enthusiastic feeding to deadly dour in the blink of an eye, and you must take time to develop the right tactical frame of mind for this magical place. It is here the thoughtful not to say crafty angler does best.

Remember the bottom feeding on these lochs is ultra rich with big caddis (some almost two inches long!), snail and shrimp predominating and you must plan your campaign for all four waters carefully around a flexible mix of fly lines and assorted patterns. Whether in the boat or on the bank I use a tip to middle action 10–11ft rod to be able to work droppers effectively and I suggest you do the same. Apart from their lack of distance, short rods are very hard work in the high winds often experienced here. Select your line weight and patterns according to what the trout are doing (or at least what you think they are doing!) and use nylon of 4lb double strength. Hatches when they do occur can be sustained or brief and, apart from their lush bottom feeding, the trout will snap up a wide range of emerging insects including sedges, midges, caenis and olives. When fish are active on the surface your tactics should revolve around smallish dry flies and floating line. Looking back over my diary reveals an assortment of flies but I see Wickham's Fancy, Greenwell's Glory, Red Sedge, Black Gnat and Ginger Quill have all done well in size 12–18 in reasonably calm conditions. When the lochs have fallen to a light ripple I have found most success coming from when the dry flies (size 14/16) are fished singly on a semi-static retrieve.

In more breezy conditions when the trout sometimes tend to show themselves more freely I have used slim line point flies notably the Grouse and Green or the Silver Invicta and added one or two droppers

Gin clear water on Caladail.

featuring Pennel, Bibio, Soldier Palmer, Kate McLaren and Olive or Claret Bumble. I use these in 10s and 12s and fish traditional loch style floating line with medium to fast retrieve and dibbled top dropper. I guarantee there is nothing more exciting than that crashing thump through the waves as a muscular Durness trout charges down your fly – fabulous stuff! Alternatively when the trout are not showing at all, and this happens quite frequently, I will try an intermediate line with a weighted nymph on the point Cove's Pheasant Tail, Olive nymph or a GRHE with a twist of copper wire at its head. I fish the flies on a slow retrieve around places I have caught fish in the past and just occasionally this tactic works. From experience I would suggest you use intermediate or slow sink lines only where you have seen fish rise before and therefore local knowledge is important. Simply fishing your flies randomly without prior observation rarely seems to work at Durness.

When bank fishing any of the four lochs approach with extreme caution. The water is so clear you can bet all your actions are being carefully watched! Look out for the shelves that ring the edges of the lochs for this is where those leviathans lie. If you have to wade do so very slowly and carefully as a) in lochs like Borralie you can tip yourself into forty feet of water if you step off a ledge and b) the trout often lie very close in and you can spook and/or line them before you know it. On dull days I have seen huge trout rise in less than two feet of water only a yard or so from the shoreline. Equally it is possible, if you creep out early morning, to espy huge trout apparently resting up in the shallows. On Borralie, the shelf between the island and below the cliff is a good place to watch haunting monsters lying up, their grey shadows almost motionless in the depths. However, before you think any of these trout are 'easy meat' I must warn you that, unless you possess the lightest of touches and the most deft of casts, you have little chance with them. Usually you just aerialise your first cast and they melt away, mammoth secret shadows in the green water. Similarly you can march all the way round the lochs several times without seeing a thing and then just as you reach a pit of despair, nature throws a switch, a hatch comes on, and the trout rise like magic.

It is both the degree of uncertainty and the proportion of difficulty in the fishing

Big winds on Borralie.

which sets the Durness waters apart. You know there are leviathans there but also you realise there is no guarantee of catching them. To try and lessen the odds many experienced devotees carry on their main fishing activities late at night when a phenomenon known as the 'slurp' occurs. This is actually a late night midsummer hatch of sedge which the trout suck down with a sort of a kiss (hence the descriptive title 'slurp'). While some of the largest trout are indeed taken off the lochs during the hours of semi-darkness, the success of night fishing is by no means certain. The bigger fish may feel safer and less conspicuous after nightfall but they still need a mighty hatch to spur them into activity and therein lies the rub. Durness insects are no different to any other Scottish insect and are particularly sensitive to changes in temperature. Though it is highly fertile, Durness is a very exposed locality and you can frequently wait all night for one rise or even none at all. Do try fishing through a midsummer night once however, for it is a dramatic and slightly eerie experience and that 6lber may well show and 'slurp' down your fly.

Alternatively if you need some sleep to recharge the batteries you can rise early to meet the dawn instead. To see the sun come up over Borralie or Lanlish has got to be one of the most magical fishing experiences anyone can have, making contact with one of those monsters who have slipped inshore to feed is another. Before the bright light of day arcs down into the shining waters, the trout are still foraging close in. Sneak up on one of them with a small dry or a single wet and you never know what might happen. Catching Durness trout is a spectacular, bewitching gamble no matter what time of day, month or year you choose.

The essence of fishing the limestone lochs of Durness is the ever present prospect of spine tingling trout. Just occasionally you are bound by destiny to encounter a truly fabulous fish, the trouble is you never quite know when that is going to occur. After about a decade of fishing here you might just get the hang of it, if not, no matter for the trout just grow bigger while you try. One of the best descriptions I have ever heard about the Durness lochs is that they are like the 'Catwoman' character in the Batman movies. One minute all very 'come hither' and seductive and the next completely brutal and unforgiving. Still, if like myself, you're a glutton for this type of angling punishment, you'll keep coming back for more!

Chapter 20

Loch Ericht, Pattack and Spey Dam

Badenoch Angling Association

*'The wind suddenly seemed to increase from a moan to a whistle
blowing down the side of Ben Alder in a perfect hurricane.'*
McDonald Robertson

OS Map Nos. – 35 and 42
Nearest Town/village(s): – Dalwhinnie, Newtonmore, Kingussie and Laggan.
Accessibility of fishing: – Good. Badenoch AA Permits which cover Ericht and the Spey Dam and various other waters (see also River Spey) are widely available in localised outlets including Ben Alder restaurant (Dalwhinnie), Laggan stores, Spey Tackle (Kingussie) and Ashdown Stores (Newtonmore). For Loch Pattack, additional permission for access is essential from the local estate keeper. Note: Pattack may not be available for fishing after 31 August because of stalking interests.
Best times: – Early May to late August for Ericht and the Spey Dam (water levels fluctuate according to rainfall). Pattack produces fish for most of the season.
General: – These waters are covered by the Upper Spey Protection Order and it is an offence to fish without a permit, however, visitor tickets are very reasonably priced and cover many more waters than you could possibly fish in a day. Traditional wet and/or dry fly is the norm. Ericht and Pattack are quite a hike depending on how you approach them. Spey Dam is easily reached with little walking involved.

★

I have taken the liberty of grouping these waters together as they offer the visitor the chance to fish in superb scenery with the peaks of Ben Alder, Carn Dearg and the Aberarder Forest never far from view. This area is stirringly wild and rugged with ventures to Loch Ericht and adjacent Pattack allowing the angler to experience some of Scotlands finest landscapes. As long walks over some rough terrain can be involved in exploring this area, I have therefore added the easily accessible Spey Dam to make up a trio as I fully realise not everybody enjoys lengthy tramps over hill and heather.

Let us explore *Loch Ericht* first because there is so much to this loch you would need a week or so on it even to get a small idea of its lengthy fifteen miles. It lies at over 1,000ft above sea level and stretches from Dalwhinnie, south west towards Rannoch moor. At its deepest point the loch plunges to a depth of over 500ft. This great chasm of a loch is the direct result of glacial action when massive ice flows scoured out a way between the surrounding mountains on either side. Though it looks like Ericht is a uniform sheet of water it actually is made up of two deep basins with an unseen separation across its narrower part in front of Ben Alder Lodge. Here the water is only 100ft or so deep compared with the great depths on either side! Ericht's shores are narrow, steep and plunging and consequently better fishing

High winds at the head of Loch Ericht.

results often come from near the edges and/or where little promontories reach out into the loch. In this respect things are little changed since P. D. Malloch's book *Life History and Habits of the Salmon* was published in 1909 (don't let the title mislead you as it contains a great deal of information on trout as well). He refers to Loch Ericht as being mainly deep water where 'the trout only average five to the pound' whereas its shallows contained fish of 'nearly three quarters of a pound'. Interestingly he does not mention ferox trout at all, perhaps they were not being fished for much in Ericht at that time.

The slightly shallower bays therefore fish best, notably the bay below Ben Alder cottage (a convenient basic shelter bothy if you require an overnight stop) and also the bays around the afforested southern end. Ben Alder bay is also sometimes known as McCook's Bay after a keeper/stalker who lived with his family in Ben Alder cottage. On the hills behind

the cottage you can find a cave once thought to have been used by Bonnie Prince Charlie in his flight back to France. However, it is also said the current cave, now much visited by walkers, is actually one dug out by McCook when he was too frail to take tourists up to the real one much farther away in the hills behind! Whatever the legend, 'McCook's Bay' still has excellent trout in it of up to 2lb plus and is well worthy of your angling attention if you can make the hike in.

The Badenoch AA fish Ericht out from the Northern reaches near Dalwhinnie and tracks run a goodly way down each side of the loch from here. The local hotels at one time had several boats for hire on the loch, but as I write in 1999 there seems to be no boat hire available at the Dalwhinnie end, a sign of changing demand I presume. I was first inspired to fish this loch some years ago after reading McDonald Robertson's accounts of it in *Wade the River Drift the Loch*. Robertson writes in descriptive terms of the grandeur of this wild area and its fishings and also of a strange legend concerning the disappearance into the loch of a parish known as 'Feadail'. Apparently all the inhabitants of this village were engulfed in Loch Ericht when 'a terrific convulsion of nature' submerged the village underwater. It is said that for some time after 'the church and several other prominent objects' could be seen 'far down at the bottom of the loch'. Whether this legend is true or not we can only speculate, however it adds further drama to the landscape.

The trout are wild as wild can be and fight with great vigour. There is a reasonable head of fish in the ½lb class with a number much larger caught each season along with ferox which come in at the 7lb plus mark. In the 1940s and 50s Ericht was famed for its large trout caught on the troll, however the demand for this seems to have lessened. The water has a tea stain of peat to it and the natural feeding does not appear particularly rich (midge, stonefly etc.) However, the trout do fine in the well oxygenated water. For best results from the bank, fish Ericht on a calmer day as, speaking from experience, any gale racing up or down the loch can be very intimidating. Concentrate on anything which breaks up the uniformity of the bank such as an inflowing burn, underwater spits, boulders or small promontories – the challenge here is very much to think small trout habitats rather than miles of windy water. While wading take care not to tip yourself into any of Ericht's many sudden holes and ditches which can be hidden from view when loch levels rise and fall. As the water deepens relatively quickly it is not usually necessary to cast far out to be amongst fish but they do have specific territories so do not linger too long in the one spot.

Cast and walk, cast and walk is very much the order of the day here. A 10ft rod, floating or intermediate line and traditional flies like the Soldier Palmer, Zulus and Coch Y Bondue are adequate along with

McDonald Robertson's recommended fly selection of Grouse and Claret, Teal and Red, March Brown and Woodcock and Yellow. Traditional loch style angling with medium paced retrieve is usually all that is required though do change to dry fly if a hatch comes on and trout are seen rising well on the surface. Spinning is also allowed and though I am not a fan of spinning for trout, it disturbs the water and can be brutal on small fishes' jaws, I think there is something of a place for it here, especially in gales which blow your fly everywhere but where it should go.

If Ericht is proving too tough in blustery conditions then ask permission of the keeper at Ben Alder estate to visit *Loch Pattack* which is a much softer option even on a gale lashed day. Pattack is reached by a reasonable track which wends its way up from the back of the newly built/renovated 'fairytale castle' of Ben Alder Lodge, below. Occasionally permission may be granted from Ben Alder estate to take a car along the track to Ben Alder lodge but unless you obtain this permission it is walking all the way on a long forestry track. Allow yourself a few casts in Ericht first before you turn and walk up the hill path to the loch. Pattack is a most unusual high hill loch, being relatively shallow with a bottom of sand, shingle, weed beds and stone. I presume the sand is a glacial deposit akin to the sand and gravel spits found in Ericht. This is an inspirational water to fish on several counts. First, the situation has the hall markings of a hill walker's paradise with massive peaks to the South and West, indeed the area is renowned for those who enjoy yomping up mountains. Also the trout fishing is fast and furious with obliging trout smacking into flies wet or dry with great vigour. On most days this is undoubtedly the place to boost flagging confidence or introduce comparative beginners to the sport of wild trout angling. The trout may not be much more than half a pound but just treat

Pattack as a place to experiment and learn in tranquil 'away from it all' surroundings.

Travel light and pack a travelling rod, floating line and a few wet and dry patterns like Bumbles and Zulus or similar for this loch. A great deal of matching the hatch is not a prerequisite, simply cast out a team of two wet flies 'loch style' in the normal way. The trout seem willing to take wet flies in most conditions though if the wind drops it is worth experimenting with a few small size 16 dries like the Greenwell Spider or the March Brown. Trout rise all round the loch and the clean gravel streams which flow into it allow profuse and some would say, rather over abundant, natural spawning. The natural feeding is predominantly of the midge family (including a lot of biting ones so take the repellent) and most dark flies do the business.

A cast on Loch Pattack.

I loved the markings of the small Pattack trout, some were golden, others had a green sheen and some 'parr marked' trout were also present. Though the Victorians named the latter to differentiate them from their brethren, modern thinking now puts parr markings on trout as a sign of territorial aggression. The fingerprint markings along the flanks often fade when caught but whatever the reason for their presence, they make for a particularly lovely trout. Do not however expect monsters. As far back as 1866 this loch and its adjoining river have only held smallish brown trout, too many trout and not enough food I fear. That famous angler of old, Tom Stoddart, fished the nearby River Pattack (apparently known as 'Pattaig' at that time) and he too only produced small trout, so its character has changed little since that time. Treat Pattack as an interesting diversion away from the rigours of Ericht and it should appeal to most wilderness trout enthusiasts

other than those who (for one reason or another) prefer or are not able to walk long distances, which brings me to the *Spey Dam*.

This is an easily reached loch lying at the end of the minor road (originally built by General Wade) which runs out from the small village of Laggan. The surroundings here are much more lush and green, with agriculture and some forestry very much to the fore. The Spey Dam lies at just over 1,000ft above sea level and provides an anchor point for the headwaters of the famous River Spey. It is a popular and well maintained water with a number of club boats for hire. I am not normally the greatest fan of 'dam' waters, I just do not find their massive grey walls and scarred banks that appealing, however the dam here is relatively small and unobtrusive and does not give the feeling of bleak exposure that some others do. Once you are past its small wall at its junction with the Spey, the loch opens out to reveal a pleasant scene of farmland and moor with some attractive rolling hills behind. A road runs along one side of the loch and everything is easily reached, a great plus for the fishing enthusiast who wants to fish without too much effort!

There is a good mix of sizes amongst the trout population here, the local club has made brown trout stock additions in the past, and some excellent trout in the 1lb plus range can be caught amongst the ½lbers. The fish rise well around most parts of the loch and the natural feeding is good with midge, olive, sedge and caddis present. On warmer days, bank fishing can be just as productive as the boat, though to gain quick access to the far side, a boat is normally required. I fished the Spey Dam during one of those prolonged summer heatwaves and found the water level had dropped somewhat, however the trout were still active quite close to the shore. During any hatch I had spirited responses from some fine browns on the dry fly. Dark

The Spey Dam.

flies did best in the clear to faintly stained water and I found a small black Hopper fished dry produced crashing takes on the surface and wet flies like the Kate McLaren, Greenwell's, Rough Olive or Invicta also did well. Again this is largely a traditional water with 10ft rod, floating/intermediate line and 4lb nylon all that is required. It usually fishes best from May to the end of July and evening sedge rises are particularly productive.

Though the Spey Dam may seem something of a 'soft option' compared with the drama of the hill lochs it is by no means a pushover. It can provide the wild trout enthusiast with plenty of challenges as well as respite from long walks in mountainous country – what more can you ask?

Chapter 21

The Shieldaig Lochs of Gairloch

'One must care about a world one will not see.'

Bertrand Russell

OS Map No. – 19
Nearest town/village(s): – Badachro and Gairloch.
Accessibility of fishing: – Good at present though this may alter in the future. Permits and information are freely available from the Shieldaig Lodge Hotel by Gairloch. Numerous other trout lochs in the area can be accessed through the Gairloch AC.
Best times: – Normally from late May onward, variable according to local temperatures as many of the lochs are at high altitude.
General: – Long walks are involved for some of the lochs though there is a stalkers path part of the way. You will need a fair degree of physical fitness here. Take warm and waterproof clothing, light loch style tackle, a compass and a camera, the scenery is superbly wild and rugged.

★

The Gairloch area of Wester Ross is noted for its fabulous sandy beaches, its magnificent back drop of vast mountains and some top notch wild trout fishing. This is a popular, much visited tourist area yet, get yourself a little way off the beaten track, and you can feel a million miles from anywhere. Like so many 'wilderness fishing' venues, the best angling lies away from the roads which thread their away along the coastal fringes and across to Kinlochewe. Sadly some of the more easily accessible roadside lochs in this area have been heavily targeted by illegal set line/multiple rod worm fishing and, after

such sustained abuse, many local trout populations take a long time to recover if at all. I am not denigrating this area in particular, far from it for it is one of the most spectacular parts of Ross-shire, it's just I want you to go in with your eyes open and your hiking boots firmly strapped to your feet!

To reach the lochs which still retain a good head of trout, a stout pair of legs and equally robust lungs are required but at least in the Shieldaig area which I now describe, there are some reasonable starting off tracks to follow. The lochs of the Shieldaig and Flowerdale Forest's lie to the south of the village of Gairloch and have been under the auspices of the Shieldaig Lodge Hotel for as long as I can remember. They fall into three distinct groups. The first are small lochans collectively known as the *Fairy Lochs* and they lie below the hill 'Sidhean Mor' (Gaelic translates as the big Fairy Hill). The second group are a trio of remote larger lochs clustered in a dramatic wild valley below the heady peak of Baosbheinn (pronounced 'Boshven' – popularly thought to be Gaelic for the 'Hill of the Wizard' but actually an old Norse name meaning the Hill of the Hunt). The third cluster comprises more accessible waters near the coastal hamlet of Badachro. All the lochs command exceptional views of the virtually trackless interior of the Wester Ross wilderness considered by ardent naturalists, mountaineers and roving fisherman to be one of the finest in Britain.

I start first with the lochs in the Badachro

Shieldaig lochs.

area for these offer slightly easier reached wild fishing and give you but a pleasant enough taste of much better to come. Of these waters, dark peaty *Loch Clair* surrounded by rough grazing and moor, is usually the most productive. I first discovered Clair when Andrew, my first son, was a baby (he's a strapping six-footer now!) so this loch and its satellites hold some good memories for me. There is a reasonable head of brightly speckled trout in the ½lb class here and traditional floating line and dark coloured flies like the Kate McLaren or Bibio do well. Clair is not a 'run of the mill' loch however as the fishing is often challenging and it can take sustained warmth to make the fish rise. The natural feeding is predominantly from the shallow loch bottom, caddis, snail and the like and this tends to make the trout seem dour and hard to move. Big baskets are not common and for any success you must choose a dull day with a good wind and concentrate your efforts close to the southern promontories and bays. Evening fishing can also

prove more useful than struggling on in hard bright sunshine. There is normally a boat on Clair but bank fishing is adequate enough. If you have time after the walk out from Badachro (which takes about half an hour or so on sheep tracks) go on past Clair to its two little 'satellite' lochans which contain reasonable trout and then work back the same way casting in each one. Personally I find these kind of relatively accessible lochs fish better earlier rather than later in the season, when they have been well bombarded with both legal and sadly, illegal methods.

My favourite group of lochs at Shieldaig are undoubtedly the mystical *Fairy Lochs*. These lochs are steeped in legends both modern and ancient and references to ghosts, wizards and fairies surround this imposing rugged area. The approach to them starts off easily enough along a stalkers path to the south of the hotel, the same track which leads out to the glorious trio of waters below Baosbheinn. Once you gain height you will notice a prominent valley running up to the bluffs of Sidhean Mor (pronounced Sheehan More). You can either approach the lochs this way or by going further along the track to the end of Loch Braigh Horrisdale and then cutting up the hill to arrive above the *Diamond Loch*. Whichever way you choose it is a steep 'pech' (good Scots word for hard work on the lungs!), however once you arrive at around 220 metres/800ft above sea level, stop and drink in the view for without doubt, you have arrived in Fairyland. The mighty peaks of Ben Alligan and Baosbheinn dominate to the south and the twinkling lochs of the Fairies beckon and bewitch your senses. There are five main clusters of water nestling in the steep dips between the rocky hills and first up is the excellent *Fairy Loch* with its enchanting islands and rocky coves. This loch is clear and quite deep and the best fishing lies near the edges of the promontories, weed beds, ledges and around the islands. The localised natural feeding is of the caddis, sedge, midge, beetle and heather moth variety and the trout though occasionally dour come in at around the ½lb plus mark with a few much larger taken each year normally in May or June. It is possible with care to walk around the whole loch casting as you go and the usual traditional gear is normally all that is required. Switching from floating to intermediate line will sometimes produce trout which are nearer the bottom and vary your flies from dry fly (if fish are showing on the surface) to celebrated wets like the Zulu, Dunkeld, Soldier Palmer, Invicta, Greenwell's and Blae and Black (size 10 to 12). This can be demanding fishing at times but there is always the odd chance of a real biggie of 2lb plus taking hold.

If the Fairies are thwarting your efforts on their loch, wander up and across the separating bluff down to *Loch Sgeirach* where some beautifully marked trout with small black speckles and flanks of burnished gold await your fly. Dark patterns normally work best in the slightly darker water and the Kate McLaren has brought me some lovely trout in the ¾lb class from here. This is another typically enigmatic Ross water but, largely because of its prolific hatches of midge and sedge, it tends to be slightly more obliging than its immediate neighbour. From here it is another short hop across the tops to '*Spectacles*' (two small lochs adjoined by a tiny stream) and the long narrow loch of '*Diamond*'. Both these lochs contain little islands and you should direct your casting efforts towards these important features. The trout hug the sides, as islands always help provide essential food and shelter in these high lonely places. Again it is hard fighting trout in the ½ to ¾lb class with some much larger occasionally hooked. Loch style tackle and dark flies do the business.

All the lochs in 'Fairyland' have a definite eerie feel to them greatly accentuated by the constant echoes of voices around the rocky cliffs. None more so than the last water in this group, the '*Aeroplane loch*' which contains the sad twisted wreckage of an American bomber which crashed there on its way back home at the end of World War II. All the returning servicemen passengers were killed outright and a plaque cum small shrine dedicated to their memory has been placed on the rock face above the loch. Though some anglers fish this lily padded water, indeed it is said to contain a reasonable head of ½lbers, I personally could not bring myself to do so. Too many ghosts haunt this hillside loch which technically is a war grave, indeed there has been a least one strange inexplicable sighting of an airman standing alone by this water. I may be superstitious but I feel the souls of the dead should be left in peace amid the melancholy wilderness where fairies skip and wizards might cast their spells.

If you fancy a good walk, two – three hours out and the same back, visit the wonderful remote lochs of *Gaineamhan* (Sandy loch), *Ghobhainn* (colloquially known as 'Gowan') and *Bhealaich*. As I write this in early 1999 the exquisite trout in these waters remain undisturbed as does the magnificent wilderness surrounding them. This may all change however if the owner of the surrounding land gets the go ahead from the Scottish Secretary of State for a controversial hydro scheme he wishes to site on these lochs. The scheme involves damming the lochs, raising and lowering water levels, disrupting the spawning redds, joining the lochs with a pipe to loch Bad an Scalaig which contains predatory pike, and also the possible bludgeoning of a car/lorry track into this remote untouched area. The events surrounding the landowner's application for this scheme, which is likely to make use of a large amount of tax payers' money/government funding under the 'Scottish Renewable Energy' tag, border on

The Shieldaig wilderness is under threat.

the unbelievable. I recount the case now as an example of the lengths some people will go to in order to exploit water assets at the apparent expense of the environment in general and angling in particular. I beg you to learn from this scenario for in the years to come there are likely to be many more such schemes. Be on your constant guard for it is of little use moaning about the loss or deterioration of wild trout angling after the damage has been done.

Initially there were so many objections to the environmental and ecological effects of the Shieldaig hydro plan – Highland Council, SNH, SANA, British Mountaineering Council to name but a few – that a public enquiry was held. This became a desperately protracted affair due to the applicant landowner asking for delays and postponements in order to submit 'new' evidence on the development. Incredible manoeuvrings continued apace when the enquiry finally got underway. The applicant suddenly transferred the land on which the lochs are sited (leased for 21 years by the Shieldaig Lodge Hotel) to a Trust of which he is sole beneficiary. This action it was claimed, annulled the terms of the existing sporting lease granted to the local hotel and would allow the

developer (a contracted Hydro company) full access to the lochs to do their work at the apparent expense of the angling hotel guests. At the same time, The Scottish National Trust who own land bordering the Gairloch estate, inexplicably did a U turn on their original stance of opposition to the development and withdrew all objections to it. Later it was learned that the chairman of the SNT's Council had without warning, suddenly overruled his committee's unanimous decision to oppose the scheme. This single-handed reversal of an already public objection, brought widespread condemnation in the press. The U turn appeared to directly oppose NT policy of championing the unspoiled nature of this magnificent area. What prompted the chairman's decision to intercede in already established NT conservation policy was never made clear. To their credit Scottish Natural Heritage, another principal objector, stuck rigidly to their environmental guns and declared the River Kerry, part of the watershed involved in the scheme, a new SSSI and submitted it to be ratified as a SAC (Special Area of Conservation).

I find the idea of siting a hydro scheme capable of producing a mere 2.1 megawatts of power in such a fabulous wild land area smacks of extreme ecological exploitation for mercenary purposes. One wag neatly summed it up when he said it was simply to generate income not electricity! Though it may create in the long term, one or two jobs in maintaining the weirs and generators it will be at the expense of many more tourist related jobs in the angling and hotel accommodation sector. The anglers visiting the Shieldaig area do so because of the immense stature of the wilderness and the unique wild trout populations contained within the lochs. Hopefully the new Scottish parliament will see this environmentally destructive hydro plan for what it is worth and anglers will still be able to fish these wonderful waters in all their splendid solitude. Unfortunately government led 'Scottish Renewable Energy' (SRE) schemes which purport 'green energy' are gaining ground in popularity in some political quarters. These same SREs throw huge amounts of public money after ugly windmills disfiguring hills, crass wave machines which sink in the sea and power-poor hydro schemes which threaten the future of game fish. Beware the 'green energy' tag. What seems eco friendly is often at the complete expense of the local environment and in direct contradiction to the green ethos. You have been warned!

Climbing off my high environmental horse now, I do still urge you to visit this trio of prime Shieldaig waters if you can. To reach the lochs, which lie at approximately 300 metres above sea level, follow the winding stalkers' path up past the 'Fairies' and down to the first water, the shallow *Sandy loch*. This is easily fished by wading the weedy margins. Trout here are free rising spirited individuals a little on the small size from too much spawning in the intervening burns but good 'uns nevertheless. A trout of 1lb would be a monster in this loch but the fish fight well on light traditional tackle. Silver Invicta, Dunkeld and Kate McLaren do well here. The central loch '*Gowan*' is the jewel in the crown of all the Shieldaig lochs holding magnificent, beautifully marked trout in the 1lb plus class. This remote loch has somehow managed to strike a balance of size amongst its trout population, producing large fighting trout of exceptional quality without much physical hands on management at all. It is suspected their successful flourishing is due to the trout feeding a lot on their own fry and small sticklebacks. This seems to self regulate their population size with unerring accuracy and Gowan has a self sustaining trout population with fish of 2lb to 3lb coming from here quite regularly. Gowan usually has a boat on it but bank fishing can be very productive

Afoot in Fairyland.

especially around the shallower edges. Brora Ranger, Kate McLaren, Bloody Butcher and Silver Invicta account for a lot of fish here. The Alexandra is also recommended by the locals. Fish if you can, at the feet of the statuesque bulk of Baosbheinn and you will truly fish in paradise.

The furthest away loch from the road is *Bhealaich* and on a clear day this is probably one of the most dramatically situated lochs anywhere on the West coast. The great peaks of Alligan, Baosbheinn and the Torridon hills dominate the southern vistas and the trout, though darker than their immediate neighbours, offer great sport coming in at a good ½lb–1lb plus. This loch is shallow at its northern end and falls to 66ft or so in its southern bays. Midge figures predominantly in the natural feeding and dark flies do well here on traditional floating and/or intermediate line.

If you do get the chance to visit the Shieldaig lochs, impending hydro schemes permitting – take it. You will not be disappointed and, if by the time you reach them, the trout have not been affected by ugly, so-called 'green' exploitation so much the better – surely this wild magical land and its lochs deserve better treatment.

Chapter 22

The Lochs of Kilmelford and Oban

'A single fly fished properly is worth much more than a tangled team.'

Colonel Oatts

OS Map No. – 55
Nearest town/village: – Oban, Kilmelford.
County/district: – Argyll
Accessibility of fishing: – Very good. Trout fishing permits can be had through the Oban and Lorn AC (OLAC) who have permit outlets in Oban and also at the roadside hotel in Kilmelford village. For Loch Avich boat permits can be obtained either from OLAC or from Loch Aweside Marine, Dalavich.
Best times: – Generally from May onward. Some of the smaller hill lochs can become weedy later in the season but there is a good selection of waters to compensate for any loss of fishing.
General: – Traditional loch style is the norm (wet and dry) but be prepared to switch line density as sometimes the trout go down and intermediate or sink tip is used. The Loch of Avich is protected under the Loch Awe Improvement Association Protection Order and you must obtain a permit before fishing there. Some of the more remote waters above the Kilmelford area take a good bit of walking. Be prepared to read map and compass as various small lochs are easily missed in hollows and dips. Beware of boggy ground at some waters. Boats available on some larger lochs, otherwise it is bank angling by fly only.

★

Kilmelford is a small village lying to the south of the bustling harbour town of Oban and roughly 15 miles to the north of Lochgilphead. It is often famed more for its marina and extensive sailing facilities than for any connection with brown trout fishing. Dig a little deeper however and a fascinating past develops. It is from near here that the redoubtable Colonel Oatts wrote his timeless book *Loch Trout* and from here that generations of trout anglers have ascended the steep winding road to fish the Kilmelford hill lochs. Nowadays these waters are mainly administered through the Oban and Lorn AC and access is relatively easy. Take care however on that tortuous 'Loch Avich road' which runs between Loch Awe and Kilmelford. There are some hair raising blind corners and sudden bends to contend with, driving

Wading in the shallows – Loch Avich.

Loch a Phearsain, Kilmelford.

here is definitely not for those of weak constitution!

This is a part of western Argyll I love as it is not quite the rugged merciless terrain of say nearby Lochaber, yet it still has a grandeur all of its own. The seaboard is dotted with splendid harbours, coves and green agriculture and then, as you ascend the 170 or so metres toward the hill lochs, the vistas change to huge forests, rolling moor and rough grazing. The Kilmelford area has a tamed yet still beautiful wildness to it, very 'Argyllshire' in fact and its subtle charms are unique and inspiring. I begin with the string of little lochans which dot the hillside near the Avich road. These are reached by rough tracks across grassy moor and though they are small, some excellent trout come from them every now and again. *Loch a Phearsain* is the largest of these and on its day, this is a cracking loch. It lies at the bottom of a steep hollow and has a perfect mix of weed and reed beds, some insect holding bracken and birch and a block of maturing forestry down one side. In Oatts's book *Loch Trout* there are two fading black and white pictures of the Colonel fishing corners of this loch in the 1950s. Inspired by these photographs I tried to look at what has changed here since then. Fifty years on the trees have all grown considerably, nouvelle forestry has appeared, fishing pressures undoubtedly have increased and the trout population has over time, had various stock additions made to it. In fact it rather mirrors the development of its much larger 'neighbour' Loch Awe, though at least Phearsain has not had a fish farm stuck in its midst, that dubious honour belongs to roadside Loch Losgainn Mor. Unfortunately because of its cyclical nature, the exact quality of wild trout angling in Phearsain, or indeed any similar hill loch, is always a terribly difficult thing to quantify. Often subjective judgments are made from anglers' perceptions rather than by following hard scientific fact. Fishing at Phearsain, fifty years after Colonel Oatts cast his fly there resplendent in mackintosh and plus fours, I could have taken the easy way out and claimed 'things ain't what they used to be' however I have to be more honest than that. Frankly I remain uncertain whether there had been any significant decline in angling there or not. Perhaps fifty years is not long enough; ask me after another fifty if I'm still around! Of one thing I am certain however and that is it was a great privilege to follow in the footsteps of an enlightened angling writer who stood up for his principles and wrote about wild brown trout while others of his day merely dismissed them as small inferior pests.

Tactics for Phearsain are traditional wet and/or dry and having now fished this loch both early and late in the season it seems to fish best from May to about the end of July. If you are bank fishing take a long rod with you otherwise you will spend an inordinate amount of time disentangling flies from trees and bracken. The short travelling rod I had with me on my last visit was just not up to the task – in my rush to get there I had forgotten about those high banks behind. An ability to Spey or roll cast makes a lot of difference for bank fishers on these steep sided lochs. You still need a long rod to execute them though! The water is clear to a faint peat stain and the centre of the loch is deep enough to harbour a char population. The trout are well marked dark gold ½lbers with a good number of 1lb plus fish amongst them. The larger trout seem mainly to haunt the edges of the copious weed beds at the far end of the loch but around both the island and the lily pads are also productive spots. To reach the far sides of these, a boat is a definite advantage but you can still fish enough parts of the shoreline to fill a morning's angling. Dark hackled flies like the Zulu or Clan Chief produce a lot of fish, a Kingfisher Butcher also did well for me (size 10/12). The natural feeding here is predominantly of midge and sedge and if the latter insects are hatching profusely, a single dry Red Sedge is excellent in calmer conditions.

While in this area it's worthwhile stretching the legs and puffing up the hill and across to the nearby small lochs centred around *Loch a Mhinn* (pronounced loch 'Aveen'). There are four little waters (Losgainn Beag, Curraigh, Mhinn and Nam Ban) here and these all lie in steep

dips so mind how you go when clambering about. At one time I believe they were stocked with rainbows though there is no sign of these interlopers now. They fish similarly to Phearsain and though they mainly produce trout in the ½lb range, some much bigger to 2lb have been caught in the past. Because they are all a few hundred yards apart, this makes a delightful evening's fishing with the sun sinking in the West, especially in June when it never really gets dark. The little lochans are rather reminiscent of Scourie waters though the terrain is more grass and bracken and less of the heather and ling. Take care around Curraigh, there's a mighty bog at one end, but otherwise enjoy!

If you are more into hard walking then the ten or so lochs above *Gleann Mor* are also worth a tramp. Take a map and compass though as it is easy to become disorientated if mist or low cloud descend. Locals will tell you the waters' names and may tell you tales of mighty fish on lonely hillsides. You can safely believe them for many of these enigmatic lochans contain some excellent 2lbers. This is challenging 'small loch fishing' at its best and definitely for those who like the high and lonely places of Argyll. The natural feeding is mixed but copious sedge hatches can and do occur. Tactics should be light loch style and follow Oatts's advice of starting with some short casts close to the shoreline before lengthening line. Sometimes (usually early in the season) the trout are lying very near the bank near 'reefs' – the Colonel's term for underwater rocks and shallows. Oatts also advised when investigating new lochs 'the dry fly is of value and is a good preliminary to the wet . . . particularly on small hill lochans'. You would do well to heed this advice on these remote lochs above Gleann Mor and pack an elk hair sedge or two amongst traditional wets.

If big loch angling is more your fancy

The sun goes down over Kilmelford harbour.

then take a trip further along the high road and after many dips, twists and turns you will espy *Loch Avich*, a real gem of a water set about 300 metres above sea level. Here the trout are wild unadulterated stock and have a superb range of sizes from a few ounces to 1lb plus with the odd specimen trout of about 7lb thrown in for good measure. It is thought the wild trout of Avich fall into two distinct categories, small slow growing trout which rarely exceed ¾lb and a population of much faster growing trout which quickly attain good size. The loch is surrounded by coniferous and some natural forest notably oak and birch and it has good natural spawning facilities in its clean gravely burns. The centre of the loch is deep at around 200ft and by and large the trout are caught more in the shallow bays, off burn mouths and near the overhanging trees.

Avich is a classic example of an untamed Argyll hill water. It fishes best early and late in the season and prime months are May to early July. The water is reasonably clear over a dark base of rock, gravel and sand and it has a neutral to slightly acid pH. The principal natural feeding for the trout is of the terrestrial variety and when a hatch of midge, stonefly or sedge is on

you are in for great sport. Larger trout will also forage in the margins for snail, fry and/or caddis. The trout are a fine well spotted gold and fight splendidly for their size. Though the loch can be quite exposed in a gale, this is definitely a place where the boat is preferable to bank fishing. Angling from the bank can in part mean struggling through trees and scrub to reach the shoreline. Fortunately this same undergrowth provides a modicum of shelter and good hatches can occur close in especially at dusk.

'Loch style' is the preferred mode of angling though take both intermediate and floating line for the trout can and do feed at different depths. In common with most wild trout lochs they can be remarkably choosy or hedonistic at the drop of a cast so be prepared. I found Avich trout to be in selective mood when I fished there though admittedly this was very late in the season. A fat bodied fly fished slowly was their definite preference. A Claret Bumble or Bibio does well and other popular local patterns include the McLeods Olive, Olive Nymphs and Dunkeld. When boat fishing a 2 or 3 fly cast with a dark Bumble on the top dropper is a must.

The Avich and Kilmelford waters remain dear to my heart. Undoubtedly they will provide excitement, drama as well as the occasional chastening experience. The first time I made a pilgrimage up to the Kilmelford lochs I was left mortally embarrassed by forgetting to take the fly reel. There I was the 'visiting expert' all hot and copiously sweating from the climb to the lochs, looking helplessly down at trout rising wildly all around me. Bereft and broken I had to skulk back to the car without so much as a cast. On the way down I almost felt a firm tap on the shoulder from the Colonel tut tutting at my silly haste, though I'd like to think he had a wry smile on his face . . .

Loch Avich – a classic example of an untamed Argyll hill loch.

Chapter 23

Loch Leven

'Because fish move with the seasons and because there is such a great expanse of water, the ordinary angler is not attracted. The real loch fisher should be glad that this is so . . .'

Adamson

OS Map No. – 58
Nearest town/village(s): – Kinross, Milnathort, Glenrothes, Dunfermline, easy road links to Edinburgh.
Accessibility of fishing: – Very good but this is a busy ever popular fishery with advance booking normally required for different sessions (normally split into morning, afternoon and evening).
Best times: – Variable. Generally from May onward.
General: – At one time Loch Leven was considered the best trout loch in Scotland as it had a world renowned reputation for holding stocks of exceptionally good quality brown trout more resembling sea trout. Today however, following long term environmental degradation of the loch from over enrichment, the loch has been partially turned into a rainbow trout fishery. Though brown trout continue to inhabit the loch the first fish you are likely to hook here is usually a rainbow. Wherefore Scottish trout? The green waters of this loch usually require angling from the boat and though this is the home of traditional loch style angling you will see a wide range of tactics used from sinking lines and lures, to top of the water 'loch style'.

★

Two things made Loch Leven famous. One, its undoubtedly beautiful and prolific trout of fabulous sporting quality, and two, the fact that over time more fishing writers have chosen to record their experiences on this Scottish loch than they have over any other. Just as the Tweed is a 'literary' river, this is a literary loch of high standing etched forever into the annals of angling history. In the early 1800s this shallow rich loch was fished primarily by net rather than rod and line and in 1831 after some draining and lowering of the loch level, R. B. Begg records 'twenty-four dozen of trout at one haul'(by net) in his book *The Loch Leven Angler*. Begg also records that 'angling is comparatively of recent introduction' as there was a general assumption then that Leven trout 'did not rise readily to the fly'. The fish were assumed to be bottom feeders and even seasoned anglers of old found their bags extremely light. The *Perthshire Advertiser* in 1844 notes two Edinburgh anglers caught 17 trout weighing 13lb on the fly in Leven. This was considered the best catch for 40 years at that time! Netting of the loch halted in 1873 and to this day the loch has been a popular commercial rod and line fishery.

It is interesting to note that most past writings indicate the course of rich fertile Leven has never run altogether smooth. Right from when catch per rod records first began there have been heady peaks and disastrous troughs. Begg also wrote that in 1850 the erstwhile 'dour' bottom feeding trout of Leven suddenly changed character with fish actively rising on the surface and big baskets being taken. The change was 'sudden and complete' and catch records in 1872 noted that rod-caught trout had risen to 18,000 compared to only 2,000 in the net. However, despite this apparent turn- around in fortunes Malloch circa 1909 alluded to 'many ups and downs' with angling success or failure 'depending on the number of pike in the loch'. Malloch seemed to roundly blame these toothy coarse fish for the expansion and contraction of catch numbers. Nevertheless it is recorded in *The Trout* (Granby, 1898) that, in a day's competition in June 1888, Malloch still managed to kill 52 trout of 44lb 6oz!

Loch fishing doyen R. C. Bridgett circa 1924 comments that when it came to empty creels 'such a state of affairs may obtain more frequently on Loch Leven than it does on less famous waters' though he does go on later to describe Leven as 'the most famous trouting loch in the universe'! Adamson circa 1950 makes the observation that 'Leven is a unique natural fish–pond offering unsurpassed sport at moderate cost' and Tom Stewart circa 1964 states the lochs trout can 'rise at every cast' or 'lie doggo, gorged with the snails that litter the golden sands of Leven'. This state of fluctuating fortunes seems to have continued right to the present day with the early 60s seeing some exceptional bags, the 70s likewise but numerous blank days remained equally common. Things rather came to a head in the late 80s when the increasing over-enrichment of an already fertile loch from sewage and fertiliser ingress, seemed to threaten Leven's very existence. Dense blue green algae blooms appeared ever more frequently and this appeared to cause catches to oscillate even more wildly than before. Riparian owners called for reviews, environmental surveys and the like but apart from highlighting the need to correct the obvious environmental damage (which to a certain extent has been done) any complete turnaround of

Loch Leven – a loch of many ups and downs.

Leven's luck has never been entirely achieved. Really this is not surprising given its past 'feast and famine' history but anglers being anglers needed to blame something and over the last 20 years they have tended to curse the green algae blooms of Leven more than anything else.

However, blaming any apparent decline in fishing on overabundant algae is rather naive. The rich bottom feeding of the loch has never helped bring trout on to the surface, stocking policies (albeit with native trout from local hatcheries) have fluctuated from mass additions to none at all, predation is high, the timing of algae blooms is unpredictable and anglers' expectations, fuelled by tales of past catches of exquisite trout from Leven, are probably over high. It is a fact of life that modern anglers tend to demand more/larger fish per rod effort and to satisfy their needs and keep in business as a commercial fishery, the management of Leven decided in 1993 to introduce rainbows into the loch. While this provides a stop gap resource for the 'catch em big, catch em quick' trout aficionado, in the long term this may prove something of a disaster for the culture of Scottish brown trout fishing. I rather suspect that by the year 2050 this once world famous loch will be spoken of as just another 'put and take' and little else. Barring any unforeseen environmental

Loch Leven trout show distinct migratory tendencies.

disasters, the complete loss of the Leven brown trout is unlikely as the introduced rainbows cannot breed and the natural spawning for the indigenous trout seems to remain good. It is extremely sad that a loch with this amount of history should come to this especially when you consider the uniqueness of the East coast 'Leven' strain of trout colonised here after the last Ice Age (see also Chapter 8 on River Ken).

Loch Leven trout closely resemble those found in Loch Watten Caithness and are trout with distinctly sea trout characteristics, indeed sea trout were common in Loch Leven prior to the lowering of its water level. They are exceptionally athletic, fast growing fish with long, silvery gold bodies and black asterisk spots and their flesh is red and firm. 'Levens' have been used for restocking purposes all over the world since the late 1800s, giving sport as far afield as New Zealand, and are now common to all parts of Scotland as introduced supplementary stock. They do not tend to be long-living fish (7 years or so is the norm) and appear to 'go back' after reaching this age. Also, when introduced into a dissimilar environment, say small peaty and/or acidic waters, they tend to lose their silvery sheen and become more like the fish common to that habitat. If they interbreed with resident trout their original

characteristics are normally lost quite quickly. Average sizes of the native Leven fish have tended throughout history to average around the pound but of course there are many trout much larger than this at present. They have distinct migratory/roving tendencies preferring an open water cruising lifestyle. Malloch circa 1909 even went as far as to suggest Leven trout travelled through the water at '2 or 3 miles an hour, swimming 6 to 18in below the surface, sucking down one fly after another and usually heading upwind'. Quite how he made these calculations is unclear, nevertheless he was quite correct in assuming Leven trout have defined pelagic characteristics. Even before our forebears decided that virtually every accessible fishing loch in Scotland needed stocking whether native stocks were adequate or not (thankfully they did not manage them all!) these trout were rovers and colonists swimming out from their Eastern streams and around to the West coast to settle there.

I had a fascinating discussion on this urge to migrate with Dick Bolton who lived near Loch Leven during the 1950s and 60s and occasionally worked as an evening boatman on the loch. He told me of the placing of hakes (grids) across the spawning burns to stop the trout leaving/migrating from the loch during the fishing season. These hakes were only removed to allow spawning when the season ended, however Dick would see trout run the streams after a flood as notably early as July. If water levels rose sufficiently enough to let fish through over the hakes, say after a thunderstorm, it seems the trout showed no hesitation in following their strong migratory urges. This urge to run exists outwith spawning time in East coast trout and Dick's local observation, made over a lengthy period of time, confirms the theory. He also told me that the natural spawning on the tributaries near his home was profuse until 1967 when a horrific fish kill occurred on the North Queich either from pollution or disease. Coinciding with this disaster, the loch took another one of its serious nose dives but with the restarting of a natural hatchery in the early 80s it did pick up again, returning to its more common 'feast and famine' cycle.

The legend of Leven still remains very strong and many anglers want to fish here. The richness of its very shallow green waters, the charm of the green hills and the romance of Castle Island where Mary Queen of Scots was imprisoned in 1567, make this an attractive angling venue. Fishing is by excellent boats and the big long drifts still draw the crowds. The natural feeding is rich to the point of saturation with olive, midge, caenis, sedge and all other types of aquatic life present. Snails, shrimps, caddis, daphnia, nymph and other types of small fish are all on the trout's menu and Leven fish are generally spoilt for choice. Interestingly Malloch made great play of Leven trout consuming vast amounts of the larvae of the bloodworm (chironomid midge) which dwells in the bottom silt though he makes no attempt to define an imitative fly for trout thus feeding. This food, which we would now call midge larvae or 'buzzers' undoubtedly still plays a huge part in the feeding cycle of Leven but it is not until comparatively recently that any exact imitations of this were thought necessary. Tom Stark, a famed boatman of the 60s, recommends little other than traditional attractor patterns like the Teal and Green, Peter Ross, Grouse & Claret, Black Pennel, Greenwell's and Bloody Butcher and it is only when reservoir fishing really took off in the late 70s to the present day that we see midge imitative patterns creeping into the Leven repertoire.

Today, Leven browns may feed on much the same as they have done in the past but the fact that they go through intensive periods of consuming daphnia (this eutrophic water has these microscopic creatures in super abundance), is better recognised. The trout tend to follow these clouds of nutrients up and down according to the intensity of sunlight and consequently if daytime fishing, sinking lines and lure-like attractors have been employed in order to catch fish. Rainbow introductions are sometimes blamed for this break away from traditional loch style but the truth is that seasoned Leven anglers were forced into using these unconventional brown trout tactics long before any American imports were introduced. I fished Leven in the early 90s (pre rainbows) in a ladies' competition where most of us drew blanks. The best and biggest trout came in at about 3lb and won the entire competition. It was caught on Hi D sinking line and a Green and Black spider or was it a Cat's Whisker, my memory escapes me!

Persistent eutrophication calls for unconventional tactics but if you don't want to use a hefty Hi D line, try what the Orkney anglers do when fishing here in competitions. Use a 20ft leader with weighted nymph or similar to take the point fly down to sufficient depth, fished slowly it sometimes works. If you prefer modern traditional tactics, and are lucky enough to hit a rise of trout, there is an across the board choice with anything from Dawson's Olives to Sedgehogs, Mallochs Favourites to Buzzers and Doobrys to Muddlers (amongst numerous others!). Really, 'you pays your money and you takes your choice'.

By 2000 it is hoped that a National Centre for Game Angling will be established at Loch Leven and I wish this enterprise all success. Some recognition of angling as a sport is better than none at all, and it is vitally important to pass on fly fishing skills to our youngsters. However, what the old Leven stalwarts would make of today's tactics for this once great traditional trout loch, I shudder to think!

Chapter 24

Loch Morar and Satellite Waters

'There are all sorts of days on the loch and many moods of the trout, and we need them all . . .'

R. C. Bridgett

OS Map no. – 40
Nearest town/village(s): – Mallaig, Morar.
Accessibility of fishing: – Good. For Loch Morar, the garage Morar Motors issue day tickets, Loch Morar AC has boat hire at the lochside. The Morar Hotel also arranges fishing. For the satellite lochs of Nostarie and Ghille Ghobaich and their extensions, permission is not required.
Best times: – Usually May to September depending on the severity of the winter.
General: – Loch Morar is covered by a Protection Order making it an offence to fish without a permit. Traditional loch style tackle is normally required. Wellies are the norm as the lochs of Morar are very deep close to the edge and a lot of wading is not required. Some very rough walking is involved in this rugged area and the ability to use map and compass properly saves time and effort.

★

If you do meet with good clear weather, I guarantee there is no more dramatic an angling setting than the stunning hills of the Morar peninsula. This is an untamed wilderness of sentinel peaks, transparently clear rivers and great chasms of lochs all of which give the appearance of being very much unaltered since time began. Morar is a land for the adventurous angler who relishes remoteness and does not mind putting a bit of physical effort into his or her fishing. Even getting there is a demanding task as the road to Mallaig, despite some long overdue improvements, is still one of the most tortuous on the West coast. Sharpen up your driving skills (or take a valium if you are the passenger!) and strive to reach Morar if you can however, for once you arrive the surroundings are quite unsurpassed. Silver sands, aquamarine seas and a rocky backdrop of huge mountains, secret glens and fabulous trout lochs await. Often they never reveal their true glory being shrouded in mist or rain but if they do, the views across to Rum and Eigg and down the length of Loch Morar are quite breathtaking. 'Awesome' is how my youngest described this area and I'm inclined to agree with him!

I was first inspired to visit the Morar peninsula some time ago when I read a chapter of V. Carron Wellington's book *Adventures of a Sporting Angler*. Wellington (see also Chapter 16 on Assynt Lochs) was one of those rather eccentric pioneering anglers of the 30s and 40s who relished exploring some extraordinarily remote areas in search of golden trout. His account of a disastrous, marathon trek to the chain of lochs above Mallaig including *Nostarie* and *Ghille Ghobaich* (the latter loch translates from Gaelic to 'the loch of the silly wee boy') makes fascinating reading. He had set off on a day when 'conditions were not at all promising for the good creel I had in mind' first to Loch Nostarie and then onward to its adjoining lochs and across the ridge to Ghille Ghobaich. He experienced little success in any of the waters though he thought he was 'covering

Loch Nostarie. Following in Wellington's footsteps.

good trout' the whole time until finally in some desperation, he stripped off, clenched his rod between his teeth and swam across to the island in the centre of 'Ghille'. Here he did at last capture a few fine trout of around 1lb or so in the fading evening light. However he thought this bag was not enough for his waiting friends and for some unfathomable reason added an injured cormorant to his creel having throttled it first to put it out of its misery (this was prior to the days of protected species). Quite why he did this I do not know unless chronic fatigue had addled his brain. Cormorants are inedible, oily, smelly birds at the best of times! By now night had fallen and he spent several hours staggering around the hillside in darkness before making it back to Mallaig at two in the morning in a state of total exhaustion.

Bearing all this drama in mind we set about recreating some of Wellington's walk, hopefully without the trauma and the cormorant, but perhaps with a few more fish in the creel at the end of the day. We were, if you like, modern pioneering anglers following in his long gone footsteps, albeit much better equipped with OS Map and compass and lightweight gear. It would be fun to see what the trout lochs still held whilst avoiding past pitfalls. We planned to reach Nostarie in bright but not impossible conditions down an apparent track from Glasnacardoch near Mallaig. However, after half an hour's plodding through foul bog, shades of past pioneers' experiences were already looming. At last Nostarie appeared (take a tip from me and keep to the high ground when approaching this loch, you will reach it in half the time) and we paused to drink in the spectacular vista. It was interesting to see the wooded island still very much as it was described over 50 years ago, a fitting monument to the Northern Highlands as they were before being denuded of vegetation by man, sheep and deer. Also in evidence on Nostarie was the gull colony mentioned in Wellington's

Morar hill lochs cry out for the traditional approach.

book so things did not appear to have changed that much. Wellington alludes to these birds as being a disruptive influence on the fishing as he says 'no self respecting trout would suffer the indignity of such an intrusion'. I am not sure whether this is fact or opinion as there are a number of top notch trout waters in Scotland with large gull colonies including Loch Borralie in Sutherland and the River Tweed in the Borders. The only real problem with gulls I do know of is their ability to carry parasitic worm infection and pass it into the food chain and thence into the guts of trout. There is an indirect truth therefore, in Wellington's observations on these noisy scavenging birds.

The Morar hill lochs positively cry out for traditional 'loch style' tactics with plenty of weedy bays, islands, promontories and skerries all providing good trout holding areas. The water deepens close to the edge and wading is not too necessary or advised except where you can see the bottom clearly. The base of the loch is dark and the rocks

are covered with a fine brown silty layer. Wellington had fished Nostarie in daylight with a Peter Ross on the tail and a Shaggy Whaup (a brownish hackled fly resembling a Bumble) on the dropper without much success at all so I plumped for a more natural approach. As the water is relatively clear to a light tea stain and the natural feeding in the midge, stonefly mould I chose instead a size 10 Black Pennel on the tail and a size 14 'multi purpose' Greenwell Spider on the dropper. I had with me a light travelling rod, floating line and 4lb nylon and, having got my breath back, I busily plied my trade around a few of the promontories. Only small trout were my reward for this more subtle tactic however and I switched quickly to some more traditional fare with a Zulu on the tail and a Clan Chief as dropper. The day was hot, hard and bright however and it was some time before a nice trout of around ½lb obliged. Still, I felt proud to at least have matched Wellington's success on Nostarie for he too had only one ½lber from there!

The indigenous trout of this chain of lochs fight exceptionally well and are of the dark golden variety, heavily speckled with black and red spots. I suspect just like Wellington, that the lochs contain trout much larger than ½lb, but it does seem conditions must be dull with a good hatch on to make the bigger fish move close in within casting range. Early season fishing on any warm days in May should also be spectacular for the trout will not yet have migrated out towards the centre as is common in many high hill lochs. Exploring the chain of lochs does take some time however and the walking requires calf muscles of iron so do allow yourself time and be prepared with good warm waterproof clothing and plenty of sustenance.

In the end, Ghille Ghobaich was only given a cursory glance by us though I am told by the locals that the trout rise very freely there and have no reason to doubt that as plenty of tell tale rings were in evidence. Discretion proved the better part of valour and, rather than risk the ignominy of being benighted like Wellington, we squelched our way out from this enigmatic chain of lochs tired and hot but with very happy memories. As

A view to take your breath away – Loch Morar and the Lochaber hills.

we wandered back the thought struck me that 'Ghille Ghobaich' probably got its name from the many 'silly wee boys' past and present who have clambered about in the Morar hills in a spirit of adventure seeking out wild trout in a fabulous wilderness. And why not!

Magnificent *Loch Morar* is an altogether different proposition. This is the deepest loch in Scotland, dropping to over 1,000ft in places and it is reputed to hold its own monster 'Morag' akin to Loch Ness. Speculation exists that it is either a colony of huge eels (unlikely I would have thought as bottom dwelling eels are rarely seen on the surface unless they are migrating in thin water to the sea for spawning) or perhaps otters or seals. I'm inclined to fall in with the idea of a large dog otter creating a stir as it is said the monster has a small head yet leaves a great wake behind it. Otters can do this when swimming powerfully in calm water, still on the other hand, dreams of hooking 'Morag' add a touch more drama! Monsters aside, the trout taken from the clear limpid depths of Morar are of excellent calibre and each year fish in the 2lb category are caught. This loch gained a Protection Order in the 1990s and this seems to have cut down the

Loch Morar, the deepest freshwater loch in Scotland.

amount of illegal fishing it was experiencing earlier (multiple set lines along the shores accessible by road etc). Overall the PO looks to have had a beneficial effect on Morar, that and the general slump in the tourist industry which has cut down the number of tourists using illegal set line fishing methods (wittingly or unwittingly) along its magnificent banks.

Interestingly the disappearing sea trout of Morar were the subject of a 5 year research programme started in 1991 after catches of these fish had fallen from 1,000 per annum to nil in 1992, 93 and 94. Mortalities during passage through nearby electricity generating turbines was thought to be the cause though worryingly the scientists at that time seemed to shy away from damning the more likely culprit, sea lice infestation from nearby fish farming interests. Why?

The better times to visit Loch Morar are normally from late May to September and traditional loch style from the boat is the norm. Bank fishing can be productive but this is a vast water often steep sided and overgrown with tree and scrub and the best way of covering a reasonable amount of water is by going afloat. The Loch Morar AC provide boat hire half way down the winding road to Bracorina and

from there most craft head out toward the prominent group of islands at the loch's western end. Dapping (that method of wind assisted fly fishing with long rod and floss line) is very popular here and though I personally am not a fan of this method – it can be downright cold and boring sitting static without casting a fly – it is one to consider in a good wind. Both wet fly and dry fly are equally effective and popular local patterns include the traditional range of Zulus, Bumbles, Invicta, Soldier Palmer, Clan Chief, Silver Sedge and those of that ilk. The natural feeding is of the sedge, stonefly, beetle, olive, midge and nymph variety. Parts of the gravel and rock shoreline here are very exposed and battered by wave action and this does not encourage minute algae to grow in great quantity. Consequently invertebrates have to seek shelter where they can and where they are the trout will also lurk. Fishing over little sheltered trout habitats is therefore essential if you are going to have any success and on my visit, the island studded western end definitely looked the most popular.

Wherever you fish on the Morar peninsula you can be assured of two things. Rugged scenery which will take your breath away and spirited trout which buck the rod and set the adrenaline going. When will you go?

Chapter 25

Loch Talla and Fruid

& the waters of 'East of Scotland Water'

'Make happy those who are near, and those who are far will come.'
Chinese Proverb

OS Map Nos. – 72 for Loch Talla; other waters 73, 66, 67, 58 and 59.
Nearest town/village(s): – Edinburgh, Moffat and Tweedsmuir for Talla and Fruid. For other EoSW waters, Edinburgh, Gifford, Glenrothes, Crieff, Stirling are also nearby depending on your choice.
Accessibility of fishing: – Very good. For Loch Talla and its sister Loch Fruid, the famous Crook Inn at Tweedsmuir supplies inexpensive permits. Information on all other EoSW fishings and how to obtain permits is available from a central 'Fishing Desk' at the East of Scotland Water offices in Edinburgh. In addition there are permit providers in situ on various other outlying waters controlled by EoSW.
Best times: – Varies, but May and June are normally the most productive months for the wild trout.
General: – Loch Talla is an unusual semi-remote wild trout/Arctic charr reservoir style water situated in pleasant Border country to the south west of Edinburgh. Traditional loch style is frequently used on Talla but there is scope for nymphing and/or dry fly according to the prevailing conditions. Boats are available for hire and bank fishing is allowed. Little walking is involved, you park by the loch. To all intents and purposes this is 'central belt' fishing being so near Edinburgh, yet Talla and Fruid offer a complete escape from the city hubbub. They form two of a number

of lochs/reservoirs carefully maintained by East of Scotland Water who have a structured management policy in place for the different types of fisheries in their control.

★

Loch Talla is an evocative water set in a deep narrow valley high in the rolling Tweedsmuir hills. In the early to mid-1800s when Stoddart roamed these parts, Talla was little more than a burn crossing the bed of a boggy glen however, once the

Victorian technology on Loch Talla.

then 'Edinburgh Corporation' converted it to a reservoir in 1895, the loch assumed its current splendid if slightly austere character. Situated above the upper reaches of the Tweed, it has an ornate Victorian dam at the Tweedsmuir end and is fed by a cascading stream at Linnfoots at the other. You may drive all along its narrow 2.5 mile long shore and up and across the high road to nearby Loch Megget if you so choose. *Megget* is also administrated by East of Scotland water and has a fine history of some excellent trout. Stoddart in *The Angler's Companion* mentions 'killing with the fly, three panniers full of trout, each containing a stone in weight' from what was known in his time as 'Megget Water', a stream later converted like Talla, to a reservoir. Such huge bags of fish would be somewhat frowned upon today but it does show the abundance of wild trout generally available in this historic area.

Loch Talla itself has a fine head of wild unstocked brownies in its dark based but clear waters and they are traditional yellow bellied trout with lovely pink flesh. There is a good spread of sizes in the loch from approximately 5oz to 2lb plus. Most of the better fish come in at around the pound mark with a reasonable number of larger trout caught each year. Char are also resident. Talla trout tend to be canny cautious beasts and you will need a fair degree of skill and good prevailing conditions in order to tempt them. The loch is quite exposed lying at some 346 metres above sea level and consequently the better months for angling are usually from May onward when temperatures warm up a little. Boats are normally the best mode of transport around the loch, which does has rather steep banks in places, however fly angling is available from the shore if you prefer.

Despite the depth of water contained in Talla, normally 70ft plus at the dam, the natural feeding is good with a healthy mix of invertebrates being consumed by the trout. Olives, midge, stonefly, shrimp, cased caddis and hatched sedge are all happily taken as are any terrestrial insects blown over the water. Daphnia blooms can occur in warmer weather and the trout can become fixed on these for a time following them up to the surface in duller weather and down again in bright sunshine. The Talla trout also show tendencies to migrate on or offshore according to reservoir water height fluctuations. It follows therefore that different areas of the loch can become productive at different times. The southern end, away from the dam, sees a lot of the action especially where the burn runs in and the loch is less precipitous. As a very general rule when boat angling, you should stick to drifting the course of the shoreline, working in and out to try and pick up feeding fish.

Seasoned Talla aficionados tend to use smaller flies especially in calmer weather with 14 to 18 popular. In a good wind however, loch style from the boat demands traditional 10–14s with Grouse & Claret, Soldier Palmer, Bibio and Zulu all doing excellent service. Floating and intermediate lines are principally put to good use here and there is plenty of scope for nymph and dry fly angling when the trout are, respectively, lying deeper or visibly rising on the surface. Buzzers are sometimes fished on a slow retrieve with some success, so there is room for all styles of fly fishing. Nearby *Fruid* fishes in a very similar way to Talla though its trout are longer and darker in colour and no less sporting for it. Care should be taken on Fruid as its banks are steeply inclined.

The management of Talla, Fruid and Megget is particularly good with these waters forming part of a network of fisheries under the care of East of Scotland Water. Drew Jamieson and his team have worked tirelessly to produce a co-ordinated strategy for managing the 17 or so busy waters now under their direct

Loch Talla provides quality trout angling high in the Tweedsmuir hills.

control. The principal aims of the management policy, first established from 1975 onward, involve the conservation and enhancement of the local fish populations including brown trout, the endangered species of charr in Talla and Megget, the powan of *Carron Valley* and the significant populations of pike and perch in *Rosebery*. Also, management aims to provide a variety of fishing experiences (wild, stocked, rainbows, boat, bank etc) and maintain public access to the waters subject to safety and water quality. To attain these goals the division of the waters into classes, i.e. wild, supplementary stocked or hatchery maintained was deemed essential as was scientific based management with appropriate research and 'customer' co-operation. Restocking of waters with no previous history of introduced fish is avoided and stocking is only undertaken in specified waters where customer expectations are high. Interestingly up to 30 per cent of all stocked browns are recovered and 80 per cent of all rainbows. The management policies are broadly speaking successful, though sadly there are still a number of greedy anglers who do not follow the local rules to the detriment of fellow anglers.

The lochs and reservoirs which are designated 'wild', i.e. unstocked, encompass Talla and Fruid; 'supplementary stocked' involves Carron Valley or *Gladhouse*; and 'hatchery maintained' are waters like *Castlehill* or *Glencorse*. From this anglers can then make an informed decision as to which type of angling they desire and management plans appropriate to each fishery can be devised to meet their needs. When angling pressure looks to be having a considerable effect on resident stocks, EoSW will sometimes take the bold but necessary step of 'resting' that fishery for a year or so to allow stocks to recover. In a busy central belt where demand for angling is high this is a brave but laudable step in conservation. Funds derived from anglers permits are put back directly into the fishery network to help offset costs in maintenance, stocking, environmental renewal and research into brown trout behaviour.

Setting long term objectives for the fisheries is very much a two way business with anglers actively encouraged to make direct contributions to the running of the waters by making detailed catch returns. These inform of fish sizes, time spent fishing, numbers taken out and/or put back, any unusual fish caught for example a tagged fish, note stomach contents of trout for food analysis, report pollution or poaching incidents and so on. In this way anglers feel they are doing something worthwhile for 'their' fishery and the organisation

Early season – when water levels are high, trout will often lie close in.

60s visits any change has been for the better. Today Carron Valley is not only an excellent supplementary stocked fishery but also the site of an important project looking into the long term effects, if any, that stocked trout have on the resident population. Aspects such as competition between stocked and wild fish for food and territories are being assessed as are the effects on future survival rates when wild and introduced trout spawn together. Studies of movements of introduced trout are also underway. Again co-operation with local anglers is of key importance, for they are being asked to record the position of any tagged trout caught in relation to its release point and also detail stomach contents of any trout taken. The information they return enables the scientists involved to look at any different features of stocked/wild trout behaviour, how quickly stocked trout adapt, any potential spawning problems and any differences in their diets. The long term aim of all this research, which is being conducted by the Universities of Stirling and Glasgow with sponsorship by the Wild Trout Society and East of Scotland Water, is to provide insight into practical aspects of wild trout management in Scotland which can then be used by any fishery with a similar interest.

East of Scotland Water have done a notable job of managing and maintaining high amenity waters in areas where trout angling is in big demand. Their management strategies provide a model system for busy waters and we can learn much from them. Equally the softness of the border and Trossachs country in which many of these well cared for waters lie makes for wonderful respite from the busy cities they encircle. I let Stoddart have the last word on this though – *'to my fondness for scenery, taken by itself, I fear I am too far implicated in the piscatorial mania to do proper justice . . .'*

Give these waters a try and see if he was right!

involved with the water can make decisions according to the (usually reliable) information amassed. EoSW have also been instrumental in producing some excellent informative leaflets on the care of the environment surrounding their fishings, protecting the wildlife, safety for the angler and of course, descriptions of their fishings. This exchange of information is seen as a key part of the management plan.

Research also forms an important part of the remit and exciting projects are underway notably on the popular *Carron Valley* reservoir (known in my day as the Carron Dam) near Stirling. As a very small fry in the big pond I accompanied my Dad on a trip or two to this water and can still remember its high productivity (so much so my mother used to groan 'Oh no, not trout again' when we returned!). Though the management has altered since those

Chapter 26

Tomich Lochs

'Every age needs men who will redeem the time by living with a vision of things that are to be . . .'

A. Stevenson

OS Map No. – 26
Nearest town/village: – Tomich, Beauly, Inverness.
Accessibility of fishing: – Good but book well in advance, this is a very popular place. Guests resident at Guisachan and/or the Tomich Hotel have priority but day fishing permits can sometimes be arranged.
Best times: – Usually late May to August.
General: – The lochs are small well cared for waters with some supplementary stocking of wild trout brought in from good quality sources. All the lochs require the absolute minimum of walking and are popular with those who like easily accessible hill lochs in beautiful settings. Boat and/or bank fishing, not much wading required to be amongst the fish.

★

Nestled together on a hillside of the famous Guisachan estate near the historic village of Tomich lie an enigmatic cluster of small hill lochs. Collectively known as the *'Tomich Fishings'* these waters have a long illustrious history stretching back to the time when the estate was a grandiose affair of cultural and sporting interests.

Tomich sets itself apart from other trout loch fishings by its quite extraordinary sense of place. To walk the hills and forests of the Guisachan estate once owned by the benevolent Lord and Lady Tweedmouth, is to follow in the footsteps of King George V, Gladstone, the Duke of Marlborough, Landseer, Churchill and many others. At one time Tomich was one huge sporting landscape where no expense was spared and its lengthy history mirrors the rise and fall of many of the more glamorous Victorian estates. In the hands of the Tweedmouths, huge improvements were made to the estate from around 1850 to 1900. These included the building of the lavish Guisachan House (now in ruins), the farm steading and the construction of the neat stone houses and school within the village of Tomich. The estate was run as a grand 'huntin shootin' concern until the demise of the Tweedmouths and from the early 1900s on, it changed hands on several occasions before being split up and sold to among others, the Forestry Commission. Guisachan today is a much smaller concern comprising the farm, a tourist orientated accommodation complex and a small acreage of hill ground on which lie those delightful Tomich trout lochs.

Tomich is also in something of a league of its own regarding its careful on-going management of small high hill lochs begun in the 1940s. To be frank, the standard of dedication and care the Guisachan trout receive is normally only found on waters with exclusive salmon interests. Trout loch management at Tomich really took off when a Mr Michael Waddel took control of the much smaller Guisachan estate around 1945. Mr Waddel, a dedicated trout fisherman, spent long hours on the Tomich lochs and it was he

Kyle Laidlay doing what he loves best.

who originally had the raised boathouse and dam constructed on *Loch Gretal (Ghreidlein)*. This boathouse was more of a good quality summerhouse on the loch complete with panoramic glass windows and furniture. By all accounts he was a colourful character who loved whisky and trout lochs in equal measure. After Waddel's death in the 1960s the Frasers took over ownership of the land and its lochs and have continued astutely to maintain the trout waters under the guidance of Kyle Laidlay.

Various 'textbook' management ploys carried out at Tomich include surveys of aquatic life, fertilisation of waters, restocking, reductions of fishing pressure and so on. Because of a long uninterrupted strategy of conservation and care both trout and anglers have reaped the benefits and today

the Tomich waters have a justified reputation as exceptionally well maintained trout lochs. It is worthwhile looking at some of the methods in this managerial process. Surveys of the lochs were first carried out in 1969 and *Loch Gretal* in particular was found to be an exceptionally rich water (pH 6.9) containing abundant shrimp and caddis along with claret dun, alder fly, olives, mayfly and numerous sedge varieties. In the early 1970s experiments with fertilisation were undertaken on some of the lochs over a 3 year period, under guidance from Pitlochry Freshwater Fisheries lab. The results of this fertilisation produced some large well fed browns and under scientific guidance, 'liming' has continued on and off to the present day. Today's fertilisation practices involve powdered lime being emptied into the waterline of various lochs where the wind and waves then disperse it.

Interestingly artificial enrichment has been tried on other Scottish lochs with mixed results. Apart from its expense, often a great deal of effort goes into it to produce one or two bumper years and then if it is not kept up, the newly cultivated invertebrate life falls away and everything reverts back to normal. It is not recommended as a 'quick fix' method but then what is? While the scientists of the 70s put superphosphate into the Tomich lochs it is sometimes more satisfactory to place limestone chips in the feeder burns so that any acidic run off from surrounding areas is largely neutralised. Even this method is not failsafe however as gravel can get washed away or silted up. Still, long term fertilisation can work if you think your loch is in too acidic a state to support good trout growth.

Another long standing management practice at Tomich has been the tight control of fishing pressure on the lochs and today they are operated on a system of 'beats'. Too much angling on small lochs can mean stocks are depleted to dangerous

Loch Gretal.

levels; too little pressure however and too many trout become stressed competing for the same amount of food. It is all a question of balance and Tomich has done this well. Supplementary stocking was begun on various lochs in the early 1980s and fertile Gretal in particular achieved some interesting results from fry additions. For example 100 x 5in fry were added in 1982, the loch was rested for 2 years (how many of today's commercial fisheries would do this?) and then in 1984 the trout were fished for at around 2lb plus in weight. The care lavished on the Tomich trout is exceptional and this tradition has been carried on by fishery manager Kyle Laidlay who determinedly pursues brown trout interests just as his predecessors did. You know when you fish here you are safe in the hands of true trout enthusiasts!

Tactics for Tomich vary slightly from loch to loch but you should first mount your campaign with some traditional wet flies like the Kate McLaren, Claret and Olive Bumble and Soldier Palmer (size 10 to 14). Add to this a good selection of dry flies in preparation for surface feeding fish. Go for G&H Sedges, Wickham's and/or Silver Sedge for those balmy evenings when the trout rise in gay abandon to the bigger hatching insects. Elk

Hair Sedge will also do the business when the sedges are about as will any dry fly which sits up well in the water (size 12–18). A rod of 10ft or so should suffice with floating and/or intermediate line used 'loch style' from the boat or bank. Kyle will direct you further on this in his own inimitable way so I shall not delve too much into techniques other than to say the lochs are challenging but not impossible – as always, a lot depends on the local conditions!

Taking the clear waters of Gretal first, remember that its trout are extraordinarily well fed for an exposed hill loch some 400 metres above sea level. As previously indicated, trout here thrive on fat caddis, shrimp and snail and can tend to hug the rich bottom feeding rather than appear on the surface. This is therefore the place to experiment with wet fly and nymph, size 10–14 Invicta, Greenwell's or GRHE or similar, but be ready to switch to 'dries' as soon as you see a rise. The later into the season it gets, the more the trout seem to want to rise only in the evening rather than during the day. In this respect Gretal behaves like many Inverness-shire waters which seem only to produce big trout in the dusking hours of mid summer. Still, even if the fish are playing hard to get, Gretal is gorgeous fishing with superb views of the Affric hills. The loch is small and easily fished by boat with Waddel's dam and (now renovated) boathouse along one side. The trout here are of superb quality and size with a goodly number of 2lb plus trout caught each year. For best results you will need to concentrate efforts around the edges of that shrimp holding weed and look out for that thunderous swirl – there's some big 'uns in there!

If you are lucky enough to be guided by Kyle do let him tell you some of his marvellous tales for he is a rich fund of fisherman's stories, most of them far too libellous for me to repeat here! However I can relate one about the awful day when Kyle found a dead pike on the shores of his beloved Loch Gretal. In a state of shock not to say high dudgeon, he rushed to tell village friends and angling colleagues of the ghastly trout-eating intruder he had found lying on the bank. How could it have got there he mused in abject horror, and his chums looked equally aghast. The ruse went on for several days with Kyle's blood pressure ever rising at the thought of incoming pike devastating his lovely Gretal trout, until finally one local wag quietly owned up and said he had 'planted' the pike having caught it elsewhere. On this occasion the normally perspicacious Kyle had been well and truly hoodwinked!

Lying beside Gretal is the much larger 30 acre water of *Beinne Moire* and its satellite the *Root Loch*. Though not quite scaling the heights of the profuse natural feeding found in Gretal, Beinne Moire nevertheless has excellent olive and midge hatches along with shrimp, snail and caddis. The trout here are slightly darker than in Gretal, however this is classic hill loch fishing with some very good trout coming to the fly here. A typical cast for Beinne Moire would centre around a bushy top dropper dry sedge or similar, a Greenwell's mid way and perhaps a Kate McLaren or Silver Invicta on the tail.

Expect crashing takes of trout averaging around ¾lb with a good few much bigger. For newcomers to this loch, Kyle has devised some clever psychological boosts to raise flagging spirits in times of difficult fishing. Each little land feature has been given a name and thus when out in the boat on Beinne Moire you know that you are sooner or later going to approach the 'Bay of Plenty', the 'Cape of Good Hope', 'Monster Point' or 'Guaranteed Point' or even the 'Bay of Last Resort'. They may only be names dreamed up for sake of encouragement, however you would be amazed how much of an effect they can have on weary fishers!

Other small lochs Kyle will direct you to include *Upper* and *Lower Fiodhag*. These are reached along winding forest tracks (these are a bit of a maze so follow the appropriate coloured posts) and a short walk of around 25 minutes. There is a boat on Lower Fiodhag and this water which has some shrimp present, produces good trout in the ½lb to 1lb class. Upper Fiodhag is unusually clear and will produce a specimen trout of around 1lb 8oz from time to time, however it is not a loch for beginners. The Fiodhag waters are testing and demand some subtle tactics especially if the golden trout are not rising. Use similar tactics to the waters earlier mentioned and cast carefully for sometimes trout are feeding tight to the shore and you can line fish unnecessarily. Note that complete novices should not be deterred from visiting Tomich for Kyle also has other waters suited to beginners new to the art.

Tomich has something for everyone and is quite unique in terms of its history and its long devotion to the cause of the brown trout. Virtually all the textbook techniques for managing and improving trout waters have been tried here and it is a great learning ground. Fish cannot be absolutely guaranteed, but a fabulous trouting experience laced with wonderful quirky tales and spiced with the occasional monster trout, can . . .

Chapter 27

The Whitebridge Lochs – Loch Knockie, Killin and Ruthven

'I hope within these pages to be able to show that the loch fisher is not the mere machine he is so often represented to be . . .'

Hamish Stuart

OS Map Nos. – 34 and 35
Nearest town/village(s): – Whitebridge, Fort Augustus, Inverness.
Accessibility of fishing: – Good. Whitebridge Hotel offer permits for Loch Knockie and most other hill lochs in this area. Permits for Loch Ruthven can be accessed through Grahams Tackle shop in Inverness.
Best times: – Generally from May onward once water/air temperatures improve.
General: – These lochs are relatively easy to reach lying off quiet minor roads to the east of Loch Ness. They make a grand change of scene from the winding touristy A82 which rumbles up the other side of Loch Ness. Traditional loch style equipment will suffice. Boat fishing only on Loch Ruthven (an SSSI and bird sanctuary). Boat and bank on Knockie though note here the banks are heavily wooded and make for difficult walking in places. Bank only (with wellies or waders) on Killin.

★

This trio of excellent hill lochs lie dotted in the Eastern fringe of hills above the glacial trench of Loch Ness. Their surrounds are of pleasant wooded hill and glen with farming and forestry making up the principal land use in this quiet backwater of Invernesshire. That famous Scottish walking/mountaineering buff, Tom Weir once described this picturesque area as a 'country of strange little lumpy hills' and I would echo this apt description. Many of the smaller lochs lie in peculiar little pits, deeply indented into the fertile rolling landscape and each possess a charm and character all of their own. Around fifty years ago all the waters off the minor road running from Inverness to Fort Augustus were known collectively as the *'Whitebridge lochs'*, however time has now eroded their original title and they have become known only by their individual names. Fortunately the Whitebridge Hotel retains much of its original character as a fishing inn and from here all the lochs can all be easily reached.

In off the bank at Loch Killin.

Island studded *Loch Knockie* is roughly one mile long and lies in a rocky hollow just to the SW of the hamlet of Whitebridge. Many trees and much scrub surround it and, with the added shelter from those unusual knobbly hills, it takes all but the roughest of days to deter the boat fisher here. The water is sweetly clear and there are plenty of fishy looking bays and indentations as well as weed beds and small islands. Despite its resemblance to a corrie loch Knockie is comparatively shallow with a mean depth of around 24ft. Consequently the natural feeding is quite rich with sedge, daddies, midge, olive, snail and caddis to the fore. Shrimp are also reputed to dwell around the weeds and gravel and these further add to the richness of bottom feeding. The trout have flourished in Knockie for centuries and the loch sustains a healthy population of fish. These come in at anything from a few ounces to two pounds or more in weight and all are capable of boldly snatching your fly and putting a grand bend in the rod. Boat fishing is definitely the more

Loch Knockie – shallow and rich with good weed beds and islands.

productive as the bank vegetation is dense in places and makes casting difficult. Knockie is best approached with traditional loch style and black/dark flies such as the Kate McLaren, Zulu and Bibio do particularly well here. Floating line, 4lb nylon and a rod of 10ft should suffice and a medium to fast retrieve with wet fly is predominantly used. Opportunities for dry sedge or similar will arise however should the loch fall calm. Evenings can see some intense activity in the summer months when the sedges are prolific and Knockie has been known to produce some of its best trout around the witching hours of dusk. However, trout rise readily to the fly on most occasions and what makes this loch really exciting is never knowing what will come to your attention next. Be warned, there are some goodly trout of the 2–3lb class amongst the smaller ones and late June is the most popular time for the larger fish.

At one time Knockie and all its surrounding little lochans had boats and were ardently fished (roughly from the Victorian era until around World War II). After that the trout fishing became slightly less frequented and though present levels of visitors are reasonable they are far from excessive. This makes an interesting counterpoint to the apparent overall decline in Scottish trout angling sometimes purported in the national press. Here the trout have not really suffered any fall in quality, it is simply that, in real terms, fewer anglers appear to fish for them and/or make less effort to report their catches! Remember the trout's ecological balances can be just as upset when too few anglers visit a water as compared with too many. Infrequent fishing can actually have something of a detrimental effect on remote wild waters as, with good natural spawning and no 'culling' taking place, trout start to reproduce willy nilly and stressful competition for food is intensified. In this situation average sizes can

Loch Ruthven, a jewel of a trout water complete with its own mayfly hatch.

often fall from lack of fishing – the classic scenario of too many trout and not enough to eat. Thus one must always be cautious in declaring Scotland's wild trout under threat – every area and every water is so different and each needs very careful long term assessment before making any sweeping statements on productivity.

Nearby little *Loch Killin* is a great option for those who like uncluttered easily reached bank fishing for the shores are open and wide without the abundant vegetation of Knockie. This water has a spectacular setting at the head of the River Fechlin and is accessed by a winding single track road. It is a high breezy dark loch proudly overlooked on one side by a statuesque crag where the buzzards circle and the ravens cry. Though Killin can look grim and foreboding it is an enigmatic place to fish with real touch of 'away from it all' class. The shoreline is of rock and sand and there is a deep centre where that unusual class of char 'The Haddy' is said to lurk. This particular char is darker than its brethren with large fins and smaller scales and it adds a touch of further mystery to this already unusual water. The trout of Killin rise freely almost without exception and though small they offer great sport on light tackle. Dry or wet fly is taken with gay abandon and it does not seem too important what pattern you select (size 10/12 Bumbles of any darker colour worked fine for me). As long as you

follow the simple rule of thumb for 'wild' trout and walk and wade quietly, covering new water all the time, Killin should reward you. Lingering in the one spot for too long is unproductive as you simply disturb everything that's there. Wade with caution as parts of the sand bar are a little soft and also below the crag is a long way down! Great subtleties are not required here, just refresh your loch style skills with lovely speckled trout up to ½lb or so and enjoy the fabulous scenery.

Loch Ruthven is the jewel in the crown of the 'Whitebridge lochs' though today it is more associated with the nearby city of Inverness rather than the tiny hamlet of Whitebridge. Its fishing quality sets it apart from the other waters as it lies on a particularly rich seam of land possibly with a limestone/shell sand derivatives as this is also found in its bigger neighbour Loch Duntelchaig. In 1999 an application for a Protection Order on this water was placed with the Scottish Office so if this goes through, you may well be fishing Ruthven under PO regulations. No harm in that however for the area is already an SSSI of some note with rare bird colonies already protected here.

Ruthven's surroundings are of a rich agricultural nature and it has a legendary mayfly hatch of some repute. Indeed Ruthven is one of the few waters around this Inverness-shire area to harbour these luscious insects. The bottom of the loch is sufficiently malleable to allow the mayfly nymph to make a successful burrow in its base. Mayfly cannot exist in intensely

Loch Killin where the 'Haddy' is said to lurk.

rocky or extremely silty habitats, the nymphs need specific conditions to allow them to survive over a lengthy period safe in their burrows before they hatch (see also Chapter 18 on the lochs of West Caithness). As far as I am aware the Ruthven mayfly are rather an isolated population in this region, probably only existing because of the unusually high fertility of the surrounding environment. Do note however that these insects are the 'real thing' (Ephemera) and not what the Americans sometimes call mayfly, i.e. large olives.

The water of Ruthven is very clear with excellent feeding and a broad spectrum of invertebrate life is present with nymphs, caddis, olive, sedge, mayfly, snails, daphnia and midge all there in good quantity. With the depth of water roughly around 11ft, apart from the deeper hole below the crag, the trout enjoy an excellent diet and the 'average' weight some years can be as high as 1lb 8oz. However the water clarity does not make these canny fish easy game, especially when they fix themselves on daphnia, midge and/or caddis. Thankfully during the mayfly carnival the odds fall more in favour with the angler and

lovely wild trout up to 4lb or so have been frequently taken. In a good wave, Green Drake imitations can work spectacularly here in size 10–14 as can all the traditional bushy patterns. Conversely when the loch has fallen still try small size 16 dry flies like the Greenwell Spider. I have also enjoyed considerable success in the dusk light with the dry Daddy (size 10 or 12) fished on a dead slow, twitched retrieve. Daddy Long Legs imitations are something of an enigma here, sometimes they work astoundingly well, particularly in a good breeze, and other times they are totally ignored. I suspect the times when they are dismissed coincide with the more abundant blooms of daphnia but despite their hit and miss appeal, Daddies are always worth a throw.

Budding fly tyers should note that this loch has its own fly of repute, the 'Ruthven Palmer' tied by Jimmy Newlands. It is worthwhile reiterating the dressing here as it does the business on most Highland waters when the browns are rising freely.

Dressing of Ruthven Palmer
Tail – yellow floss
Body – yellow seals fur
Rib – medium flat gold
Body hackle – red game cock hackle
Head hackle – light furnace hen

This dressing bears more than a passing resemblance to Kingsmill Moore's Golden Olive Bumble (without the blue jay throat) but either choice will do great execution at mayfly and sedge time.

Summarising the pleasures of three great trout waters like these is not easy but once you have sampled their charms do not be surprised if you feel the need to return to the quiet green land of Whitebridge complete with lumpy hills, tranquil lochs and wooded valleys. Without question the trout here will provide you with challenging fishing in delightful settings . . .

Part Four

THE ISLAND TROUT WATERS

The islands surrounding Scotland are universally recognised as wonderful untouched havens for the wild trout. Many, like Shetland, are so speckled in trout lochs it would take from here to eternity to fish them all, hence I have had to make but a small selection of what could be considered the cream of island fishing. Really, all the islands dotted around Scotlands coasts are pretty wonderful for trout but space does have its limitations! Enjoy . . .

Loch Harray, Orkney.

Glen Lochs, Mull.

Chapter 28

Isle of Mull

'The loch fisherman is liable to become a creature of habit with the wet fly.'

Colonel Oatts

OS Map Nos. – 47, 48 and 49.
Nearest town/village: – Tobermory.
Accessibility of fishing: – Very good. Tobermory AC distribute permits through A. Browns the ironmongers in Tobermory. Tackle and Books handle some other lochs and boats on Frisa can be had through Forest Enterprise. The Ross of Mull AC also do visitor permits for the southern half of the island. Visitors are made welcome, fly only on most lochs.
Best times: – Mull enjoys a temperate climate with the Gulf stream along its shores. Anytime from early May on can be productive.
General: – It is traditional 'loch style' here but do experiment. Some waters are a short step from the car, others require a reasonable hike into the hills but there is a selection to suit all tastes. Boats available on various lochs otherwise it is bank only.

★

Baby-shaped Mull is an enigmatic island lying off the Argyllshire coast. It is dominated by the prominent Munro 'Ben More' which towers 966 metres over the island's south western half. To reach Mull you can take the main ferry from Oban or, alternatively go on the short hop across from Lochaline. This is an island of contrasts with reasonably rich agricultural land along the coastal fringes, much mature forestry inland and its all topped off with great swathes of high hill and heather moor. Also prominent on the island are strange rock formations sometimes known as

'Steps and Stairs'. These are the remains of lava flows from ancient times when Mull formed part of a cluster of volcanoes along Scotland's west coast fringes. Nowadays the main activity on Mull is the tourist rather than the volcanic kind as this is a very popular visitor haunt in the summer months. Most visit Mull to make a pilgrimage to the adjacent holy island of Iona, admire Fingals Cave on nearby Staffa island and/or go to the impressive Duart Castle, seat of the Clan Maclean. Many tourists are greatly surprised at the size of the island and the length of time it takes to travel from one end to the other. Roads are winding, mainly single track affairs and it is slow progress for most of the island's 50 mile length. Still it is fabulous scenery providing you don't mind the crazy Iona bus drivers and the manic camper vans!

Mull's trout waters are roughly divided between the Northern half of the island with Frisa and Mishnish, and the southern quarter with the Glen Lochs and the waters of the Ross of Mull. The most well known of these lochs has got to be the famous *Mishnish* chain which lies off the twisting road between Tobermory and Dervaig. These are productive waters which have seen a considerable (some might say rather over zealous) amount of restocking in the past. Because of these frequent stock additions it is a little hard to tell what the original Mishnish trout strain looked like. I suspect it to be a typically heavily spotted gold as I have mainly caught this 'West Coast' kind, however a few thick set silvery 'Leven' type of trout have also impaled themselves on my fly here. These trout bear close resemblance to their nearby cousins, the Frisa trout, so it is by no means clear what type of trout came first. Bill Currie in *Fishing Waters of Scotland* declares the Mishnish trout in the 1950s were well spotted and a 'glowing yellow' so perhaps my West Coast theory is correct.

Though there is obvious genetic strain dilution, the resident trout manage to retain a hardy character and fight exceptionally well. The waters of Mishnish are clear to a faint peaty tinge and the trout come in at around the ¾lb mark with a good number of much larger fish also taken. There are three lochs in the chain and the most easterly water, *Loch Peallach* which has a small dam at its eastern end, has some real biggies in its midst. My best from here came in around 1lb 8oz and it had been predating on the copious stickleback fry that haunt the shallows. All the lochs have ideal trout habitat with abundant weed beds, skerries and ledges and the natural feeding is rich with caddis, damsel fly, shrimp and snail present. As freshwater shrimp can only survive in neutral to alkaline water this would indicate a limestone derivative being present in the underlying ground, perhaps in the form of the soft clay like deposits around Peallach. Certainly growth rates have always been good here with several trout to 2lb plus being taken over the years.

At Mishnish the adjoining little lochs of Carn an Amais and Meadhoin (boggy loch) also hold fine trout, not perhaps as large as Peallach but they still give you a good run for your money. Boats are available on all the lochs but I found bank fishing very productive around the loch margins, especially with a dry Red Sedge when a hatch of the naturals was occurring. Fish all the Mishnish chain carefully however as the big trout are nearer to you than you

would think, especially on the side furthest away from the road. One of my visits to Mishnish coincided with an extraordinary summer heatwave and as I fished on through a shimmering haze of heat and flies, I dreamily contemplated how certain skills in trout fishing change very little. I had just finished reading the old angling book of 1888 *How to Catch Trout* by 'Three Anglers' which offered this advice on loch fishing: '*Angling from the (loch) shore is in many respects like river fishing as the trout lie beneath trees, near reeds, boulders, etc; and these places must be carefully fished'*. Looking around the Mishnish lochs which have all these environmental features in abundance, I simply followed the three old sages' words of wisdom to the letter. Despite my sun-induced stupor a brace of strong butter-fat trout was secured around the shallows and I speedily concluded that there's nothing really new in the world of wild trout angling. It has all been done before though not perhaps in a state of near collapse from heat exhaustion!

Traditional flies doing well throughout the season on Mishnish include the Invicta range, Zulus, Soldier Palmers and the Kate McLaren. Once insect life is more prevalent and surface hatches are reasonable, try a change to dry fly. Elk Hair Sedges are very good in 10s and 12s as are dry Wickham's and Mini Muddlers. Floating or intermediate line is most commonly used and all in all, these lochs offer easily accessible traditional hill loch fishing at reasonable cost.

Next up is nearby *Loch Frisa* (pronounced Freeza) which contains a wonderful strain of silvery liveried, torpedo shaped trout. This is the largest water on Mull, being some four miles or so long and plunging to a maximum depth of around 200ft at its widest point. Frisa is a glacial loch made up of three deep 'basins' each over 150ft deep and these are separated by shallower regions of water. Forestry came to Frisa in 1925 and the hills

Mishnish in the height of summer.

surrounding it are partly clad in wall to wall conifers however, whether this afforestation actually changed the character of the angling by acidic run off, is not clear. Certainly records from the 1970s (50 years after the first forestry developments) show Frisa trout still to be maintaining their excellent quality being red fleshed, beautifully marked and fighting fit. Though the loch must surely have contained larger fish, earlier records show mean sizes varied from 'three to the pound' to about 12 ounces at that time.

This state of affairs continued until the late 1980s when a fish farm operation was established on Frisa. Suddenly the Frisa trout turned into Pavlov's dogs and learned to expect and gratefully accept, food coming to them by way of the fish farm pellet waste. Growth rates exploded with trout now regularly coming in at between 3 to 10lb. Whether Frisa fishing can still be called 'wild' angling when the trout are feeding on artificial food, is open to some debate. A similar thing happened on Skye a few years back (see Chapter 31) and really, providing the fish farm is not disrupting, harming or polluting the wild trout habitat, I feel we have to tolerate it and not nit pick too much. Even if the trout are smart enough to forage on dropped pellets we still have to be smart enough to catch them and that's not always easy. It will also be interesting to see what happens to trout growth rates on Frisa in the future, as just now (early 1999), the fish farm has been closed down during an outbreak of the farmed fish disease 'ISA' and its future is somewhat uncertain.

Traditional loch style from the boat is the accepted norm on Frisa but bank fishing is also allowed. Trout mainly hug the margins and like Mishnish, it is not necessary to be too far out to be amongst fish. Around Ledmore seems to hold a better class of trout and the shallows there make a good starting off point. The smaller residents are all very smash and grab rather like small finnock which they physically resemble, however the bigger fish often need a degree more subtlety. Best times for the larger trout are dull days when there is an abundant natural hatch of midge or sedge and their attention is drawn away from bottom and/or pellet feeding. Flies here vary from the usual Zulu, Pennel, Soldier Palmer type to a deeper fished Dunkeld or Invicta. I also found mention of a useful fly the 'Mull Mite' tied by Malcolm Goddard, a regular visiting fisher on Mull. This fly design makes a good universal shrimp/olive/midge representation worthy of any hill loch fishers' fly box. The dressing is as follows:

Mull Mite (size 10 or 12)
Body – blend of yellow, black and red seals fur
Hackle – light partridge or teal wing
Rib – flat silver tinsel
Head – varnished orange thread.

Malcolm Goddard apparently tied this fly especially for Mull and as far as I am aware, it is at present not being made commercially. Making it yourself is relatively easy however so get your fly tying kit out and get going!

Less popular but equally dramatic fishing can be had on the southern reaches of Mull. I visited the lovely *Glen Lochs* which lie off the winding Glen More road and these provide good sport when there has been abundant rainfall. The Glen Lochs are another chain of interlinking lochs rather like Mishnish. At one time excellent sea trout were very common here but since the rapid expanding of fish farming around Mull's coastal waters, their numbers appear to have decreased. Salmon too were regularly caught in the Glen Lochs and after spates some still appear to run. The brown trout should be your main concern however and they are 'bonnie fechters' coming in at the ½lb to 1lb weight. The first and most visible loch here is *Loch Squabain* (or Sgunbain), however its proximity to the albeit single track road and a large camp site development makes

for some rather public fishing of both the legal and illegal kind. If this rather puts you off, as it did me, put on your hiking boots and head out toward the *Crun Lochan* and the top loch of *Airdeglais*. These waters are in superb settings of rugged remote hill and a more peaceful day out would be hard to imagine. Some cracking trout up to 1lb or so come from these lochs too. Use traditionals as for Mishnish and Frisa concentrating first on dark patterns like Kate McLaren or Grouse and Claret.

If you can make it all the way down to *Loch Assapol* near the small village of Bunessan without being tipped into a ditch by the Iona bus drivers, James McKeand provides the local angling 'know how' here and he will supply you with permits and advice as required. Assapol has had rather a disturbing history as at one time it had an excellent head of sea trout and salmon as well as browns, however an ill thought out dam on the loch and its burn effectively put paid to the runs of migratory fish. The resident browns (generally of the ½lb class) may have benefited from the dam altering water levels, but any long term good may be short lived. Raising and lowering water levels nearly always produces a 'feast and famine' effect on fish populations. Assapol brown trout respond to traditional patterns with a Greenwell's or those Irish Dabblers doing particularly well. Also, if you don't mind lengthy plods, there are a number of small hill lochs on estates in the Ross of Mull area and these offer real 'away from everywhere' trout.

Mull does not perhaps have the classy and prolific amount of fishing of say Orkney or Shetland, but it does possess a unique charm and character all of its own. Visit it in 'Spring', i.e. May early June before the buzzing hordes of midges (and tourists) arrive in huge numbers and enjoy its unfettered charms . . .

Chapter 29

The Orkney Isles

'So the exile – remembering – takes hope that some time he will see that green valley again, and the heat and the burden of the day is lessened . . .'

'BB'

OS Map No. – 6

Nearest town/village: – Kirkwall, Stromness.

Accessibility of fishing: – Excellent. Under ancient Viking law all fishing on Orkney is technically open without charge, however paying a small fee to join the Orkney Trout Fishing Association (OTFA) who work tirelessly to maintain the fishings, is common courtesy.

Best times: – Usually from early May right through to early September but different Orkney waters come on at different times. Bumper months are normally May, June and July but really Orkney is great all season except in conditions of extreme cold.

General: – Orcadian anglers are acknowledged experts in 'loch style' fishing and they use a wide range of traditional and modern patterns (wet, dry or nymph) on floating or intermediate line. Do as the local fly fishers do and you won't go far wrong. The Isles are very exposed windy places with little or no real shelter and you must be prepared for some quite arduous fishing in gales.

★

Fishing on the Orkney Isles is synonymous with fabulous trout and extraordinarily fertile lochs. There are no rivers of any size here and over the centuries, a huge tradition of loch fishing has developed. Consequently when you first leave the boat or plane and head out on those wonderful lochs, in angling terms you are fishing over hallowed ground. The green

Orkney mainland harbours most of the major lochs but there are smaller waters on nearby satellite islands like Rousay and hilly Hoy.

It is hard to know where to start when describing these historic isles and their superb lochs. I could fill a page with superlatives but suffice to say Orkney is a richly atmospheric land, quite different to any other you may visit, and its lochs are simply gorgeous! I was first converted to these waters at the beginning of the 1980s when I was lured over the water on the pretext of a cycling holiday. However, once I discovered the charms of the Orkney trout, ably introduced to me by friend and expert angler Ed Headley, not much more went on in the way of cycling! Ever since then, I have tried to make an annual pilgrimage across the choppy sea. Unfortunately, though I'm technically only fifteen miles from these islands as the crow flies, the storm tossed Pentland Firth is something of a deterrent in getting there, especially if your sea legs are not too hot!

Let's start this homage to the islands with the largest, *Loch Harray*, also probably the one best known to the casual visitor. Harray represents roughly five miles of exceptionally productive trout water, some of the finest in Britain, and it's a trout fisher's dream with its sparklingly clear shallow water and many bays, small islands and skerries. Overlooked by the startling Ring of Brodgar, Maeshowe and

Standing stones of Stenness – Orkney.

Canadian pond weed. However, being so large and windswept, Harray has always tended to eventually 'cleanse' itself of any environmental problems.

Although some very large trout of 3lb plus do occasionally come from Harray, the fish here mainly tip the scales at just below the 1lb mark. The trout are a wonderful mix of silver and pale gold and with their deep red flesh they make excellent eating. They also have matchless fighting qualities, their characteristics much resembling the open water 'Leven' strain. OTFA have a long established management strategy for Harray (and other local waters) and this sees occasional supplementary restocking of the indigenous trout. Sea trout also come into the loch via Stenness, being caught here principally in early May and September. The migratory trout are usually captured as finnock of around ¾lb and sometimes they so strongly resemble the resident Harray fish it is difficult to tell them apart. With all the trout generally very free rising, it is rare to return from Harray without at least one fish in the bag. It is more likely to be the gales that will defeat you than the trout.

The natural feeding of Harray is abundant with shrimp, caddis, snail and daphnia forming the bulk of the sub surface diet and midge, olive and sedge giving the principal fly hatches. Wind blown terrestrials like the cow dung fly and daddies also add to the excitement. Fishing tactics for Harray naturally revolve around traditional loch style with floating line and considerable emphasis is placed on top dropper techniques. A good deal of this method of angling is from the boat, however Harray also provides an exceptionally good wading environment and you can be assured of good fish around most if not all of its lengthy shoreline. Merkister Bay, Ling Holms, Joesy's Bay, Kirk Bay and Ballarat are just some of the many favoured trout spots on Harray – you will quickly develop your own 'hot spots'.

the stark Stones of Stenness you get the feeling this loch and its lovely trout have been around since time began. Harray is very shallow, probably only 10 to 14ft at maximum depth, and with its surrounding green field agriculture it provides an excellent trout habitat. Occasionally the loch falls foul of over enrichment produced by agricultural fertilisers, and in the 1980s there was also an overgrowth of

Fishing Harray even in the height of a busy summer, is rarely anything other than a joyful experience. The red fleshed trout come at you all smash and grab through the waves and for their size they are truly exceptional fighters. Whether boat or bank fishing you should aim to cover the darker blue water channels which appear amongst the paler shoreline shallows. These are actually pockets of deeper water rather resembling small trenches and they are great food collecting trout holds. Casts around the numerous skerries are also good and trout rise here with extraordinary power, apparently from only inches of water. Most of my fishing on this loch has been done from the bank while in the company of my Orkney mentor Ed Headley and what times of drama and of laughter we have had amid the trout laden corners of Harray. Soldier Palmer, Coch Y Bondue, Muddlers, Loch Ordie, Pennels and Invictas are all used to great effect here and specialist flies like the Shredge and Coch Zulu are also effective. Just occasionally the intense summer daphnia blooms cause the trout to feed consistently sub surface and in this case intermediate or even slow sinking lines are sometimes used. Harray can be testing but in general it is much kinder on the angling system than its adjacent neighbour of Stenness.

Loch Stenness has to be one of the most frustrating lochs in the Northern Isles. On its day it is capable of producing some fabulous trout from its limpid brackish waters. I have to admit I have never enjoyed tremendous success from here for though I've seen the odd monster follow on the fly rather like a rainbow trout, I have rarely connected. Perhaps I should have been less impetuous in anticipating the take for it is said that Stenness trout like to chase the fly some way before snatching it. Apart from brown, sea and/or slob trout this loch also contains a variety of fish from flounders to pollack and from mullet to coalfish. There is an abundance of fish fry from these species and others and the larger trout appear to concentrate their feeding efforts on their smaller brethren. Nowadays the loch is mainly fished for sea trout from July onward and there are some real experts at this game of cat and mouse amongst the bladderwrack strewn lower shoreline. The finnock easily access the loch from the wide mouthed exit into the sea and they are game, bonny creatures not usually enormous (about the 1lb mark is common), but full of spirited fight. Choose really wild dark windy days to try and tempt the sea trout. These are the same trout that Orcadians fish for directly into the sea and your tactics should mimic those used in the salt with Teal Blue and Silver and other lure-like flies put to good use in size 8–12.

I suppose the large Stenness brown trout should technically be classed as slob trout as they live in that 'half and half' environment akin to an estuary mouth of a river. Consequently it sometimes pays to follow tidal river tactics fishing two hours before high tide and two hours after. This tactic should allow you to cast to the fish in a more active phase, however they can still be damnably difficult! Floating or intermediate lines are normally used with a selection of patterns geared more toward sea going trout than browns. Flies such as the Dunkeld, Butchers, Blue Zulu, Teal Blue and Silver are often used on the point with Bumbles, Pennels and Soldier Palmers for droppers. Natural feeding is almost always from the rich loch bottom and flies fished fast so as to resemble small fleeing fish do best. Superb trout haunt Stenness and fish in the 4lb plus range do come occasionally to the fly, it is just getting them to take which is the problem!

Swannay Loch with its rolling moor and low hills has a much more familiar traditional Scottish loch appeal. This slightly peaty water contains some quite extraordinary trout and if you are specimen hunting, this is a water which can and does provide the goods. Two-pounders are relatively common but whatever their size, golden Swannay fish are supreme fighters. The natural feeding here mainly centres around midge, olive, cow dung and sedge and the trout can go through periods of fixation on one insect variety and not another. Sometimes profuse sedge hatches scatter across the water only to be ignored by the trout in favour of say, small black midge. Consequently Swannay is often regarded as an 'experts' water' as it can be a demanding, exhilarating challenge. This loch fishes slightly better in the early half of the season with May and June normally being exceptionally good. Bushy size 10s are usually in use here with Bumbles, Mini Muddlers, Ke Hes and Zulus popular choices. Incidentally, Kemp and Heddle, Orcadian inventors of the Ke He, devised it to imitate a heather fly (bibio) which came off the local moors here in late August/September. If you look at the Ke He, it is a superb imitation of the heather fly complete with upper red leg joints. However, through the mists of time it was often claimed to have been created to imitate a small black bee. Natural bibio flies have fat bodies, flat wings and a dark outline and from a distance do indeed resemble small bees, so the mystery of the Apis connection has more or less been solved. Swannay is principally fished from the boat as the shore can be devilish with sudden soft holes and drop offs. Around its southern end is the most popular site with the island of Muckle Holm being a favourite spot. It is not easy fishing by any means but if you do contact a Swannay fish it will usually be a good one, full of fire and fight.

Boardhouse and *Hundland* also provide the angler with fabulous sport. These lochs lie side by side in the N.W. corner of the mainland isle. Boardhouse has a dark peaty base with soft margins here and there and it is better fished from the boat. Midge, olive and sedge form a lot of the natural feeding and this loch is noted for copious hatches of caenis, those tiny white flies which get everywhere from in your eyes to down your neck! Caenis are so small it is impossible to imitate them but a large white fly like the White hackled Invicta fished fast will sometimes distract the fish long enough for you to sink the hook. The Boardhouse trout average around ¾lb but as with all Orkney lochs much bigger are sometimes to be had. This loch favours traditional methods and Greenwell's, Muddlers, Ke He and similar do the business on floating or intermediate line. Of these two lochs I personally favour nearby Hundland which has a more interesting shoreline of skerries and boulders, shallows and weed beds. Local legend also has it that Hundland will fish well even in the brightest of sun but as it fishes best in the early half of the season before the sun is at full height and the weed gets excessive, this could just be coincidence. The trout population here much resembles those of Boardhouse, indeed the fish are thought to share the same spawning burn, however some much larger browns also come from here. Trout of 2lb plus have been caught in the past and the specimen hunter often does well here. Again, it is not easy fishing but similar traditional tactics to Boardhouse usually pay off.

Two other waters I must mention are *Skaill* (open to OTFA members so do join) and the little loch of *Clumley*. These smaller lochs hold some real monsters of trout. In sweetly clear Clumley I was briefly connected to something in the 4lb range before we parted company by the old stone wall that runs into the loch. Both waters offer difficult challenging fishing and the big resident browns come on and go off almost in the blink of an eye. Profuse midge, olive and sedge hatches do occur but sometimes the fish fix themselves on nymphs or other sub surface feeding like

Orkney splendour – wading on Loch Harray.

shrimp. To a man they stubbornly refuse to rise and subtle changes of fly retrieve and depth are often needed. Rich agricultural land surrounds these waters and the natural feeding is superb, so are the trout, but don't hold your breath in your attempts to attract them. Dull warm windy conditions are best and take along Silver Sedge, Greenwell's, Soldier Palmer and a sparsely dressed Pennel or two. Be prepared to scale up and down in fly size according to the conditions. Big waves demand bushy Size 10 flies while calm conditions may need as small as a 16 on 3–4lb nylon. Wade quietly and cautiously along the shoreline and just occasionally you will get the take of a lifetime when one of those leviathans (which resemble the bigger trout of Durness) rips away with your fly clamped in its jaws. Great stuff!

Orkney has a wonderful timeless feel to it and the Orkney fly fishers are an extremely dedicated lot, knowledgeable and friendly, always ready with a bit of cajoling advice whenever you need it. Many visiting anglers come once and then return annually until they are no longer fit enough to make the journey, such is the magnetism of these lovely isles and their sparkling lochs. Ed Headley summed it all up beautifully when he remarked *'There's so much good trout fishing on Orkney, I don't really need to fish anywhere else!'* Try it and you will see what he means . . .

Chapter 30

The Shetland Isles

'There are so many lochs which are known but to a few individuals.'
Charles St John

OS Map Nos. – 1, 2, 3 and 4.
Nearest town/village(s): – Lerwick, Brae, Scalloway.
Accessibility of fishing: – Excellent. Shetland AA have around 360 lochs on offer spread right across the islands. Permits are available from the Tourist Information Office and/or the Rod and Line Tackle Shop in Lerwick. Shetland AA have also produced a super booklet *Trout fishing in Shetland* which is compulsory reading 'afore ye go'. Copies of this can be ordered in advance from the Shetland Times or purchased while on the islands.
Best times: – May to September with the best month normally being June.
General: – Shetland is one of those places where around every corner a new lochan beckons. The amount of water available for trout angling here is quite unbelievable for such a small area of land and you really need at least a fortnight to even faintly scratch the surface of it all. It's not all quantity either. There are some top quality, exceptionally fertile lochs mixed in amid the more peaty variety and trout will grow to several pounds in weight given the right natural feeding. Take your waders for many of the lochs are shallow and you need to get that little further out. Also take plenty of traditional tackle and flies, a float tube if you have the space, sun screen for occasionally exceptionally bright days and lead boots so you don't blow flat in the gales!

★

Magnificent Shetland where the sun never sets.

In loch fishing terms, Shetland is Scotland in virtually exact miniature. From fertile limestone waters to sandstone and granite based lochs, and from high peaty tarns to limpid machair waters, the Shetland Isles have got the lot. They may not be on the scale of some of the mainland's huge expanses of water, but they still are as diverse a selection as any trout angler could desire. There are some 360 lochs here (it is said one for every day of the year but

I think that's for the tourists' benefit!) and over its 60 mile plus length the island provides some terrific contrasts. The southern half of the mainland from the airport at Sumburgh northward toward Lerwick, is exceptionally rich with the islands' principal machair loch, the *Loch of Spiggie*, nestled in its midst. The general environment of this part of Shetland is very similar to Orkney.

Travelling north past Spiggie you arrive at the lush green hills of the Tingwall valley containing its popular lochs of Tingwall and Asta. From there the terrain changes dramatically and you can either head west to numerous peaty tarns dotted among heather moor and stony hill or alternatively you can go north to where some secret lochans indent a barren, oddly lunar landscape. For a change of 'mainland' scene why not head over by ferry to the little outlying lochs on the islands of Yell, Unst or Fetlar for there you will also find trout. There are no rivers as such on Shetland, however think numerous small waters on a par with say Durness, Gairloch and Assynt and you will get the general idea.

Shetland has an interesting history as a select angling destination. Right from Victorian times prolific sea trout in the islands sheltered salt water inlets (Voes) were the principal quest of local and visiting anglers. Huge bags were common with some large fish of 5lb upward amongst them. Brown trout angling was also pursued with vigour though it has to be said that it was the excellent sea trout which got most of the attention. In the early 1900s a number of hotels thrived on visiting angler trade and, from the numbers attending, it seems Shetland was once a very popular haunt of church Ministers holding 'seminars'. The fact that lines of waders and rods leant against the Kirk wall on a Sunday hinted that the Almighty was not the only thing on the minds of the visiting men of the cloth!

Many sea trout were taken in those days, sometimes running into the 10lb class and the Isles remained a top drawer sea trout venue until the late 60s/early 70s when a slow spiral of decline began. Changes in sea temperature, seal predation, netting out of the wild fish for resale and finally the coming of the fish farming industry, put many nails into the sea trout's coffin. While national sea trout losses are blamed predominantly on fish farming, Shetland shows a salutary complex structure of decline which some local anglers say appears to have begun prior to mass aquaculture development. Commercial netting of sea trout apparently made inroads into stocks, past anglers may have slaughtered unnecessarily large bags containing prime breeding stock and predatory seals, which used to be mercilessly culled by shooting, are now protected and enjoying the life of Riley! When the fish farms arrived in bulk in the 80s, many were sited over the main feeding grounds for the young sea trout and/or on the underwater routes which they use when returning to their native burns. The deadly tide of sea lice greatly accelerated what was a slow downturn in wild stocks to the point of near collapse. The fact that Orkney and Shetland sea trout catches are not recorded in overall national catch statistics (unlike most fishery board records on the Scottish mainland) has not helped in bringing a case for reversing this decline. If no records exist to say what was there and what is now not, government bodies can easily ignore any anglers' calls for conservation of this wild fish. However, it should not be thought that all of Shetland sea trout angling has gone forever. There are still one or two places where they can be caught on the fly straight from the sea and once you are on the islands, local anglers are generally most helpful in pointing you in the right direction.

While the localised migratory trout have suffered a downturn, the resident browns seem to have gone from strength to strength. The Shetland Anglers Association came into being in 1920 and over the last 80 years members of this enthusiastic and able group have worked tirelessly to enhance the fishings. Fry and fingerling restocking is undertaken periodically on waters thought to have poor natural spawning and/or to be under some angling pressure. In tandem with restocking, various pristine waters like Spiggie are left untouched to maintain genetic integrity. In recent years a number of sea trout locations have also been supplementary stocked in an attempt to revive numbers. Perhaps because of the nature of the island way of life (this is an isolated community where Shetlanders, when they do meet up, like to enjoy the 'crack') the club has gone out of its way to bring brother anglers together. They have a neat little clubhouse complete with bar in the centre of Lerwick and visiting anglers are made most welcome. The club also masterminds various serious and not so serious competitions throughout the season and details of these can be had from the Secretary.

Recommending lochs to try on Shetland is a daunting task, however one which does stand out above the rest has got to be *Spiggie*. This is a naturally regenerating, free rising water which has a good supply of wonderful native creamy gold and silver trout ranging from ¾lb to 1lb 8oz plus, with the occasional fish coming in at around the 3lb mark. As the loch holds sea trout as well as browns I suspect some cross natural spawning has occurred to give the fish their remarkable colour, that and the fact that the water is gin clear over a light sand and rock base. This is classic 'machair' alkaline clearwater environment, indeed the loch is only yards from the sea, and in this respect it closely resembles Loch Harray on Orkney. The feeding is exceptionally rich and trout happily gobble down copious amounts of shrimp, midge, olive (but not mayfly), sedge, cow

Creamy gold and silver trout from Spiggie.

dung flies, snail, daphnia and bloodworm. The fishes' flesh is red and firm indicating a predominantly crustacean diet and they make excellent eating.

Spiggie is a delight to fish. Marsh marigolds colour the loch shoreline, lush pasture clothes the low hills and trout rise like jet rockets from their holds amid the boulders, weed and off the calcium rich shell sand. Wading is on the whole a simple affair as the loch is so shallow. Trout can be attracted from all over this water and off the north sands (known locally as the Deeps) is a favourite local wading haunt. When working the shoreline you should avoid the nesting bird areas which are clearly marked on the map at the boathouse at the Northern end but this is only a small part of the loch, the rest is yours. Petrol engines are not allowed on this RSPB owned water, however the wader does exceptionally well as does the float tuber. This is essentially floating line country and traditional flies with a flash of orange in them like the Dunkeld, Partridge and Orange or Orange Ke He do well. Also try out a Bibio, Soldier Palmer and a Red Sedge or two. Dry fly works fabulously

Loch Tingwall.

when the trout are on the surface and hooking one of these beauties is like being attached to a whirling dervish such is their inherent strength. Spiggie reeks of quality and I cannot recommend it too highly.

Tingwall Loch is another popular local venue being only a short drive from Lerwick and this clear neutral to alkaline water has some good sized browns present. Here the trout enjoy a similar diet to those of Spiggie though the deep shore off its East side, where a depth of over 80ft has been recorded, makes for a slightly different environment overall. This water sees some restocking with browns and trout generally average ¾lb to 1lb with some bigger taken each year. Boat and bank fishing here and traditional methods using floating, intermediate or even (whisper it) sinking lines will do the business. At times this loch sees profuse midge hatches and Connemara Black, Black Pennel and Bibio do good things. Occasionally this loch can be rather dour, windswept and foreboding but the chance of connecting with a good Tingwall fish makes it worth a throw. It divides into two halves the southern part more famed for larger trout and the north half said to

contain smaller fish. Around the islands and the narrows is also a good spot. There is an unusual promontory at its north end where in ancient times a Norse Parliament (the Lawting) would meet to discuss the affairs of the day. The walkway out to this parliamentary seat is still visible, indeed this promontory makes for excellent angling. Fishing there, I idly wondered if the Norseman dropped a line over the side when proceedings were slow!

The neighbouring loch of *Asta* (lesser fished but no less clear and fertile) is also worthwhile even if you have to duck the stray golf ball or two. I saw some grand trout move in here though the average might be said to be closer to half a pound. Silvery specimens can come from Asta as well as the gold bellies and fishing methods are as for Tingwall.

Heading NE from Lerwick you will pass the *Loch of Girlsta* where the islands only known population of char and possibly some ferox haunt the bleak depths and then you hit another limestone strip and the small demanding *Loch of Benston*. This is an alkaline loch rather similar to the Durness waters. It has large shy trout in its clear limpid depths and most locals fish off the gravel and rock shoreline out toward the islands. The feeding here is rich with shrimp, corixia and sedge all taken. There is a profuse weed growth on this shallow loch and it does fish best from early on. Excellent trout up to 3lb plus are caught but it is not easy fishing. Some locals fish sunk lines and goldheads, others try floating line and buzzers or dry fly. Try everything and you might just be rewarded.

As you travel north from Lerwick you might want to give the tough 'big fish' waters near Echaness (pronounced Ayshness) a whirl. This area holds a collection of small demanding lochs made to make your toes curl but if you do connect with a fish it may well be a 4lber! Amongst the lochs to try are the picturesque *West Loch*, dark mysterious *Gluss Water* where the bonxies whirl, also *Houlland* and *Gerdie*. Most Echaness waters range from gin clear to a tea stain peat colour with stone and granite bases but the feeding is adequate with shrimp, snail, and caddis present along with cow dung and stonefly. Some olives look to be around but Graeme Callander, who kindly guided me around this area, is still investigating their presence as it seems numbers vary. Mayfly, i.e. Green Drake are not found on Shetland, however some dedicated local anglers are trying to introduce them by 'importing' them from Caithness or Sutherland where they are of course profuse and indigenous. This has been tried before in other areas of Scotland with reasonable success and if they get the environment right (alkaline water and some clay like soil suitable for larvae burrows), you never know! Flies for the Echaness lochs mainly concentrate on the dark varieties, Zulu, Pennel, Clan Chief or Claret Bumble are good. The waters seem to fish better in the evening when a sedge hatch comes on. Bright sunshine and cloudless skies make for exceptionally difficult fishing, these trout are shy monsters!

While here you should also make a trip out to the 'Wild West' past Bixter toward Walls and Sandness. If you want wilderness waters more on the par with say Scourie or Assynt this area of Shetland has them in abundance. Most are neutral to acidic peaty lochs with correspondingly darker fish but there are some large specimens amongst the typical eight ounceers so be prepared. This is an area of Shetland which lives up to its name and the angler can spend days wandering from loch to loch amidst moors thick with golden plover. Dunlin squeak and flit along the loch shores and red throated divers cast a haughty glance your way. Out with Gordon Williamson of the Herrislea House Hotel we tried *Hulma*, *Hollarin* and a number of hill lochs near the Papa Storr ferry. Peace and solitude await you in this grand barren land. If you fancy a real 'expedition' style of fishing holiday, bring your tent and go to the North of the island mainland to fish the lochs of *Ronas Hill*. Big trout and little trout lie in wait, traditional hill loch fishing at its best.

Shetland has so much top quality angling in such huge variety it is difficult to do it justice in words alone. Better you get out there and enjoy the whole experience. My memories of Shetland are happy and glorious. I guarantee that once you fish here you may never want to leave . . .

'Wild West' of Shetland with its abundance of lochs.

Chapter 31

Isle of Skye

'I never found the companion that was so companionable as solitude.'

Henry D. Thoreau

OS Map Nos. – 23 and 32.
Nearest town/village: – Portree.
County/district – Inner Hebrides.
Accessibility of fishing: – Very good. Portree Angling Association issue permits through Jansport, Portree as do various local hotels. Portree Tourist Office is also very helpful with advice on where to obtain fishing.
Best times: – Normally May and June and again in September but any time when you get a sustained warm dull patch of weather can be good.
General: – When I first fished Skye twenty or more years ago, the trout angling seemed largely ignored in favour of the excellent hill walking available there. Consequently the number of anglers on the lochs apart from hardy locals was insignificant. Nowadays the fishing is that much more promoted and organised and Skye has become quite a popular haunt for the touring angler. Loch style flies and floating and intermediate lines are de rigueur.

★

Of all the islands lying off Scotland's West coast, this is probably the most famous with a lengthy history encompassing everything from prolonged Clan Wars to Flora McDonald and from infamous Clearances to bloody battles for crofting rights. Virtually all Scots have an inkling about Skye however vague. As a babe in arms my mother sang me the 'Skye Boat Song' and this family tradition was upheld when I too hummed the same air to my sons. Ask kids to name any Scottish island off the west coast and it is odds on they pick Skye. This misty isle has long been acknowledged as the most romantic of the Inner Hebrides, yet its past is turbulent and even in modern times it attracts a fair share of controversy. In the mid 1990s Highland Council decided a bridge was required to the mainland and in one hideous construction, they shot down forever the quaint historical glamour of going 'Over the Sea to Skye'. No more 'speed bonny boats' and you even have to pay a toll to drive over the concrete monstrosity!

Despite its now permanent joining to the Scottish mainland, Skye remains a powerfully enigmatic land with the jagged black Cuillin hills dominating its skyline. These stark mountains of rough gabbro rock are the hills every climber dreams of conquering and a substantial amount of Skye's tourist industry is geared toward this demand. Here and there the rugged coastline is indented with sea lochs and rivers and, prior to mass fish farming developments akin to those on Mull, a goodly number of sea trout used to run these spate streams. Brown trout are also relatively common in the lochans which dot Skye and during the post Victorian era their stocks were added to with imported Leven trout brought over from the mainland. Over time local angling interests have periodically placed additional stocks of wild browns in some of the lochs and today the visiting angler can expect a reasonable if not excessive number of good quality trout waters on which to cast his fly.

The island divides roughly into two large halves, North Skye with its principal waters the Storr Lochs and the cluster of lochans at Staffin, and South Skye with remote Loch Coruisk and the lochs of the Isle of Ornsay/Sleat area. From the wild trout enthusiast's standpoint, the Northern half contains most of the better angling with the *Storr Lochs* now rightfully acknowledged as having some of the finest wild trout angling off the West coast. I first discovered these wonderful lochs in 'self defence' in the early 1980s when my mountaineering husband was busy exploring the delights of the nearby basalt pinnacles known as the 'Old Man of Storr'. Whilst he set off in conquest of these stark hills 'because they are there', I turned my attention to Loch Fada, Storr Loch and Loch Leathan because they too were there! The three lochs interlink to form the Storr Loch chain and boat and bank angling is the norm. I have to say that from the road, especially on one of those all too common driech Skye days, the waters look relatively uninspiring. They are surrounded by rough peat moor and a few small hills and overlooked by the southern reaches of the jagged Trotternish ridge and those rather severe looking rock pinnacles. At the northern end the lochs are harnessed into a gravity feed dam complete with tunnel running down to a small power station at the foot of the nearby sea cliffs. In this area particularly, there is a definite bleak reservoir feel and on wet days it all looks rather gloomy.

Do not let first appearances fool you however, for the Storr Lochs are an absolute Nirvana for the trout angler with gin clear pools containing some superb trout in the 1lb to 5lb plus range. One of my first and largest from here scaled in at just under 3lb and, when I had recovered from the shock, I found such good trout are relatively commonplace here. The local average is now around the pound mark which gives you some idea of the rich feeding available with caddis, sedge, olives, midge, snail and shrimp high on the menu. The carrot rich colour of the trout's flesh gives away a high degree of crustacean feeding and the fish I caught were beautifully marked with black asterisk spots and silver/gold flanks. Incidentally when a fish farm was sited at the northern end, some (though not all) of the local trout assumed different feeding patterns cruising up, even from the other end of the loch, to feed on the farm detritus. Just like Mull's Loch Frisa, a goodly few of the trout took on leviathan proportions of 4lb plus from gulping down the pellet waste. Unfortunately, in doing so, they tended to lose their free rising characteristics and lay up in deep water near the fish cages. This led the local angling club to bring in the Pitlochry fisheries scientists to see what if anything might be done. In the end there was little anyone could do other than try and enhance surface feeding by planting alder here and there along the foreshore. It was thought if the bushes grew they would harbour more insects which would then be blown onto the water and encourage fish to rise. The Storr Lochs are a big windy place however and though the bushes were indeed planted a few years ago, it is not clear if they made a great deal of difference.

The situation of deep feeding wild trout finally resolved itself in the late 1990s when various economic constraints forced the closure of the fish farm. Large freshwater fish farms not only alter trout feeding habits, they also flood the immediate area with escapee smolts. On Skye the farm appeared to bring down the average size of trout caught in the vicinity of the farm, and escapees (small salmon in this case) were frankly a nuisance. Thankfully, with the removal of the farm this problem

The Old Man of Storr towers above the Storr Lochs.

seems to have righted itself. Fish farms in the sea are forever attracting bad press, but siting them in freshwater systems does not do the wild trout any more favours. When will the government ministers supposedly controlling the fish farming industry ever wake up to their detrimental environmental impact?

Fishing on the Storr chain can be had at very reasonable cost with permits from local outlets and boat or bank angling is allowed. Most of my fishing here has been done from the bank and, apart from being a long tiring walk, the indented shoreline is easy to fish and normally very productive. Be warned however that these waters are no pushover and you need dull mild days with plenty of insect activity to make the trout move. May and June are the most popular months, after that you can be driven insane, not only by difficult trout, but also by the Skye midge which hatches in black biting clouds from late June onwards reaching a peak in July and August. Take copious amounts of midge repellent and a hooded face net. Nerves of steel are also useful. What makes it even more frustrating is that the Storr Loch trout

often rise madly during these huge midge hatches. Many a good trout is missed while you cower, a helpless whimpering wreck, beneath the merciless fangs of the harpies!

Despite being apparent 'non fishing' weather, summer becalmings seem particularly good times to fish here and all the occasions that I have contacted 2lb plus fish from the bank have been during conditions of virtual flat calm. Evening sedge hatches can also be particularly glorious on Skye. I recall one balmy night when the Storr Lochs appeared to positively heave with trout. Everywhere you looked fish were rolling and sploshing and this is one of the few lochs apart from Durness where you can actually hear the 'Slurp' as great trout rise slowly and deliberately to suck down sedges. (see also Durness Lochs Chapter 19). Parts of the Storr Lochs fall away quite steeply and the most productive areas tend to be the narrows, around the island in *Leathan*, and in the scattering of little shallower bays. Beneath and opposite the hill of Armishader is particularly good. Most fishers seem to use floating or intermediate line and standard patterns like the Invicta, Zulu and Pennel do the business. Soldier Palmer is also useful and dry sedge patterns are vital for

Hill lochs of the Quiraing – Skye.

those eagerly awaited hatches. Boat fishing requires a similar armoury but it really has to be done in a good wind, Storr trout are fickle beasts in their gin clear water habitat. Do make an effort to fish these waters, for on their day they and their resident trout are simply stunners!

Going North from the Storr lochs you eventually arrive at a cluster of small lochans below the impressive 'Quiraing' with its weird and wonderful rock formations like the 'Table', the 'Needle' and the 'Prison'. The nearest port of call is the hamlet of Staffin and these waters are also controlled by the Portree AA. They make for demanding sport amid some of the most unusual scenery in Britain and are lightly fished when compared to numbers visiting the Storr Lochs. If peaceful solitude is your game, these small lochans provide it in abundance. As ever, the longest walks provide the biggest fish so

strap on the boots and get going, it is a bit ankle twisting and boggy but trout up to 1lb or more are there. You can't really get lost because the great Trotternish ridge dominates the skyline, not as big as the Cuillins of course but still very impressive with its sharp cliffs and buttresses. Tackle should be as light as possible, you have to carry it all that way and dark traditional patterns like the Kate McLaren and the Black Pennel are fine. Wild trout in the most wild of places . . . great stuff.

Other notable waters on Skye which you might like to visit are those attached to the Ullinish Lodge (*Connan* and *Duagraich*) and the cluster of lochs of Southern Skye centred around Sleat and the Eilean Iarmain Hotel. Trout are more of the order of ½ to ¾lb here but it's lovely traditional loch style fishing nevertheless. Beware of sea mists in this district, they suddenly roll in from nowhere to envelope everything in their cold clammy tendrils. I've been caught out a few times with this curse and though mist is basically a swine in trout fishing (it puts everything into an opaque white light which appears to make it almost impossible for the trout to see the fly) I have two tips to offer. The first is to continue fishing but change to a size 10 Blue Zulu which you must fish on as fast a retrieve as you can muster. It's not a foolproof tactic but it does sometimes attract fish in misty conditions when all else fails miserably. The second tip is to have a compass with you and know how to use it to get yourself safely back to the road. You would be surprised how many anglers never take this hill loch essential or even if they do they cannot take bearings having never bothered to learn.

I could rabbit on forever about those magnificent red and black Cuillin hills and the secretive trout which haunt the clear lochans. Instead I suggest you find out about the magic of Skye for yourself. Ghastly bridges aside it's still a magnificent angling hideaway.

Part Five

Just as there are threats to Scotland's wild trout there are also some positive actions which can be taken to counter them. Part Five looks at these concepts and offers food for thought on the best way forward in conserving Scotland's trout resource . . .

River Thurso, Caithness.

Anglers mull it over – Assynt.

Chapter 32

Scotland's Trout Scene

'To the angler the common yellow trout is by far the most important fish that swims, for more people capture it than any other living thing.'

P. D. Malloch

In the twenty-first century, the pressures on our wild trout waters continue apace. More and more complex burdens are being placed on the loch and river environment from many differing directions. Whether it is recreational water-based pursuits (including angling) wanting their 'space', or whether it is commercial land or water enterprises desiring their share, the wild trout's environment is always in demand. Add to that the insidious long term effects of global warming and its attendant changing weather patterns and the picture looks uncertain. Worryingly, an overall national strategy for the management and conservation of Scotland's brown trout is not in place to meet these pressures. Yes, there are excellent long standing examples of trout fishery management in Scotland but the overall scene is fragmented rather than cohesive.

Despite the fact there are an inordinate number of differing organisations with a direct or indirect involvement with trout and trout habitats, nationally the wild trout appears to remain a considerable way down the list of conservation priorities. Anglers and Angling Clubs, individual riparian owners, Fisheries Trusts and Foundations, Scottish Anglers' National Association, Salmon and Trout Association, Freshwater Fisheries Research Services, Wild Trout Society, World Wildlife Fund, local Fisheries Boards, Scottish Sports Council, RSPB, Scottish Natural Heritage

and the Scottish Environment Protection Agency are just some of the agencies whose remit can cover trout and his loch/river habitat. Yet, despite the apparent strength in voices capable of speaking up on issues affecting Scotland's trout and the important angling industry which the fish support, the global view often appears to be splintered into factions. Anglers can be their own worst enemies as, far from raising the profile of wild trout in terms of conservation, they often keep quiet about their trout fishing only speaking up about it if something goes drastically wrong. Worse still, apparent bickering between what should after all be like-minded individuals and/or bodies, allows central government to dismiss anglers' claims that much more easily.

Even when we do make united representations on sea/brown trout related issues, it is often a huge uphill struggle to make our case heard where it counts, i.e. in central government. We seem to be kept in the dark about the appropriate environmental concerns affecting trout right until the last moment. More often than not we can only reply after the damage is done. Rather than be proactive we are simply reacting to events affecting our angling world after they have happened. Equally, anglers are often seen by the public at large as not being in any way involved with conservation. We kill fish therefore we cannot possibly want to conserve them.

Wild trout usually come last on the list of management priorities.

It is also a rather depressing fact that wild trout usually come last on the list of priorities in the general management of any water system. By the time the diverse needs of (to name but a few) salmon and coarse fishers, canoeists, wind surfers, jet skiers, white water rafters, commercial water users such as aquaculture, ramblers, bird watchers and general sightseers are met, the wild brownie can sometimes get very little attention in terms of quality managerial time. Though there now appears to be moves afoot for a more unified strategy to manage Scotland's salmon stocks, the same cannot be said for trout. Current Scottish legislation does not help the trout's case one iota when it states that a 'trout is a wild animal which belongs to no one until it is caught'. Sometimes it is argued that our beautiful but unseen trout do well when left alone in a clean river or loch habitat and that the wild trout therefore need no supervision in pristine waters. This is ultimately detrimental to their case however as it encourages laissez faire management and keeps the profile of wild trout well away from the public eye. Though the argument that rainbow trout fisheries take the pressure off wild fish is a worthy one, these fishings are a cultural disaster for Scottish trout. Youngsters starting angling in the central belt these days are brought up on American imported rainbows and may have little or no idea what a real Scottish trout looks like. But how can we hope to better conserve the species *Salmo trutta* when they are rarely brought to the public's attention other than when a disaster occurs in or near to, a particular water?

While researching the waters in this book I travelled the length and breadth of Scotland to both familiar and new trout territories. The experiences I have had have been wonderfully joyful, with many new friends made in the process. To a man (or woman!) these fellow trout angling aficionados have been open and honest about their fishings, eager to present a true picture of its current state. On certain waters, declines in wild stocks are indeed there but they have been truthfully described as have any measures taken to try and make amends. To try and give you an overall view of the Scottish wild trout scene in its current state, it is worthwhile clarifying the principal threats to our wild trout drawn from the research amassed and then offering some solutions for the future.

CURRENT THREATS TO WILD TROUT IN SCOTLAND – THE NEGATIVES

Where there has been a defined downturn in wild trout angling, it is usually brought about by a complex chain of events rather than one particular incident, nevertheless certain major problems have been highlighted throughout the book and are summarised below . . .

1.

One of the principal threats to wild trout in Scotland is its constant Cinderella image. Without true recognition of its status as a species, our trout continue to be oft neglected, playing second fiddle to all and sundry from salmon to rainbow and from canoeists to naturalists. This lack of recognition means that when it comes to potential funding of improvement projects, research and changes in by laws, trout are all too often ignored. Unfortunately the trout resource of Scotland is still largely unquantified. Though we know that trout populations generally increase in density the further north we travel there has been no real evaluation of the resource as a whole. Club/district records are obviously helpful but even if you put them all together on a map of Scotland, huge unknown quantities still remain.

2.

Pressures on trout arise from prolonged over-exploitative land practices within any river or loch system. These can be highly damaging to fish. Intensive agriculture, industrial use, forestry and/or overgrazing can produce many unwanted problems. Significant degradation and/or destruction of spawning and fry habitat from over grazing, intensive ploughing or pollution ingress near to nursery burns usually leads to a reduction in trout recruitment, sometimes to dangerously low levels. Over enrichment of rivers from fertiliser run off leads to similar 'clogging up' of clean trout habitat and acidification of lochs by poor forestry drainage (which places significant stress on fish biosystems) can occur on land with acidic soil. All these unwanted effects are very long term and insidious and are not usually greatly noticed until after the damage is done. Persistent neglect of native brown trout by

In the modern world natural spawning is a risky business.

riparian owners in favour of more lucrative 'cash crops' be that in agriculture or aquaculture, does little to help. It is a sign of the times that anglers today have to be political animals attending enquiries and debates on land use with a ready argument for wild fish conservation.

3.

The random unregulated introduction of any non-native species, and I would include everything from rainbow trout escapees to introduced ruffe in this category, undoubtedly puts the existing trout populations at some risk. Imbalances in fish populations within a water system, such as a chronic over abundance of pike, cause significant problems which only emerge over a lengthy period. Any excess competition for space, food, spawning sites and safe shelter means excess hassle for brown trout, and if one species begins to over-dominate in numbers, then disaster can result. Many unnecessary fish introductions could be avoided by proper legal controls for introducing alien species, but these do not appear to be in place as I write.

4.

In the freshwater, estuarine and marine environment serious threats to wild trout come from over-intensive fish farming practices. Along parts of the west coast of Scotland, migratory trout have all but disappeared from local rivers, killed off by the fish farms deadly by products, sea lice. These lice, which float in clouds as tiny larvae beneath the waves in estuarine waters, are indiscriminate, attaching themselves in huge numbers to passing young migratory trout compelling them to a slow and painful death. In inland waters escapees from rainbow trout and / or smolt farms compete for the natural feeding normally only available to the native fish thereby placing the existing trout under added unnecessary stress.

5.

Frequent resorts to restocking as a 'cure all' management practice means many important genetic strains of trout are now lost forever (all native Scottish trout originally had their own set of genes designed to help them survive in their home environment). Even when angling clubs / riparian owners of wild trout waters do seek advice from fisheries consultants, it will not automatically follow that they are given the right information on whether they should restock or not. Some (though not all) fisheries consultants are either connected to or run their own hatcheries, and therefore it is always in their interests to recommend restocking as a first option to 'improve' a fishery already containing indigenous trout. Anglers themselves do not help the situation as many still lay great store on the apparent need for stock additions. First introduced in Scotland in the Victorian era, the concept that restocking from outside sources will routinely enhance a trout fishery, still holds firm in many quarters. Most emphatically it does not, and apart from the risk of diluting genes, you can waste valuable resources introducing stock which do not thrive in your waters, and / or, turn a beautiful wild fishery into little more than a 'put and take'.

Finnock are under increasing threat from fish farming.

Our indigenous trout need long term care and conservation.

6.

Increased angling demands on pristine trout waters brought about by better transport systems/quicker access can pose a major threat if there is no management system in place at popular waters to cope with public requirements. Except for a few noted exceptions, any lack of proper sustainable trout management with appropriate legal back up, is a major headache for the long term care of the wild trout in this country. At the moment trout come under three aspects of Scottish law, i.e. Civil law, some criminal statutes and in certain defined areas, Protection Orders. Clarification and reform of trout angling law to benefit long term conservation of the species is long overdue.

7.

Pressure is also increasing on various rivers and lochs from other water user groups like jet skiers, canoeists, water skiing and power boats, and white water rafters. At present there is no real universal code of conduct for these groups as regards consideration for other water users, some do, some don't depending on which water these activities are going on. There are also genuine concerns over the present government's plans to increase access to land (and water) without a clear cut strategy as to how each water user group is going to get its fair share with proper regard to all aspects of the environment.

SOME SOLUTIONS – POSSIBLE POSITIVES

Just as the problems are interlinked so are their solutions. Some may come to pass in our lifetimes some may not, but if wild trout are to survive and flourish we must go out and work for their cause now rather than when it's all too late . . .

1.

The practice of sustainable management of ecosystems, a term much bandied about in the 1990s, is being slowly encouraged across Scotland. The holistic care and management of water systems which include wild trout, is *the* way forward. Old practices of isolating one fish species from another (e.g. caring for salmon but not trout) or regulating one water user group and not another are slowly being changed. Good channels of communication between all the (government or private) bodies with water interests are essential and anglers are gaining, sometimes unexpected, allies in the fight against unwanted developments. Such partnerships need to be maintained and encouraged. All native fish in our rivers and lochs have great worth and we need unity of thought and action to conserve them. Co-operation between bodies such as Fisheries Trusts and land/environmental/nature and water user groups is a key issue. The encouragement of Forum style partnerships to devise overall management strategies for river/loch systems and the land that surrounds them, is essential. In some areas, especially those covered by Trusts, this is indeed happening and this generally bodes well for the trout of Scotland. The management policies of the River Tweed, which acknowledge the importance of *all* fish within the catchment area backed up by a Protection Order, could provide one ideal model for the future managing of Scottish trout.

2.

The quantifying of Scotland's wild trout resource has begun. With the instigation of research projects into genetically distinct trout populations in Scotland it is hoped that a true (scientifically based) value can be placed on our undoubtedly wonderful trout. This should mean that in the long term better conservation and management of trout can be instigated with vulnerable populations given better protection than at present. More attention needs to be given as to what is a wild trout and one which is native and to this end the growth of genetic studies of trout in Scotland is to be encouraged. At present any trout, even a stockie brown which goes on to reproduce in natural spawning sites can technically become a second/third generation 'wild' trout. There needs to be special recognition and conservation given to the important *native* ancestral strains of trout – these are the true Scottish trout which colonised this country after the last Ice Age.

3.

Sensible law reform will hopefully be a topic for the new Scottish Parliament for it is almost certainly needed. A streamlining and rationalisation of the current mishmash of legislation surrounding brown trout, i.e. civil law, some statutes under the Salmon Act and the statutory requirements of Protection Orders, is required. This needs to take into account the regulation of the introduction of damaging non-native fish species into Scottish waters. It will need to allow reasonable responsible access to trout waters to continue and/or improve, whilst ensuring the balance between conserving a wild resource and increased public access is maintained. The Protection Order system tried to do this but made the most colossal error in protecting riparian owner rights rather than properly conserving all the indigenous fish species within a water. All of Scotland should be covered with a Protection Order which does the latter rather than the former. The unnecessary classification of sea trout under the Salmon Act and brown trout under civil law must stop and all trout brought under the same umbrella of control of sea lice and the siting of farms in sensitive wild fish areas. This was recommended by Lord Nickson's Task Force in 1997, so far it has not happened. We must lobby the new parliament at every opportunity as to the importance of trout in terms of an angling resource which brings valuable income to rural areas. In England the EA have come up with legislation which covers all trout, why do we lag so far behind?

4.

Public education on the intrinsic worth of brown trout as a national asset to be proud of must happen more frequently than it does at present. These are Scottish fish, a central part of our country's great angling heritage. We should be shouting this from the rooftops rather than just trundling on making do with degraded fish habitats, less wild trout and more fishing for stocked trout and/or introduced non-native species. Fish need a place in the Scottish wildlife structure as much as the (more visible) birds and mammals already well protected by current legislation. The management guidelines on trout already available from the Game Conservancy, the Scottish Institute of Fisheries Management and the Wild Trout Society need to be worked upon to allow an overall strategy for our brown trout to develop. There has been, albeit slow, progress toward better co operation between Scotland's angling groups themselves and also with various environmental bodies involved with trout habitat. We must do everything to nurture co-operation rather than confrontation for, while we fiddle, Rome burns . . .

The needs of the next generation must be considered now.

statute. Where sea trout are concerned there needs to be an independent regulatory body set up to monitor the actions of the fish farming industry in particular in their

Malloch said in 1909 that in terms of numbers fishing for it, the common trout is the most important fish that swims. Is it going to take another century to prove him correct? I do hope not . . .

A Final Word

'Fishing takes us to the most beautiful places in the country; always we enjoy our surroundings, the crisp fresh air of the loch and the stream, the music of the woods and waters, the glories of mountain and cloud. Sometimes we have grand sport besides and sometimes very little.'

R. C. Bridgett

With the new millennium upon us another century in Scotland's wild trout angling has begun. Let me share with you one last tale which says more about our wild trout angling than any scientific data ever can . . .

It is late in the season and I am eager for one last evening cast on those tranquil waters. On arrival the loch is patiently waiting like a dear friend for whom I am always inadvertently late in meeting. The day has been warm and bright and the sun, having not yet sunk below the western fringe of hills, throws a glittering pathway across the dark water. Slowly and thoughtfully I pick my way round the tiny bays, carefully following the invisible tracks of the generations of anglers who have fished this water before me. Fresh prints on the sandy shore indicate roe deer have passed this way and otter spraints on the rocks show the great hunter has been making his presence felt.

On reaching the far bank to fish I pause to drink in the last shafts of autumn sunlight and appreciate the comfort of total silence. I doubt there is another human being within several miles of me and though my wildlife companions are undoubtedly watching, they are staying quietly out of sight. Now, completely alone in the trout's world, I am the visiting huntsman and he is lying proud in his natural element. As the light begins to soften and dip, the occasional sedge stutters out, fluttering skittishly across the loch. Life sparks into the cool waters and the trout rise to meet it with tumbling splashes. I hook one on a dark top dropper, a Black and Peacock Spider and though that trout is sleek and perfect I carefully slip him back. The rapidly cooling air is signalling encroaching winter and I wish him well for the coming spawning.

There but for two hours alone at the loch, time has virtually stood still in the fishes' world and mine. As I turn to wade out replete with the simple pleasures of Scottish trout angling, an unseen brown smacks hard into the sunk tail fly. A hidden shadow, he was there and gone before I could even raise the rod tip yet I sense that sharp determined tug on the end of the line in my hands still. It was almost as if he was reminding me what Scottish trout angling is really all about . . .

Our trout fishing leaves many images indelibly stamped on our memories. It's dramatic, uncertain, challenging and sometimes imperfect angling often in beautiful surroundings which take your breath away. Having now explored many of the finest trout waters in Scotland I have come to the conclusion there is really no such thing as the 'perfect' trout water. The quality of each fishery is wrapped up inexorably in our experiences there, both tangible and spiritual. The thrill of connecting with a wild fish is what we all crave but the outcome is always tinged with exciting risk. This is central to our satisfaction.

It is just not possible to get this kind of sport on heavily stocked rainbow ponds where most things are made safe, sanitised and certain. In true Scottish trout angling you must pit your wits against creatures of instinct whose world rarely changes unless forced to by man. Scotland's wild/native trout fishing remains firmly traditional not coldly modernistic and in certain remoter areas, it is little changed rather than radically over developed. It is relaxing simplicity in a place where 'limits' do not exist. We are solitary anglers in the wild and beautiful element of fish, angling on lochs or rivers where our forebears fished well over a hundred years ago.

The question now arises whether in the next one hundred years my descendants will fish for wild trout in such similarly pleasurable, uncomplicated circumstances. Whilst I cannot look into the waters, I do know that we have the power to do something positive where it is necessary. We need to work out a cohesive strategy now to ensure our future enjoyment of Scotland's *Salmo trutta*. Let us maintain our trout angling with all its drama, beauty and challenge while allowing these wonderful fish to remain as joyfully unpredictable as they have been since the last Ice Age. Safe, ego pandering, introduced stockies they may not be, but a fish Scotland can be proud of, most certainly.

In our wild/native trout we have an exceptional and in some areas, still relatively plentiful game fishing resource, but we will all have to work to keep it that way. Concerted action must be taken now to properly conserve what we have, fight ecological and social hazards where needed and increase overall public understanding of our national brown and sea trout stocks. The trout of our lochs and rivers may remain blissfully unaware of our actions, but that is just the way it should be . . .

Select Bibliography

Various Historical References

R. C. Bridgett *Loch Fishing in Theory and Practice* Herbert Jenkins

J. Inglis Hall *Fishing a Highland Stream* Viking

P. Geen *Fishing in Scotland & the Home Counties* T Fisher Unwin

Marquis of Granby *The Trout* Fur Feather and Fin series

Henry Lamond *Days and Ways of a Scottish Angler* Philip Allen

P. D. Malloch *Life History and Habits of the Salmon Vol. XV* The Derrydale Press

G. W. Maunsell *The Fisherman's Vade Mecum* A & C Black

Charles McLaren *The Art of Sea Trout Fishing* Unwin Hyman

Colonel Oatts *Loch Trout* Herbert Jenkins

McDonald Robertson *In Scotland with a Fishing Rod* Herbert Jenkins

McDonald Robertson *Wade the River, Drift the Loch* Oliver & Boyd

Professor N. W. Simmonds *Early Scottish Angling Literature* Swan Hill Press

W. C. Stewart *The Practical Angler* A & C Black

V. Carron Wellington *Adventures of a Sporting Angler* Oliver & Boyd

Various More Modern References

Frost & Brown *The Trout* Collins

J. Goddard *Waterside Guide* Collins Willow

R. Greer *Ferox Trout and Arctic Charr* Swan Hill Press

S. Headley *Flies of Scotland* Merlin Unwin

D. H. Mills *Salmon and Trout* Oliver & Boyd

Kingsmill Moore *A Man May Fish* Colin Smythe Ltd

Mclaren and Currie *Fishing Waters of Scotland* John Murray

P. O'Reilly *Matching the Hatch* Swan Hill Press

Shetland Anglers Association *Trout Fishing in Shetland* Shetland Times

T. Stewart *Two Hundred Popular Flies and How to Tie Them* A & C Black

Tom Weir *Scottish Lochs* Constable

General Reading

J. Bailey *In Wild Waters* Crowood Press

G. Bucknall *The Bright Stream of Memory* Swan Hill Press

M. Greenhalgh (Editor) *The Complete Book of Fly Fishing* Mitchell Beazely

C. B. McCully *A Dictionary of Fly Fishing* Oxford University Press

Stolz & Schnell (editors) *The Wildlife Series – Trout* Stackpole Books

Index